Treating Attention Deficit Hyperactivity Disorder, Impulsivity, and Disruptive Behaviors in Children Using Behavioral Skill Building and Cognitive Behavioral Therapy Skills and Interventions

Treating Attention Deficit Hyperactivity Disorder, Impulsivity, and Disruptive Behaviors in Children Using Behavioral Skill Building and Cognitive Behavioral Therapy Skills and Interventions

TREATMENT AND INTERVENTION MANUAL

Reinhild Boehme, LISW-S

Benjamin Kearney, PhD, *series editor*

An OhioGuidestone Company
Berea, Ohio

Nothing contained in the manual is, or should be considered or used as, a substitute for medical advice, diagnosis, or treatment. The manual is not intended to replace, and does not replace, the specialized training and professional judgment of a health care or mental health care professional. Individuals should seek the advice of a physician or other health care provider with any questions regarding medications, personal health or medical conditions. This manual has been prepared as a tool to assist providers. In its efforts to provide information that is accurate and generally in accord with the standards of practice at the time of publication, the author has checked with sources believed to be reliable. However, in view of the possibility of human error or changes in behavioral, mental health, or medical sciences, neither the author, nor the editor and publisher, nor any other party who has been involved in the preparation or publication of this work warrants that the information contained herein is in every respect accurate or complete, and they are not responsible for any errors or omissions, or the results obtained from the use of such information. Further, the information presented in this manual does not constitute legal or financial advice or opinions. The ultimate responsibility for correct billing lies with the provider of the services. The reader should consult the current version of the relevant laws, regulations, and rulings.

The Institute of Family and Community Impact
An OhioGuidestone Company
www.OhioGuidestone.org

ISBN 978-1-7328190-6-1
Printed in the United States of America

Contents

Preface

For mental health professionals, building trusting relationships with clients and knowing which interventions will most benefit them are challenging enough. Helping clients who are also dealing at the same time with chronic conditions such as poverty, violence, and addiction can seem overwhelming. That's especially true for behavioral health service providers who have limited experience. That's why we at OhioGuidestone have developed this series of clinical manuals to help professionals develop their skills while providing effective treatment.

OhioGuidestone, the largest community behavioral health organization in Ohio, regularly trains new therapists and other behavioral health interventionists to work with clients who face severe, therapy-interfering challenges. We've brought that experience to these manuals.

In this era of managed care oversight, tight funding, and pressure to deliver evidence-based or informed care, it is essential for new therapists to get up to speed on best practices quickly. It is also essential for experienced clinicians to be well provided with effective and varied treatment plans. The manuals in this series provide step-by-step guidance on evidence-based and informed treatment modalities and interventions that can be used by both licensed and unlicensed mental health professionals—as well as by their supervisors for training purposes.

Seasoned mental health professionals will find the resources offered in these manuals useful for developing a renewed focus on evidence- and research-based interventions. At OhioGuidestone, our interventions are grounded in cognitive behavioral science and also shaped by the relational and attachment scientific advances that continue to inform the behavioral health field (especially the interpersonal neurobiology work published by W. W. Norton & Company). We understand the demands of serving client populations experiencing trauma and toxic stress. Our interventions are designed not to address discrete diagnoses (clients often have more than one) but rather the symptoms that are related to them. The series addresses a wide range of issues, such as depression, anxiety, ADHD, PTSD, and even reluctance to engage in therapy, and it provides interventions for children and adults.

We cannot "fix" our clients. But we can guide them along clear paths toward developing the skills they need to navigate the challenges they face, in their thoughts and in their lives. It's our sincere hope that the books in this series will help better prepare more mental health professionals to do just that.

— Benjamin Kearney, PhD, series editor

If you purchased this manual and want to make copies of interventions to help your clients, please do so. However, please do not share copies with other professionals but encourage them to buy manuals for themselves. This will help us continue to add to and update this series, to better equip all helpers who make a difference.

Getting Started

Who Should Read This Manual?

This manual is written to assist both community mental health workers who will provide therapeutic behavioral services (TBS) and psychosocial rehabilitation (PSR) and therapists who provide psychotherapy.

How Is This Manual Structured?

The first three chapters of this book provide a theoretical foundation for the treatment of children and adolescents with ADHD. You will learn about established effective treatments for ADHD and how they can be used in the community mental health setting.

The Interventions section contains three categories of interventions.

First are interventions for use by community mental health workers. These focus on psychoeducation and behavior management and take the form of TBS and PSR.

Next are interventions that elaborate on skill building in all settings. Community mental health workers can assist with this.

The final set of interventions are for use by therapists. These focus on building insight, acceptance, relational joy, and the capacity for co-regulation in children and parents. These interventions take the form of psychotherapy.

Please note that second and third sets of interventions are not sequential. Treatment in the form of TBS, PSR, and psychotherapy should take place concurrently if this is appropriate. Behavioral and insight-oriented interventions, as well as relational ones, need to support each other. When parents know how to attune to their child with ADHD, behavioral interventions are much more likely to succeed.

It is imperative the community mental health worker and the therapist communicate and collaborate. If a parent struggles with attunement, the therapist should let the community mental health worker know. If a parent struggles with understanding and accepting that ADHD is a biologically based illness, the community mental health worker should let the therapist know. Collaborative problem solving is essential.

What Are Therapeutic Behavioral Services and Psychosocial Rehabilitation?

Therapeutic behavioral services (TBS) and psychosocial rehabilitation (PSR) are supportive services that are therapeutic in nature and oriented towards changing behavior, but they are not psychotherapy. TBS and PSR can be provided by qualified unlicensed mental health practitioners.

Here are the categories into which TBS falls:

- **Consultation** to **assist with the individual's needs and service planning** for individualized supports or **care coordination** of healthcare, behavioral healthcare, and non-healthcare services and development of a treatment plan.

- **Referral and linkage** to other healthcare, behavioral healthcare, and non-healthcare services to avoid more restrictive levels of treatment.

- Interventions using **evidence-based techniques** (solution-focused interventions, emotional and behavioral management, and problem-behavior analysis drawn from cognitive behavioral therapy (CBT) and/or other evidence-based psychotherapeutic interventions).

- Identification of **strategies or treatment options** (assisting the individual and family members or other collaterals to identify strategies or treatment options associated with the individual's mental illness).

- Restoration of **social skills and daily functioning**.

- **Crisis prevention and amelioration** (assisting the individual with responding to or avoiding identified precursors or triggers that would risk their remaining in a community setting or that result in functional impairments; assisting with identifying a potential psychiatric or personal crisis; developing a crisis management plan; and/or, as appropriate, seeking other supports to restore stability and functioning).

Here are the categories in which PSR services fall:

- Restoration, rehabilitation, and support of daily functioning to improve self-management of the negative effects of psychiatric or emotional symptoms that interfere with a person's daily functioning.

- Restoration and implementation of daily functioning and daily routines critical to remaining successfully in home, school, work, and community.

- Rehabilitation and support to restore skills to function in a natural community environment.

Please note that, for PSR, the client must be present, as PSR is solidly focused on skill development. *You cannot use PSR to work with the parent without the client present.*

The Ohio Department of Mental Health further specifies rules regarding provision of TBS and PSR. These rules should be consulted regarding further questions about the nature of TBS and PSR. If you would like to learn more, please consult Ohio Administrative Code section 5160-27-08, which can be found online at the LAWriter website: codes.ohio.gov.

Does This Mean Any and All Services Provided by Nonlicensed Mental Health Practitioners Can Be Called TBS or PSR?

TBS and PSR must be face-to-face (with the client, family or caregiver, and/or collateral supports), and they must feature solution-focused and evidence-based techniques that address the client's treatment goals as identified in his or her individual treatment plan (ITP).

As an unlicensed mental health provider, you can use techniques from evidence-based forms of therapy, such as CBT, to help your client eliminate, decrease, or manage mental health symptoms. Keep in mind that you are not providing psychotherapy.

Working with ADHD: The Essentials

You have just received another referral for a student with attention deficit hyperactivity disorder (ADHD). Now his mother is in your office. It is evident that she is at her wits' end. She launches into a long litany of complaints while her son pulls yet another board game off your shelf, promptly spilling its contents onto the floor.

You can feel this mother's exhaustion and rising anger. The child is visibly frustrated and bored. You are worried the parent is going to "snap" right here in the office.

What can be done? What works for children with ADHD? What is different when treating adolescents with ADHD?

Evidence points to the need to help those who are in a unique position to be change agents in children's lives. In other words: Parents are change agents in their children's lives. Parents need to be empowered to use effective behavior management and to institute skill-building practice at home. Teachers, too, need to be consulted about behavior modification and skill building. And children need to have environments, both at home and at school, that are conducive to their particular ways of learning.

Relationally, there is much work to be done. By the time your client has arrived in your office, family relationships are usually strained to the point where parent and child fight daily and the frustrated child has become aggressive. Families may have lost the ability to enjoy each other's company because everything—even going to the playground—is now stressful.

Where to Start?

We begin with the parent. We want the parent to become the primary change agent, especially for young children. We use components of behavioral parent training (BPT), which is derived from the theoretical foundations of cognitive behavioral therapy, more specifically, the behavioral component of CBT. We use those components to help the parent become an effective skill-builder in the child's life.

We are not simply trying to teach the parent to "manage" the child's behavior. Behavior can be managed without the client learning new and more effective tools. Rather, the parent becomes a treatment collaborator to help the client make lasting change. We are working with the parent/caretaker to improve the child's mental health because this is the most effective way to create change. The client is always the focus of treatment.

If you would like a more in-depth overview of the theoretical foundations of CBT, as well as step-by-step practice guidelines integrated with case examples and theoretical musings, you may want to read *Evidence-Based Practice of Cognitive Behavioral Therapy* by Deborah Dobson and Keith S. Dobson (Guilford Press, 2017) and *Doing CBT: A Comprehensive Guide to Working with Behaviors, Thoughts, and Emotions* by David F. Tolin (Guilford Press, 2016).

Why Are We Using Components of Behavioral Parent Training?

The Centers of Disease Control and Prevention points to behavioral parent training as the treatment of choice for young children with ADHD (see Behavior therapy for young children with ADHD [2017]).

The latest review of available evidence (Evans, Sarno, Wymbs, & Ray, 2017) concurs. For adolescents, things are a bit more complicated. This makes sense. Developmentally speaking, parents play a different role in the lives of their adolescent children. They no longer control the environment and resources in the same way they do for younger children. Hence, intensive skill building plays a more important role in the treatment of adolescents with ADHD.

The Practitioner's Guide to Evidence-Based Psychotherapy (Fisher & O'Donohue, 2006) notes that behavior therapy is evidence-based and empirically strongly supported for the treatment of ADHD in children.

Conceptually, behavior therapy in the form of BPT offers a structured approach to treatment, which can create a counterweight to the chaos that ADHD symptoms can bring. BPT is highly structured and includes psychoeducation about effective behavior management. Psychoeducation of the parent about ADHD and its symptoms aims to correct parental (and, if needed, child) cognitive errors about symptoms and behaviors. Here is an example:

> Elijah struggles with sitting still. He is constantly on the move. His mother reminds him, often, that he needs to sit still at the dinner table. While having dinner, Elijah suddenly raises his hands to tell his mother a story but knocks over his plate, spilling food on his clothes and the floor. "That's it!" his mother yells. "You were told to sit still, and you decided to do this to me again. Go to your room. You are grounded for the rest of the month. No friends, no games, no TV. You should have thought about this." Elijah storms out of the room.

What went wrong?

- Elijah's mother interpreted his inability to follow directions as willful.

- Based on this, she punished him for not following directions.

- She personalized the incident.

- She struggled with managing her own emotional responses.

- The punishment was excessive.

Helping Elijah's mother understand that his inability to sit still is a symptom, not a willful act, could change the tone of the interaction. If Elijah's mother had received psychoeducation about ADHD and had understood that he is struggling with a symptom, she might have said this: "Oops. Elijah, it seems like you accidentally knocked over your plate. Could you fetch a couple of rags from the kitchen so we can clean up? Oh, and you may also want to grab your stuffed animal. I know it calms you down a bit when you hold it."

This response keeps the emotional intensity of the interaction low, helps Elijah problem-solve (something that can be difficult for children with ADHD), resolves the issue (things get cleaned up), and includes an attempt to prevent future problems, at least for tonight at the dinner table. Additionally, the consequence imposed by Elijah's mother is logical and immediate: He has to help his mother clean up. Ideally, she would also enthusiastically praise Elijah's help with cleaning, thus putting the focus on what he did well.

What About Medication for ADHD?

The NIMH *Multimodal Treatment of Attention Deficit Hyperactivity Disorder Study* (MTA, 2009) concluded that medication is an effective treatment for children with ADHD.

According to the study, there are reasons to treat a child with a combination of ADHD medication and behavioral interventions: namely, the presence of comorbid conditions, such as anxiety or depression and difficulties in family and academic functioning. After completing a thorough assessment of the child's symptoms, you should:

- determine the impact of the child's ADHD symptoms on family functioning;
- determine the impact of the child's ADHD symptoms on academic functioning;
- determine the impact of the child's ADHD symptoms on relational functioning outside of the family and school;
- assess for the presence of comorbid conditions (and their impact on functioning);
- assess how symptoms of ADHD translate into specific behaviors for this child; and
- assess whether any of the child's behaviors are dangerous for the child or anyone else.

When this assessment is completed, you should explore with the parent whether the child should be referred to a psychiatrist to assess the need for medication. There are many factors that come into play when discussing this with the parent:

1. Symptom and Behavior Severity

Does the child engage in impulsive behaviors that pose a danger to self or others?

Example: An 8-year-old boy with ADHD who frequently jumps of the roof of his parent's one-story home because it is "fun."

2. Ability to Learn

Is the child able to absorb the material at school? Can the child learn, or are ADHD symptoms causing the child to fall behind?

Example: A kindergarten student with ADHD who jumps from one activity to the other, is physically and internally "jumpy," and misses much instruction.

3. Home Situation

Can the parent manage the child's behaviors? How strained is the parent-child relationship?

Example: A single mother of three boys has resorted to physical punishment of her oldest, a 7-year-old with ADHD. The boy has now also become aggressive with his siblings. In this case, you may want to offer home-based behavioral services as well as a referral to a pediatric psychiatrist to assess if the child needs medication.

4. Parental Choice/Preference

Is the parent opposed to medication for ADHD?

Example: The parent of a third-grader understands that her child has ADHD but is strongly opposed to treating it with medication because she has heard from others that it will turn her child into a "zombie."

By now it should be clear that there is not a simple, "one size fits all" answer regarding the use of medication for the treatment of ADHD in children, but the evidence clearly shows that medication is effective. Treatment choices should be centered on the specific child and family. Medication and behavioral treatment can be used together effectively.

The Practitioner's Guide to Evidence-Based Psychotherapy (Fisher & O'Donohue, 2006) notes that "behavior therapy and stimulant medication may be the optimal approach for treating many children with ADHD" (p. 97). You and the parent together should always consult with your client's physician. The child's pediatrician should be made aware of the symptoms and serves as a point of entry for discussing the need to consider medication. Your client should receive a medication assessment and, if needed, management from a provider who is experienced in the treatment of pediatric ADHD, preferably a board-certified child psychiatrist. This becomes even more important if your client has other comorbid mental health conditions such as depression or anxiety. The MTA study (2009) points out the need for high-quality medication management, and participants received more detailed attention and medication adjustments than most community-based clients.

Because BPT is evidence-based and empirically supported, it must be offered to your client. You should explain that BPT is a well-researched treatment. You should also explain that it, as well as all treatment, will be tailored to fit the needs of the client and family. Using BPT does not mean disregarding client and family opinions, needs, and preferences. On the contrary, it means working with them within the BPT framework.

Additionally, you should make it clear that the treatment provided is focused on improving the client's mental health. In other words: The parent is not your client; the child is. We are using components of BPT to build client skills for managing the symptoms of ADHD.

The Association for Behavioral and Cognitive Therapies (ABCT) states that "parents are trained to become 'co-therapists'" ("ABCT Fact," 2018).

When your client's parent views herself as a co-therapist, she is engaged and invested in the treatment of her child. Treatment is not something that happens to the child, but something that is co-created in the relationship between the parent, the child, and the provider.

What About School-Based Interventions?

Generally speaking, interventions for children with ADHD are effective in the setting in which they are provided. If a parent knows how to ignore negative behaviors and reward positive behaviors consistently, over time the child will understand and adjust. If the classroom teacher, however, consistently "rewards" negative behaviors with attention, such as trips to the principal's office, the child will understand this, too. If behavior change at school is needed, Behavioral Classroom Management is needed.

Evans, Sarno, Wymbs, and Ray (2017) warn explicitly about generalization of treatment outcomes across settings. It is important to understand that treatment success in one area is unlikely to simply "rub off" into other areas. Behaviors and skills are specific to situations and need to be addressed in the situations in which they occur.

If treatment outcomes cannot be generalized across settings, what does this mean for the treatment of ADHD in children and adolescents?

Generally speaking, treatment will need to have the following components:

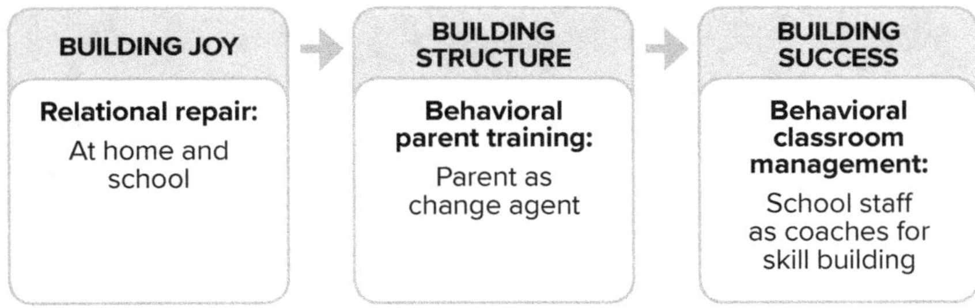

Figure 1

You are building a treatment program that wraps around the child and fits the specific child and family. If, for example, the child is successful at school without behavioral classroom management (and you have verified this), then you can skip it. If your client's parent is receiving daily calls from school regarding his out-of-control behavior, you will need to speak with the school psychologist, principal, and classroom teacher to ensure that your client receives adequate support. You should also keep in mind that a child with attention deficit disorder (ADD) without hyperactivity may not come to the attention of the teacher for quite some time, but quiet day-dreaming also impairs learning. A child who cannot focus and sustain attention still may need school-based interventions.

When you begin treatment, you want to build success as quickly as possible. Your client and the parent(s) have had ample opportunity to build resentment and frustration. Begin as quickly as possible to build moments of joy for your client and the family. Resentment and frustration can impede success.

What if your client's parent struggles with more complex thinking? Will they still be able to help their child build skills?

BPT is not dependent on a parent's ability to understand and implement a complex behavioral program. Its basic principles are simple and easy to communicate. Here is what you can say:

- *The more attention you pay to a behavior, the more you are going to see that behavior. Negative attention is still attention. If you pay a lot of negative attention to a behavior, it's more likely to continue.*

- *Praise your child if he behaves well. Go wild about how well he did. Create a record of it.*

- *Ignore behavior you don't want to see unless it is dangerous. If a behavior is dangerous, step in and help your child stop the behavior.*

- *Create a schedule and a structure that works for you and your child.*

- *Use words and hugs to tell your child how well she is doing.*

- *Talk about feelings. Feelings are not dangerous. They are just there. They can be managed.*

- *Create joy every day!*

- *Take care of yourself. Show your child that you can handle your feelings.*

- *Be kind to each other. Everyone makes mistakes.*

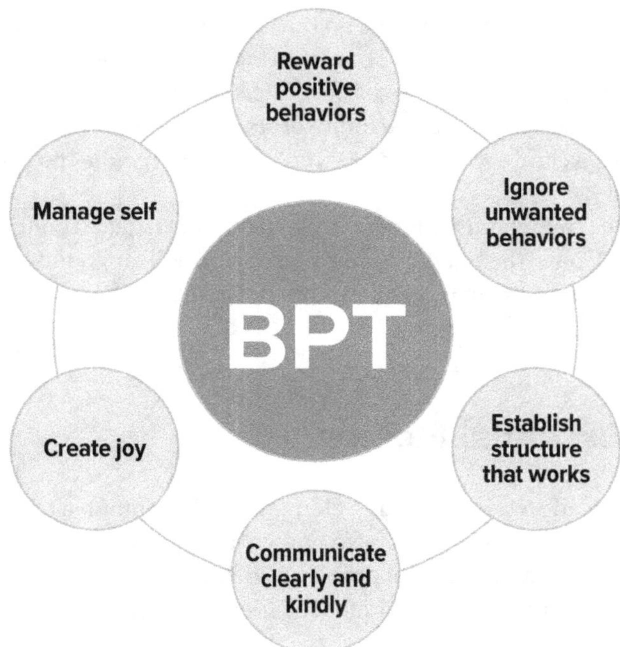

Figure 2

BPT is not dependent on using complex models and language. It can easily be adapted to fit a child's (or adult's) developmental level.

What should you tell the parent about the success of BPT and medication management?

No treatment will eliminate all symptoms of ADHD in a child. ADHD is a neurologically based illness. It is highly treatable, but it does not "go away." In many ways it can be helpful for parents to learn that they did not cause ADHD through poor parenting. They can, however, very significantly help their child manage and minimize problems. It is not a good idea, however, to raise the expectation that your client will become symptom-free. The message should be that things can become better, even much better, especially if the parent is actively involved in modeling and teaching skills.

What About Child Strengths?

Children with ADHD can be all of the following:

- funny
- creative or artistic
- full of ideas
- energetic
- unusual
- exceptionally loving and affectionate

Treatment is not meant to change who the child is. It's good to celebrate the child's unique talents and qualities. Treatment is also not meant, and never should attempt, to make children into little robot adults. Children are meant to explore their world through movement and to use their voices. Children are meant to play every day. Play creates joy, and joy develops a child's ability to handle those things that are not always joyful.

Be sure to help your client and the parent understand that all children, including those with ADHD, have the need to explore their world through movement. We are all hardwired to go into the world and explore it, to "seek" (Davis, Panksepp & Solms 2018).

CBT: The Essential Elements

CBT focuses on addressing the three elements of the cognitive triad: thoughts (also known as cognitions), feelings (also known as emotions), and behaviors (actions). CBT holds that all kinds of problems, behavioral or emotional, are rooted in unrealistic and faulty thinking that must be identified and corrected.

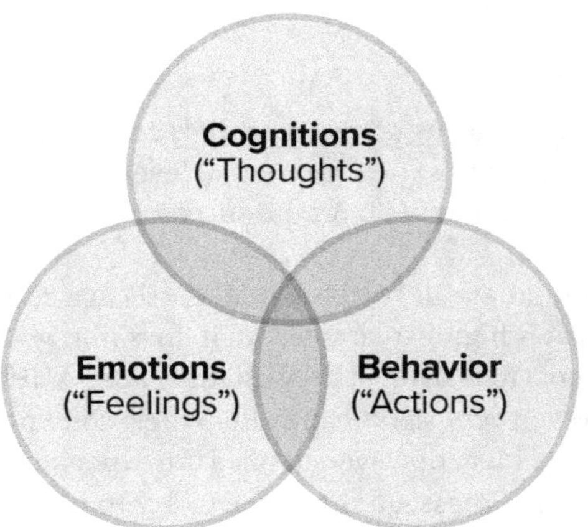

Figure 3

This conceptualization contains three components: (a) the emotional component, (b) the behavioral component, and (c) the cognitive component.

These three interact with each other. Thoughts, especially automatic thoughts (thoughts that just "happen") impact behaviors and emotions. Tolin (2016) calls them "interpretations" (p. 57) because they usually interpret what is happening in some unpleasant way. But behaviors also impact emotions and cognitions.

How Does Behavioral Skill Building in the Context of Behavioral Parent Training (BPT) Fit into the Cognitive Triad?

Behavioral skill building works primarily in the behavioral component of the cognitive triad. The parent will learn how to help the child build behavioral skills. These skills, in turn, will impact ADHD symptom intensity and effect by decreasing the role that symptoms play in your client's life. Additionally, psychoeducation about ADHD for the parent and the child will help correct cognitive errors about the causes of the child's behaviors.

What Exactly Do We Mean When We Talk About the Cognitive Component?

What and how we think impacts how we feel and what we do. But do we always know what we are thinking? Beck (1979) observed that clients often hold internal, unhelpful conversations with themselves. He used the metaphor of an intercom to bring this internal chatter into the therapeutic conversation. Beck named this uninvited and ever-present chatter *automatic thoughts*. These are the thoughts we did not ask for and are often only somewhat aware of.

Here are some examples of automatic thoughts a parent may have about the child's behavior:

- "He is doing this on purpose."

- "She is doing this to me."

- "He never listens."

Notice that automatic thoughts are judgmental in nature. They don't often compliment. If they do, they are not problematic and seldom a topic in treatment. It would be a good idea, however, to track the transformation from negative automatic thoughts to more realistic thoughts during the course of treatment.

For a child client, you may want to find another name for automatic thoughts, like "buggy" thoughts, because they bug him. You could try: "buggy thoughts" = thoughts that bug me.

But Where Do These Automatic Thoughts Come From?

In CBT, basic negative views of self, others, and the world are called *core beliefs* or *schemas*. We may hold these beliefs without being aware of them. They drive how we think about ourselves consciously and unconsciously (internal chatter), each other, and the world. Automatic thoughts are rooted in core beliefs. For the most part, we are not aware of the core beliefs we hold. Here are some examples of core beliefs:

- "I am unworthy."

- "I am a failure."

- "I am unlovable."

Children with symptoms of ADHD are at a higher risk of receiving negative messages about themselves from their parents and teachers, especially if these adults are not aware how ADHD symptoms are expressed in behaviors. Children with ADHD who consistently receive negative messages about themselves may then develop negative core beliefs. This, of course, creates a negative feedback loop like this:

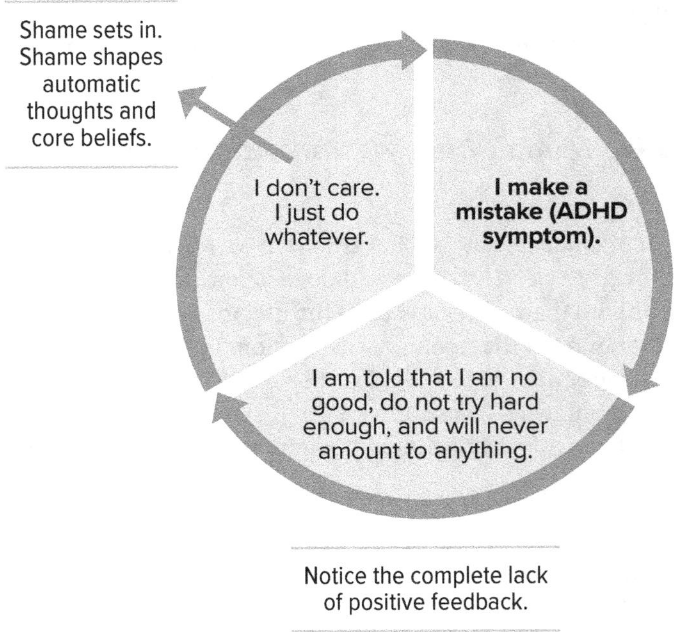

Figure 4

These, of course, are examples of unhealthy core beliefs. Here are some examples of healthy core beliefs:

- "I am worthy."
- "I am capable."
- "I am lovable."

Children with ADHD need to hear positive messages about who they are and what they can do to develop positive core beliefs. This is where behavioral skill building in the context of behavioral parent training comes in. The parent is taught, systematically, to look for and provide positive feedback for positive behaviors. Additionally, the parent is taught to provide positive messages about who the client is (not just what he does).

Here is a common parental objection to enthusiastic praise for small successes:

"He should do this because I asked him to. He should not be praised for something he just needs to do."

Here is how you can respond:

Children absorb all the messages we give them about themselves. It may seem like they are not listening, but they are. As parents we often find ourselves pointing out our children's mistakes. This is understandable. We want them to do better and be better. We do have to be careful about giving too many negative messages. If we give too many negative messages, our children may think that they are no good and unworthy of love. I know that you love and care about your child. This is why you asked for help. Let's help your child in a way that builds a sense of self-worth and ability.

Does this mean that parents of children with ADHD should never give feedback about mistakes and limitations?

It does not! Learning to own up to mistakes and accept one's limitations is part of growing up. It's good to be enthusiastic about the child's progress and successes. It's also a good idea for children to learn and accept that they don't have to be good at everything and that everyone makes mistakes. You can explain that the best way for a child to learn about acknowledging mistakes and limitations is to observe a parent or caretaker doing it.

Where, Then, Do These Core Beliefs Come From?

CBT is what Tolin (2016) calls "present oriented" (p. 8). It is not that CBT discredits what has happened to a client or disregards the emotional pain that the past may have caused. Rather, CBT insists that the client must move into the here and now. BPT focuses on the behaviors that are happening now and prepares the parent to more effectively manage the child's future behaviors.

This approach can be helpful for a parent who may have focused on negative consequences and punishment in the past. It can be helpful for the parent to explore past behavior problems of the client and their responses to them, but it is not helpful to dwell on them. You can say:

We are working on the present and the future. We are working on changing your child's behavior now. I recognize that things may have been difficult in the past. We can't change that, but we can create change now!

In other words, the faulty core beliefs and negative automatic thoughts that may contribute to unacceptable behavior can be corrected. CBT offers clarity about harmful core beliefs, such as, "I am unlovable." These beliefs are not true because they are not evidence-based.

For example:

Your client has been "hell on wheels" for several years. In response, your client's parent has yelled and screamed, slammed doors, and threatened "whoppings." The parent now feels that she has ruined her child for life.

The latter part of the statement is not a rational response. Here is a more rational way of viewing what happened:

The parent became stressed due to the child's high level of ADHD symptoms impacting behavior. Due to this, the parent did what she knew to do and what she had seen other people do. She can learn new skills to help her child respond in different ways and learn new behaviors.

CBT insists that we rationally tackle faulty core beliefs by examining the evidence for and against the core belief, then adjust to a more realistic core belief. More adaptive and realistic core beliefs then lead to more adaptive and realistic thoughts that can counter negative automatic thoughts. More realistic thoughts about self, other, and the world lead to behaviors that are a better fit for reality and produce better outcomes.

Again: The client is the focus of treatment. When we are helping the parent change the way they view the child and their relationship with the child, we are doing so in service of the client's mental health.

Here is how thoughts (cognitions) are viewed in CBT:

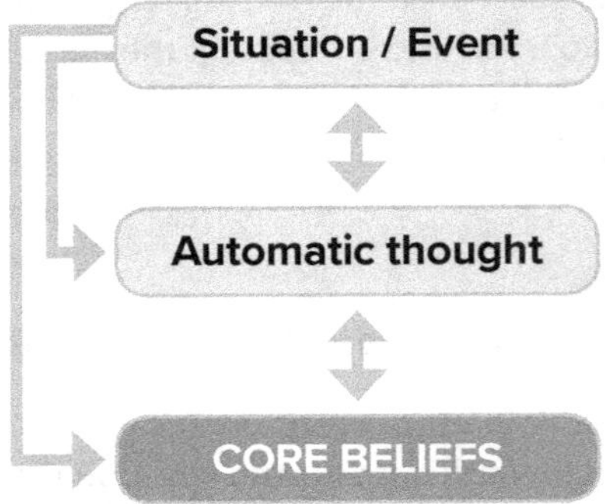

Figure 5: Note that core beliefs are much harder to identify than automatic thoughts (AT's). AT's just appear, we do not have to ask for them. Because they appear so often, they are easier to bring into conscious awareness.

An event or situation triggers an automatic thought in the parent. The automatic thought results in a negative message to the child. Over time, the child comes to believe parental negative messages, and this results in more behaviors that are not a good "fit" for the situation. The child may simply give up.

How Does Behavioral Skill Building Relate to the Cognitive Component of CBT?

Behavioral skill building addresses cognitive distortions about the child's behavior. The parent learns to think about the child's misbehavior as an expression of ADHD symptoms as opposed to willful defiance. The parent learns to disregard negative automatic thoughts about the child's behavior and instead learns to focus on sending the child positive messages that support skill building to decrease and manage ADHD symptoms.

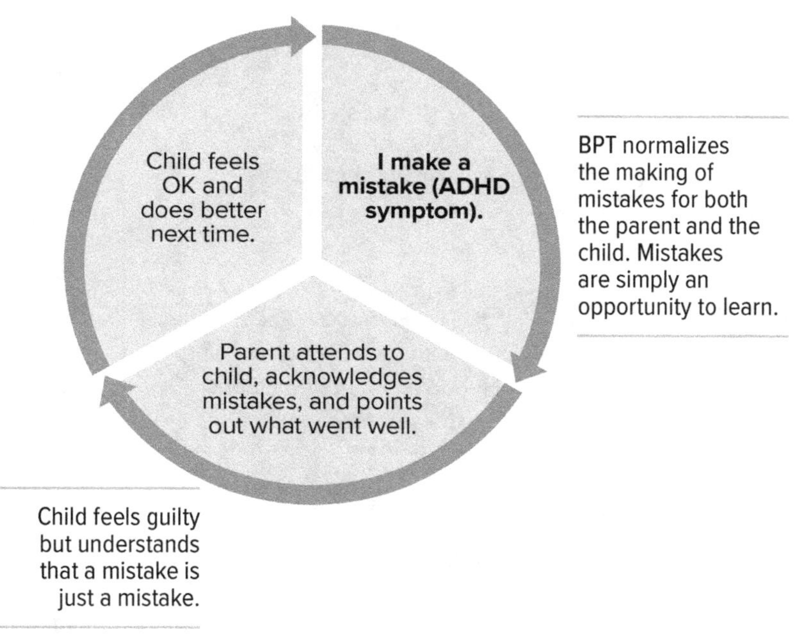

Figure 6

What About Behaviors? What Do We Mean When We Refer to the Behavioral Component of the Cognitive Triad?

Children with ADHD often engage in behaviors that are difficult for adults to tolerate. They may have a greater need to move or speak. They may not be able to solve problems or think before they act.

Because ADHD is a neurological illness, it is important to emphasize that children and adolescents with ADHD are biologically driven to behave the way they do. They really do need to move more. Their attention works in different ways. Impulsivity is not a choice but rather the default setting. For a basic introduction to ADHD symptoms, you may want to read Hallowell and Ratey's *Driven to distraction: Recognizing and coping with attention deficit disorder* (2011).

It is important to understand that ADHD symptoms are expressed in behaviors. Children and adolescents with ADHD-related behaviors that are difficult to tolerate or cause problems for caretakers and teachers are not choosing these behaviors. In ADHD, cognitive errors play somewhat less of a role in treatment because the behaviors are much more biologically driven. However, this does not mean that behaviors driven by ADHD symptoms cannot be changed. It means that interventions are much more likely to be effective when they are behavior-based, and that parents and caretakers play an important role in treatment. They become behavior coaches (using effective skill building) and function as temporary external frontal lobes, modeling thoughtful planning.

Here is a visual representation of ADHD-related behaviors:

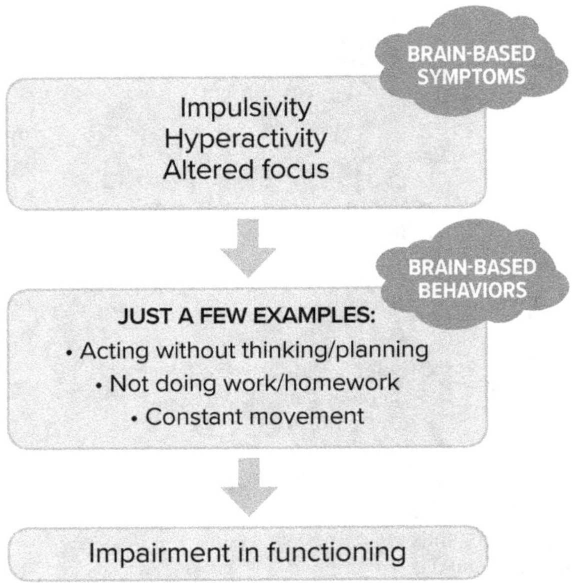

Figure 7

Here is how behavioral components relate to the cognitive components of ADHD.

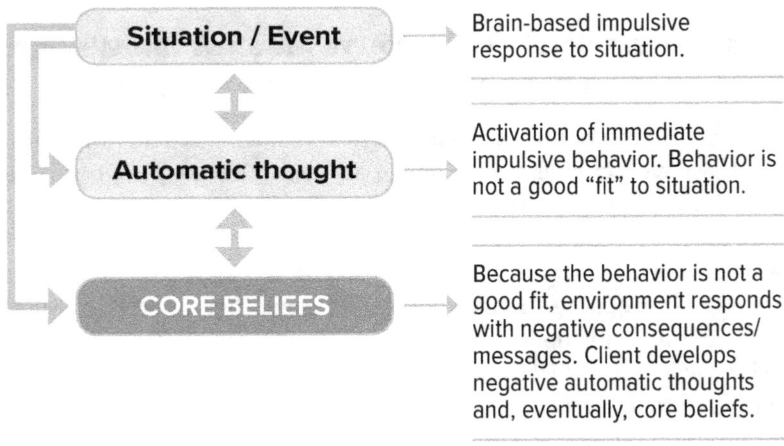

Figure 8

What About the Emotional Component of the Cognitive Triad?

What purpose do emotions serve? Tolin (2016) acknowledges that some basic human emotions are biologically based. They have a function. Fear, for example, evolutionarily speaking, is meant to keep us alive. So is love. He differentiates between "physiological sensations" and "subjective emotional states." (p. 81) There are basic emotions that we need. They keep us alive.

Children and adolescents with ADHD may find it more difficult to regulate their emotions. Their brains drive them to act impulsively, without reflection. These impulsive actions are often not a good match for the situation. This can result in shame, regret, anger, and perhaps more impulsive actions based on those feelings.

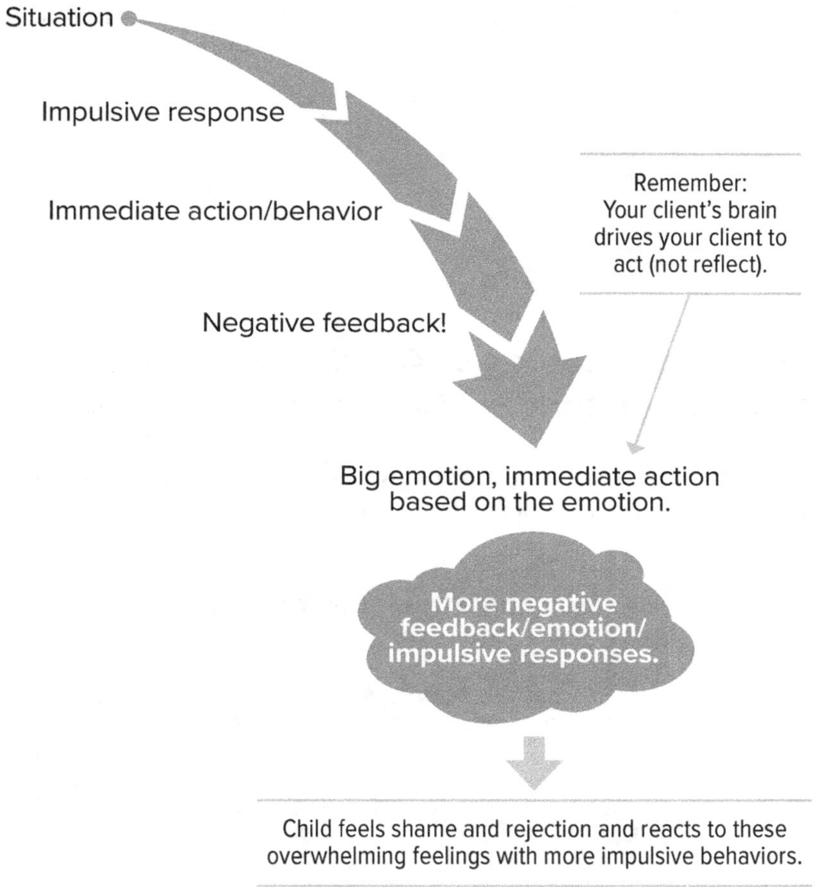

Figure 9

Emotions, behaviors, automatic thoughts (and ultimately core beliefs) are intimately connected, always interacting with each other. Emotions can be incredibly adaptive when they move us into the right kind of action. When emotions just "happen," as they so often do in children and adolescents with ADHD, they can lead to further functional and relational difficulties.

So here is how the emotional component of ADHD relates to the behavioral and cognitive components:

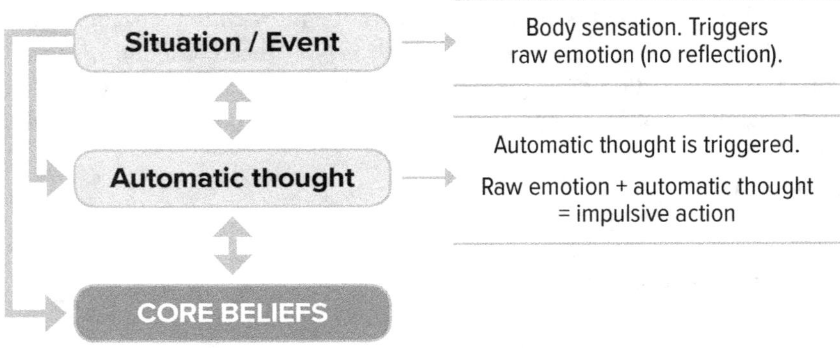

Figure 10

The Meat and Potatoes of ADHD Treatment in Children: Understanding Behavior Management

What is good behavior management? In order to practice and teach good behavior management, you have to understand the following principles:

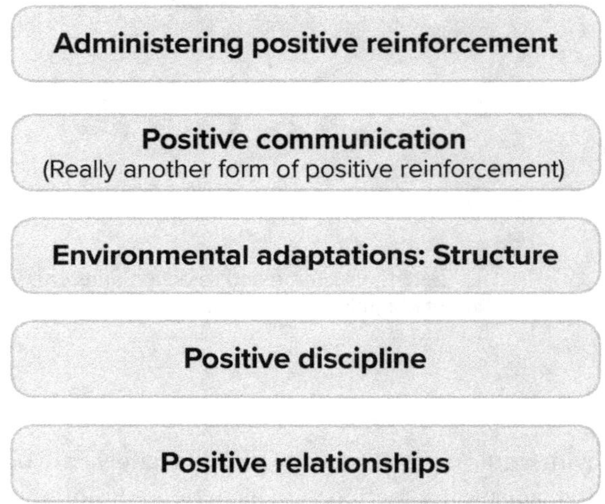

Figure 11 Adapted from: Behavior therapy for young children with ADHD. (2017). Atlanta, GA: Centers for Disease Control and Prevention.

Positive Reinforcement

Behavioral research tells us that in order to reinforce a behavior ethically, we need to do so in positive ways. Positive reinforcement can come in the form of relational rewards, such as praise, a quick hug, or additional time spent together. These are more meaningful than material rewards.

It is important that the positive reinforcement follow the positive behavior as quickly as possible. We want the child to make the connection between the two. If reinforcement is delayed, the child with ADHD may have long forgotten what happened that led to the reward.

Behavior charts are one example of how positive reinforcement can be implemented. But they should not be too complex. If they are, many parents simply give up using them and children disregard them. Behavior charts should be designed to create opportunities for success, meaning you should set realistic expectations.

Here is an example of a simple behavior chart:

Daily Dots: _____________________ used kind words:

Figure 12

In this case, every time the child used kind words (as opposed to impulsive words), the child would receive a dot or check mark on the chart. Stickers can be used if this provides more incentive for the child.

The goal should initially be low, perhaps three to five dots per day. Each should be celebrated with a rewarding gesture, such as a high-five or a quick hug. If the child reaches the daily goal, he should receive another positive reinforcement at the end of the day. Again, relational rewards are more meaningful than material rewards because they build connection.

The goal of using positive reinforcement is to help the parent become more effective in helping the child build new behavioral skills. In order to do so, parents need to understand what works and what does not work. Many parents use punishment, such as time-outs, with high frequency. Punishments may give the parent (and perhaps the child) a break, and for that purpose they can be used in an effective manner. They do not, however, help the child learn new skills. Parental positive reinforcement alerts the child, right away, that she did the right thing.

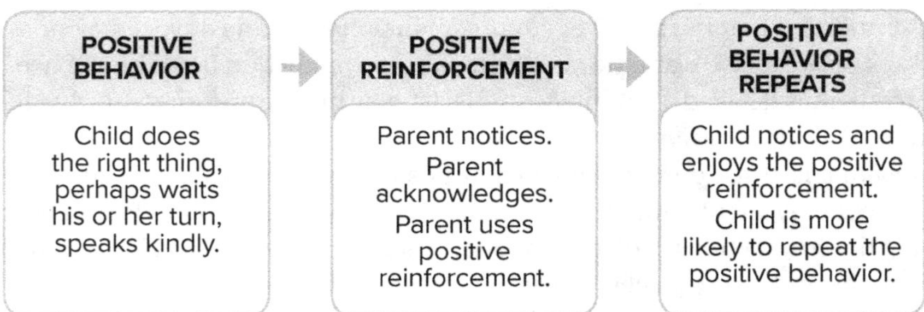

Figure 13

It's easy to see how positive reinforcement can change the trajectory of a child's behavior when used consistently over time. It is also important to note that:

- the positive reinforcement has to be right for the child and the parent. Positive reinforcement only works if the reinforcer is meaningful for the child. If it is not meaningful for the child, it not a reinforcer;

- children like material rewards, and they will respond well, initially, to receiving things. The problem is that the price of doing the right thing tends to go up over time. Hence, the child may over time want a reward that is out of proportion;

- using material rewards can send the message that the child should do the right thing just to get a reward. Material rewards can promote a materialistic world view; and

- relational rewards, such as a smile, a hug, or a high-five, send the message that relationships matter and connection fuels happiness. This is why relational rewards are preferable.

What If the Child Does Not Reach the Goal? Should the Child Be Punished?

No. If the child does not reach the goal, he should not be punished. The child learns by not receiving the positive reinforcement. If a child does not reach the daily goal, consider the following:

- The goal was too far from the child's baseline behavior. In other words: The goal was unrealistic. In this case you should review the goal and set one that is realistic.

- The chosen reinforcer was not effective and hence did not serve as a reinforcer. In this case you should explore with parent and child what may work.

- The parent was inconsistent in use of positive reinforcement and continued to use ineffective methods such as yelling. In this case you should work with the parent on understanding how skill building works and how it can sustainably impact the child's behavior.

- The child has limitations that make it extremely difficult to understand the connection between a behavior and a reward. Children with fetal alcohol syndrome seem to struggle with this more than others. In this case you should obtain a thorough assessment of abilities and limitations to explore what may work for this child.

Is it Always Wrong to Punish a Child?

It is not always wrong to punish a child, but punishment should be reserved for behaviors that are dangerous to the child or someone else, such as acts of physical aggression. It is normal for children to test limits. Not every act of physical aggression warrants a punishment. Additionally, children with ADHD and other impulse-control disorders may be less able to resist aggressive impulses because they lack the necessary skills. They need to be taught, systematically, how to express aggressive feelings in adaptive ways—and this is where parents come in. Parents model and then provide positive reinforcement. Here are some examples of behaviors that may warrant punishment, because they are dangerous:

- Pushing a sibling down the stairs. There is a real risk of injury.
- Picking up and throwing a TV or other large item.
- Hurting a pet.

When you punish a child, this constitutes a tear in the relationship between the parent and the child. The experience of relationship tear can be helpful if the parent also models the experience of relationship repair. The parent should:

- name the behavior that leads to punishment;
- name the punishment. Punishment should follow the dangerous behavior as quickly as possible and must not be out of proportion;
- make it clear when the punishment will end;
- never withdraw love;
- not lose control of their own actions;
- not use physical punishment;
- step in as soon as the punishment is over to repair the relational tear; and
- help the child return to normal activities.

What Are Acceptable Forms of Punishment?

- Time-outs
- Not being able to do something special, such as going swimming
- Not having access to a special item, such as an electronic device

Conceptually, it is a good idea to refer to punishment as a consequence rather than just a punishment. Many actions already have natural consequences and may not necessarily require additional ones. Here is an example:

Lara, a third grader, has not done any homework for the last week. Instead, she watched her favorite TV show. She failed her spelling test on Friday.

In this case Lara has already received a natural consequence. Should Lara continue to make the same mistake, her parent should:

- positively reinforce the bringing home of homework, and

- positively reinforce the completion of homework.

If Lara continues to make the same mistake even when positive reinforcement is applied, her parent could impose a logical consequence, such as restricting access to all electronic devices until (and the time restriction is important) Lara consistently completes her homework. Lara's parent should also continue to provide positive reinforcement for all steps toward homework completion.

Is There a Form of Punishment that Is Always Wrong?

OhioGuidestone strongly opposes the use of physical punishment. While physical punishment may stop a behavior right there and then, no actual learning about positive behavior takes place. Additionally, children who are beaten learn that the people who love them the most can also hurt them the most. Children who equate love with hurt may grow up to choose partners who hurt them, perpetuating a cycle of violence.

It is, of course, important to respond to parents who resort to physical punishment in a compassionate and culturally sensitive manner. Listen and understand. Many parents who use physical punishment are at their wits' end. Most parents do not want to hurt their children. They just feel like they're out of options and often are out of energy.

The strongest argument against the use of physical punishment is that it does not work. Most parents understand this because experience tells them that they often have to repeat it. Once the child reaches a certain age, physical punishment becomes impractical, as the child will no longer submit.

Sometimes parents are tempted to withdraw expressions of love and caring when a child misbehaves. This can be a terrifying experience for the child. The withdrawal of love and caring put the child in danger of developing an anxious attachment to the parent. Hence, withdrawal of love and caring is not recommended. Even when receiving a negative consequence, the child should always be able to know, clearly, that he or she is loved and cared for.

A brief relational tear can happen when a consequence is imposed. But a parent should quickly model relational repair. At no time should the parent act as if the child is not loved.

Positive Communication

In many ways, positive communication is an extension of positive reinforcement. When parents use positive communication, they:

- provide praise for doing and praise for being for their child,
- model emotional control by expressing feelings verbally and appropriately,
- are true to their word,
- do not threaten,
- negotiate in appropriate ways,
- signal that they are ready to listen and talk,
- encourage appropriate expression of feelings,
- take every opportunity they can to use words to build a positive relationship,
- use words and nonverbal communication to express love and connection, and
- communicate clearly that the child is loved for and cared about, no matter what.

Does This Mean that All Positive Communication Contains Only Positive Content?

No. Positive communication communicates all content, even difficult content, in a positive way. But this does not mean that difficult content can't be addressed. Here is an example of ineffective communication:

Robert is a third-grader with ADHD. He just got suspended from school for pushing over a peer during recess and then spitting on him. When Robert comes home, his mother opens the door and yells:

> "You are such an idiot! What were you thinking? How could you do this to me? You never do the right thing. And now I have to deal with you at home. What am I going to do? You get on my last nerve, and you are the nail in my coffin. Go to your room. I don't want to see you."

What went wrong?

- Robert's mother calls him names.
- She does not show empathy.
- She does not ask about the incident using open-ended questions.
- She lets Robert know she is taking the incident personally.
- She catastrophizes and lets Robert know she is doing so.
- She imposes punishment of unknown length.
- She withdraws, at least implicitly, love and caring.

Clearly, Robert's mother is overwhelmed. How could she have responded with positive communication? Here are some things she could have said:

- "You are home early. What happened?"
- "It sounds like you did not think. That sometimes happens to you."
- "It sounds like you were angry. Can you tell me more about that?"

- "Can you think of a better way to respond now that you are calm?"
- "How do you think you can make this better now?"
- "How can I help you get through this?"
- "I am getting upset. I am going to take time to calm down. I'll be back in five minutes."
- "That sounds tough."
- "Let's make a plan for next week when you go back to school."
- "I really want to help you find a way to walk away from these kinds of situations so that you don't get in trouble. Can we work on this together when we are both calm?"

Environmental Adaptations and Structure

Children and adolescents who are hyperactive and impulsive often require a more supportive environment. They may need more coaching by an adult to successfully complete a task. They may need a plan for recess in order to not succumb to the lack of structure and respond by acting out.

When children with ADHD require environmental adaptation and a larger degree of structure, there is often a degree of pushback. People may say:

- "He knows how to do this. He just does not want to."
- "It's a tough world. He has got to learn."
- "It's not fair to the other kids that he has a helper."

You may want to respond by saying the following:

ADHD is a neurological condition, an illness. When a child has diabetes, do you blame the child for having it, or do you feel compassion? A child with diabetes may need adaptations such as frequent snacks or bathroom breaks. Children with ADHD also need adaptations. They are just different adaptations. They may need a walking break during math class or an item to fidget with. To be fair means to meet the child's specific medical needs and to understand that they did not choose their illness.

What are some common environmental adaptations for impulsive and hyperactive children? How can you provide additional structure?

- Seat cushions that allow them to "wiggle" as a way of releasing energy.
- A timer to help the child gauge the use of time.
- Let the child sit close to the teacher.
- Use of color coding to help with focus and attention.
- Daily schedule (visual or verbal) at home and at school.
- Permission to color or doodle during lessons at school or during dinner.
- Coaching for complex tasks.

- Walking breaks. Opportunities to engage in joyful physical activities.
- Help with transitions, especially transitions to any kind of work.
- Permission to take a personal time-out at home or school with a clear plan to return to task.

How Can I Create a Daily Schedule?

Here is an example of a daily schedule. If at all possible, the schedule should be created with the client. The child and parent know best where and when the most problems occur.

Daily Schedule	Time?	Support needed:	Success?
Wake up / Breakfast / Bus			
School			
Back home: Rest and homework			
Playtime			
Activity together			
Dinner and Rest			
Nighttime			

Figure 14

You can alter this schedule in any way needed. When the schedule is done, it should be easy to understand. It's best to keep it simple.

If the schedule looks confusing, break it up into sections. You can make a flip chart and work on one section (such as playtime or nighttime) at a time. This can be especially helpful if your client needs a lot of support.

Here is an example of a section of a schedule:

Schedule: Morning	Time:	Support needed:	Success:
Get up			
Get dressed			
Eat breakfast			
Brush teeth			
Book bag and go			

Figure 15

Be sure to be specific when defining what kind of support your client needs and who is going to give it. Also, keep in mind that, once your client is successful with support, you can gradually and carefully begin to phase it out. After all, the goal is to help your client learn and master the routine. Phasing out support must be done carefully, one element at a time. You want your client to continue to be successful. Here is an example:

Rosa's mother lays out her clothes for her at night because Rosa has a difficult time making choices in the morning. Rosa has successfully gotten dressed this way in a timely manner for about a month. Rosa, her therapist, and Rosa's mother meet and decide that it's a good idea for Rosa to learn to lay out her own clothes. They agree that her mother will assist, but only if needed, meaning she will be in the room. The therapist helps Rosa's mother understand that it may take Rosa a while to pick out her clothes. The team decides together that it should take no longer than 15 minutes and that Rosa's mother will serve as a "time coach."

As a result of this change, Rosa is feeling more in control and is gaining a sense of self-efficacy that will help her make further changes in her schedule.

Sometimes parents want to stick rigidly to a schedule even when this is not necessary. Remember: *The schedule is there to support the child, not vice versa!* What matters is that the client becomes accustomed to using a schedule or routine. Clients with ADHD often struggle with creating a sense of order and sequence in their lives. Their jumpy attention may send them from one thought or activity to another with no sense of direction. Sticking to a schedule is more important for a client with ADHD than it is for everyone else. It is an anchor in a stream of jumpy thoughts.

A Word About Phasing Out Support

Providing and then gradually phasing out support is an important technique in skill building and shaping behavior. People who do not struggle with attention, focus, and impulsivity often do not understand how much support is needed to complete a behavior and how long it can take to truly internalize a new routine. Hence, many parents want to fade out support too quickly.

This is not a good idea. Children with ADHD experience failure every day. It seems like who they are and what they do is never enough. When your client is successfully following a schedule, let her enjoy that for a good while. A sense of self-efficacy is also learned. Be sure that the parent continues to provide relational positive feedback and agreed-upon rewards. In this way your client will become accustomed to expecting success.

Discipline/Consequences

When we ask parents about discipline, they often only think about punishment, specifically time-outs and physical punishment.

Discipline, however, should begin long before negative consequences may be needed. It's best to think of discipline as an extension of positive reinforcement, relationships, and parenting. You can think of discipline as part of a continuum:

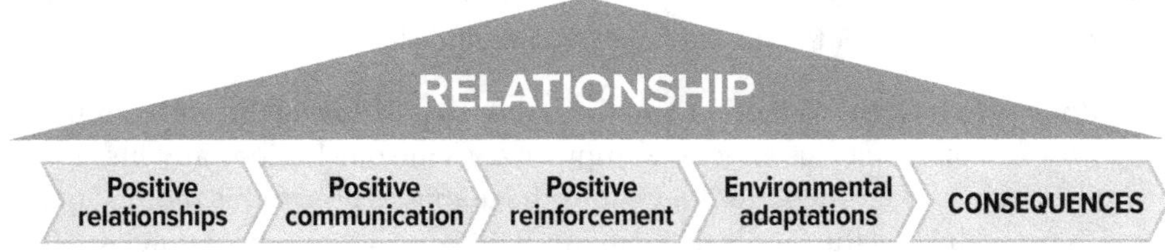

Figure 16: Discipline Continuum

All these elements work together to create an environment in which negative consequences are used very sparingly, but this does not mean that they are never needed. Even when a punishment is used, all the other elements should stay in place. The relationship between parent and child is not severed; communication (even about the punishment) remains positive; the child receives positive reinforcement for accepting the punishment; and the punishment "fits" the needs of the child.

When a child is punished (given a negative consequence), this feels like a relational tear. The child feels hurt, and it is important that the parent is taught to initiate relational repair. Many parents become confused at this point. They think that consequences include overt expressions of anger and withdrawal of connection. Nothing could be further from the truth: Consequences are likely to be more effective when parent and child remain emotionally connected. In this way the child will understand that rules are really there to protect people and their connections.

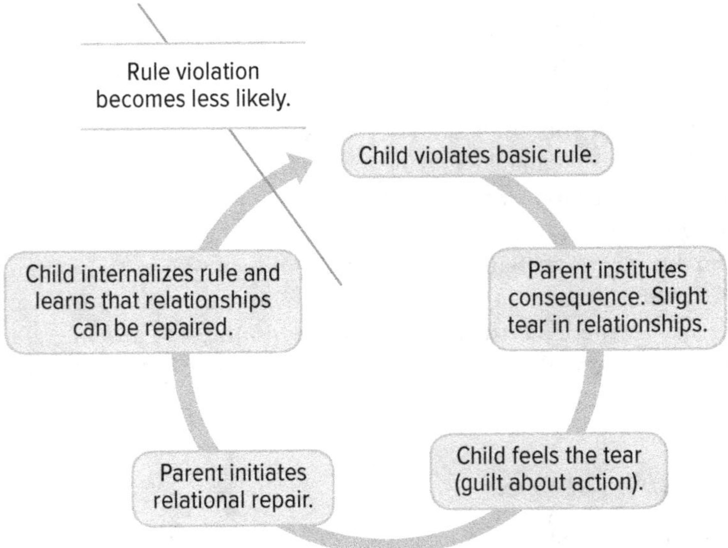

Figure 17

As a general rule for children, there should never be a relational tear without a relational repair. Relational repair can be as simple as a heartfelt hug or a few kind words. The greater the hurt caused by the behavioral mistake, the more difficult it can become for the parent to initiate relational repair. Here is an example:

Rodney lives with his mother and the family dog. He struggles with impulse control and often acts his anger out impulsively. One day Rodney and his mother have an argument. Rodney slams the door and goes to his room. Once in his room, he hits the family dog with his lightsaber. It happened quickly. He was not thinking. The dog yelps. Rodney's mother runs to his room and sees Rodney, lightsaber still in hand. The dog runs out of the child's room. Rodney's mother is very angry with him. She loves the dog. She just can't think right now. She almost yells at Rodney, but then she just looks at him and says: "I just can't even talk to you right now." She walks out and finds herself at a loss for words.

Meanwhile, Rodney is feeling the relational tear. The longer his mother stays away, the more agitated he becomes. His agitation makes him even angrier, and he begins to throw things in his room. His mother hears this, and her frustration level rises. But she does not want things to get worse. She walks over to Rodney's room and talks to him. She briefly explains that in a family, people don't hurt each other or their companion animals. That she is disappointed that Rodney hurt the dog. That he won't be allowed to be around the dog or watch TV for the rest of the day. She explains that she loves him and asks him to find a way to make it up to the dog.

Rodney's mother intermittently checks on him and finds him crying a bit later. Together, they devise a way to heal the hurt: Rodney will use his own money to get a special bone for the dog. The rest of the afternoon, Rodney draws a story about his dog and reads. At the end of the day, he gets to hug his dog. Rodney and his mother explore ways in which both of them can express their anger without hurting anyone, including the dog. The day ends with a hug and a nighttime story.

How Can a Parent Sparingly Use Meaningful Negative Consequences?

Negative consequences should only be used when all other methods of shaping behavior, such as positive communication, relationship, and positive reinforcement, have failed. Negative consequences are never the go-to method of discipline. They are the last resort and should be reserved for the violation of basic rules such as:

- hurting others intentionally. Keep in mind that children with ADHD often accidentally hurt others. Accidents are teachable moments that don't warrant punishment;

- breaking major societal rules, such as stealing from a store; and

- intentional lying that harms another person, such as falsely accusing someone of stealing.

What Forms of Negative Consequences Are Effective?

Time-outs can be effective when used in the right way. They should be developmentally appropriate in length. (A two-minute time-out feels like an eternity for a two-year-old.) Once it is over, the parent should initiate relational repair and state behavioral expectations from that moment on. The parent should do so in a kind way and offer help with following the rules.

Is It Necessary for a Child to Sit Still While in Time-Out?

Asking a child with ADHD to sit still, completely still, for any amount of time is asking the impossible. If the child is then punished again for not sitting still in time-out, a vicious cycle of behavioral deterioration ensues. It is OK for a child with ADHD to fidget while in time-out. The parent can provide a fidget item. This is an appropriate environmental adaptation for a child with ADHD.

Losing access to an item or an activity for a specific amount of time can be an appropriate consequence. Here are some examples:

- Losing access to TV or tablet. Keep in mind, however, the child needs something meaningful to fill his time. He should still have access to books, drawing materials, and simple toys.

- Losing access to an activity such as a trip to the swimming pool. However, it is not a good idea to cut off access to activities the child needs in order to function well. Many children with ADHD benefit from sports and other physical activities. It is, however, OK to remove access to a special activity such as a trip to the swimming pool with friends as long as the child is still permitted to engage in other physical activities, such as playing in the yard.

Be sure to specify the amount of time the consequence will last. If the child feels grounded for life, the consequence will simply lead to more frustration and behavioral deterioration. Additionally, the duration of the consequence must be developmentally appropriate. Telling a first-grader that she can't watch TV for a month is not appropriate—she can't understand what the time frame means. Telling a first-grader that she can't watch TV until the next morning can be appropriate if the child is allowed access to other meaningful activities.

What Can Go Wrong?

Sometimes parents confuse the removal of access to a desired item or activity with a time-out. Here is an example of how things can go wrong:

> Donte stole money from his grandmother's purse. As a punishment, he is not allowed to do anything that could be fun for the rest of the month. He can't see friends, can't watch TV, and can't play video games. He can read, but only school books. All toys have been removed from his room.
>
> Not surprisingly, things do not go well. Donte becomes increasingly frustrated and angry. He becomes argumentative with his grandmother and begins to call her names. One day he just does not come home from school.
>
> Donte's punishment may look like his grandmother removed access to activities and things he enjoys, but it is actually a very extended time-out. No child, let alone a child with ADHD, can handle this kind of punishment because it is excessive, does not relate well to the behavioral mistake, and the duration is not developmentally appropriate.

What then would be a meaningful consequence for Donte?

Donte and his grandmother should establish how much money Donte owes her. They should then determine how Donte can pay her back, using the time he normally uses for watching TV and other enjoyable activities. Depending on his age, Donte could:

- do more chores (such as clean the bathroom, do dishes); and

- earn money outside the home and pay his grandmother back.

In this way Donte would understand that the money he stole from his grandmother will need to be replaced, and that he in essence stole from both of them. By repaying his grandmother he would not only learn about the value of the money he stole, he would also learn about relational repair.

Positive Relationships

Positive relationships form the basis of all behavioral skill building, at home and in the classroom.

How Are Positive Relationships Built?

Positive relationships are built when children, beginning as infants, are provided with the things they need. This includes not just food and shelter but also nurturing care. Because we are entirely helpless as newborns, we need all kinds of care. In order to receive it, we form attachment relationships with our caregivers. Narváez (2014) identified these attachment relationships as the basis for not just future social development but also moral development. By receiving the care and support we need at an early age, and as we grow up, we learn to be relationally connected with those around us. This relational connection becomes the basis of our morality. This is why positive relationships with caretakers are so very important: because they form the basis for our moral world.

When children and adolescents struggle with attention, concentration, and impulsivity, relationships between caretakers and children can become strained early on. Children with ADHD often develop social-skill deficits. The MTA Study (2009) hypothesizes that the very symptoms of ADHD can keep a child from learning age-appropriate social skills. This makes sense. If a child is constantly distracted, the child cannot attune to parents or peers and hence does not become adept at picking up social cues. For instance, she may not notice a slight change in facial expression that signals that a behavior change is needed. The child's attention may be on an item just spotted; hence, she is not listening and following directions. By the time the child arrives in a school setting, she may be several years behind in learning and practicing the skills she'll need to get along with peers. Additionally, the parents may be very frustrated and stressed out because the child is not responding to their attention and behavioral modeling in the way they expect it.

The MTA Study (2009) points out that, with treatment, children can become more attuned to their environments and can catch up on learning social skills.

Because children with ADHD have a more difficult time focusing (and that includes focusing on social interactions and communication), it is imperative that parents and teachers take the lead in initiating, modeling, and actively managing the relationship. It is up to the parent and teacher to help the student recognize and express relational needs even when distracted. Relational interactions should communicate unconditional acceptance of the child even in the face of symptom-related misbehavior.

When working with a child with ADHD, we need to begin by strengthening the connection between parent and child because the road behind may have been rough, and the road ahead may also be difficult. In the face of this, we need to build relational joy with parents and children on a daily basis. This is also true for teachers and children with ADHD—and really all children.

Positive relationships are built through simple, everyday interactions. Here are some things parents can do to build positive relationships with their children:

- hugs
- high-fives
- verbal praise
- a smile
- a "wow" for things well done
- story time
- silliness
- dancing
- fixing something together
- walking together
- waving to each other
- eating together
- helping each other
- playing together

Play, especially, helps adults and children connect. During play, adults and children can let their guard down. They can just be in the moment. Play is not about teaching lessons, but rather about just being there, fully, with each other. According to Panksepp (2008), play should be built into every child's daily schedule.

Play, especially rough-and-tumble play, is important for all children, but it is especially important for children with ADHD who are driven to move. When adults play with children who have ADHD, they not only signal unconditional acceptance, they also attune with the child. This attunement will give the adult a much better idea of how the child feels and will set the stage for co-regulation when this is needed.

Schore & Schore (2008) put it this way:

"In play episodes of affect synchronicity, the pair are in affective resonance, and in such, an amplification of vitality affects and positive state occurs. . . . The regulatory processes of affect synchronicity that create the states of positive arousal are the fundamental building blocks of attachment and its associated emotions, and resilience in the face of stress and novelty is an ultimate indicator of attachment security."

In other words: Play strengthens the attachment bond between caregiver and child. The child with ADHD who plays with a caregiver not only learns how to experience relational joy but also how to regulate emotions through attunement, co-regulation, and finally, opportunities for self-regulation in play.

When children with ADHD are referred for treatment, there is often a rush to "fix" things. This is understandable. Building a solid foundation of relational joy between caregiver and child, however, goes hand-in-hand with behavioral skill building. One cannot work without the other. Here is a visual representation of the interconnectedness of play-based joy interventions and behavioral parent training:

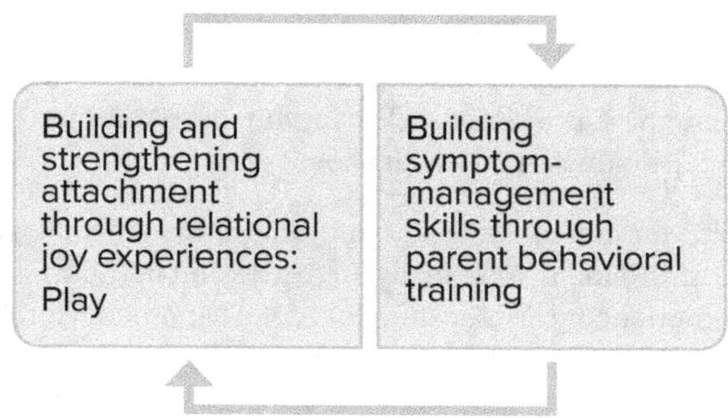

Figure 18

In order for treatment to be effective, there should be a balance between interventions that build attachment and joy and parent behavioral training. In fact, only when the child and the caregiver are able to experience joy together will the child also be able to accept parent behavioral interventions designed for symptom reduction.

Behavior Management in Action: How to Conceptualize a Case

Behavioral skill building, with parents and other adults serving as skill coaches, offers a clear path to treatment. When a child or adolescent presents with symptoms of ADHD, it is important that you engage in a thorough assessment of what drives symptoms of lack of attention and focus, hyperactivity, and impulsivity. You must rule out other factors, such as experiences of trauma and toxic stress. Etiology matters! Here is an example:

Antoine could not sit still at school. No matter how much his first-grade teacher told him to and what interventions she tried, Antoine would not sit for any length of time. He often got out of his chair, walked to the window, and looked outside as if he was looking for something and someone. At least twice a day he would simply walk out of the classroom and down the hallway to the school entrance. As a result, Antoine got very little work done. And he constantly wrote notes to his mother. In art class, Antoine produced beautiful images that he then carefully folded up and put in his shoe for safekeeping. Antoine rarely made eye contact with his teachers with his eyes always darting around, seemingly looking for something.

Antoine's teacher finally asked his mother to meet. Here is what Antoine's teacher learned:

Antoine's father was frequently abusive toward his mother, and Antoine had witnessed these assaults multiple times. His mother finally filed an order of protection. When Antoine's father was forcibly removed from the home by police, he vowed to come back and kill both Antoine and his mother. From that time on, Antoine learned how to be watchful. He wanted to protect his mother and himself. At school, he often checked windows and doors and always had an escape route planned. His mother told Antoine's teacher that she kept her escape plan tucked in her shoe.

In this case, behavior that looked like symptoms of hyperactivity, impulsivity, and lack of attention and focus were really an expression of the stress Antoine and his mother were experiencing. Medication for ADHD and behavioral skill building would miss the mark in terms of treatment. Antoine's symptoms are driven by fear. He is looking out for his mother and himself. In other words: He is not hyperactive. He is preparing for danger and preparing to move away from danger. Antoine is in survival mode.

Community Mental Health Alert for Cleveland

If you are working with a child with symptoms of ADHD who resides in an older home in the city of Cleveland or any inner-ring suburb, you must check with the child's pediatrician to see if he or she has been tested for lead poisoning. If the child has been tested for lead poisoning but has moved into another older home since then, he or she should be tested again. Be sure to ascertain that the child you are seeing is not suffering from lead poisoning. Symptoms of lead poisoning can mimic symptoms of ADHD.

Once you have completed a thorough assessment, you must develop a clear case formulation (Dobson & Dobson, 2017). Tolin (2016) calls this a "meaty conceptualization" (p. 94) of your case. Create a hypothesis of what all is causing and maintaining the problem. When you have determined that a child or adolescent is struggling with ADHD, it is clear that symptoms are neurologically driven. Of course, biology and environment interact, hence both medication management of ADHD symptoms and behavioral interventions are required and effective.

Once you have completed your case conceptualization, you are ready to identify your intervention targets and create a treatment plan. But first, you must put your case conceptualization on paper. Where does it go?

- Your case conceptualization belongs in the Clinical Summary Section of the Diagnostic Evaluation (in Evolv). When you write your clinical summary, be sure to include the neurological, behavioral, emotional, and cognitive elements that create and maintain your client's problems. Also, name what problems you want to target for your client. The problems you have identified become the basis of your treatment plan.

- When you are targeting symptoms of ADHD, be sure to include interventions that target all areas in which symptoms cause impairment. Often, but not always, these areas include: the home, the school/educational environment, and peer relationships.

Let's walk through a case:

Case Vignette: Ronald

Ronald is a seven-year-old first-grader who has been referred for services by his classroom teacher. His teacher reports that Ronald can't sit still, completes little schoolwork, is often distracted, and is very impulsive in peer relationships. He has received several in-school detentions for pushing peers and yelling at his teachers. Ronald's mother explains that he has always been like this. She says that she just can't keep up with him because he is so fast and can get himself in trouble in a moment's time. He knocks things over accidentally all the time just because he is not paying attention. He gets upset easily and may call his friends names, but then quickly forgets about what happened.

Ronald has repeated the first grade and is significantly behind academically. His teacher, informally, provides him with some interventions such as preferred seating (he sits right next to her desk so she can keep an eye on him), and he gets extra time to complete class and homework. Still, he is falling behind. Ronald's teacher believes that he is smart and tells you: "He just has to want to do it."

Ronald attends an after-school program but is in danger of being expelled from it due to physical aggression toward his peers.

Ronald's mother is tired of cleaning up the messes Ronald creates. She works long hours at a local fast-food restaurant and is exhausted when she picks Ronald up from after-school care. She feels that she is out of options and expresses that she does not know how to handle him. She admits that she has resorted to spanking him, but that this did not lead to better behavior. She explains that Ronald's father, who no longer lives with the family, was just like him. He would constantly change jobs because few things held his attention, and he lost a few due to verbally aggressive interactions with supervisors. He is currently incarcerated as a result of an assault charge.

Ronald and his mother share a one-bedroom apartment in an impoverished neighborhood. Ronald's mother sleeps on the couch in the living room while Ronald uses the bedroom. Financially, a two-bedroom apartment is out of the question. Ronald cannot play outside by himself because of frequent incidences of community violence, including gunfire. Ronald and his mother get on each other's nerves a lot and frequently yell at each other. Ronald's mother has no friends. All she does is take care of her son and work.

Ronald's mother reports frequent feelings of depression and anxiety. She is currently not receiving treatment.

Ronald's case is not an uncommon one. Our clients are often faced with multiple challenges, many of which are beyond their control. Let's call them therapy interfering conditions. Here are some examples:

- poverty
- lack of education
- incarceration of a family member
- disability
- racism
- sexism

While our clients did not choose these conditions, they are forced to deal with them. There is ample evidence that conditions of toxic stress, especially in childhood, can contribute to the development of physical and mental illness. You can find more information about the impact of toxic stress and trauma at ACES too high (2017).

How can behavioral skill building be helpful when therapy interfering conditions are present?

- Behavioral skill building can help the child with ADHD build resilience. A child who is better able to manage behavior is more likely to develop successful peer and adult relationships. Parental and other meaningful relationships can serve as a buffer to experiences of toxic stress.

- Behavioral skill building moves both the client and the parent or teacher into action. Parent/teacher and child will learn that new behaviors can be learned, increasing self-efficacy.

- Behavioral skill building can prepare the child for successful interactions with the world. A child who can successfully navigate relationships and situations is more likely to be able to move out of poverty. Additionally, parents can gain a sense of self-efficacy when they teach their children new skills. This, in turn, may prepare them for effective advocacy for those living under conditions of toxic stress.

Community Mental Health Practice Alert

What about the conditions many of our clients live in? What about poverty?

Ronald lives in poverty, as many of our clients do. Ronald's mother has few external resources. She does not have a car. She does not have savings. Her support system is limited.

Your case conceptualization must incorporate the conditions Ronald lives in. They have shaped his way of thinking and being. Ronald is growing up under conditions of scarcity. Physical and emotional resources are scarce. Ronald's mother cannot see a way of out this, and these conditions are all Ronald knows.

Incorporating conditions of toxic stress into the case conceptualization models for Ronald and his mother that not everything is her fault. Incorporating conditions of toxic stress also brings a behavioral component into treatment. When Ronald's mother is ready to do so, she may want to take value-based action and develop or increase her advocacy for herself and others living in poverty.

A Case Conceptualization for Ronald

Ronald: Assessment and Case Conceptualization/ Problem Identification

- Use the Diagnostic Evaluation (DE) Part 1 and Part 2.
- Include information about Ronald's socioeconomic status in the DE.

Here is what your clinical summary (case conceptualization) may look like:

Ronald is a seven-year-old first grader who has repeated the first grade and is struggling with symptoms of hyperactivity, impulsivity, and lack of focus. His symptoms have been present for as long as his mother can remember. He has been struggling academically and socially since kindergarten, and he struggled behaviorally and academically in pre-school. Specific problematic behaviors include: not doing work, getting out of his chair, verbal and behavioral impulsivity in the form of hitting and yelling, relational difficulties with adults and peers due to impulsivity. Ronald is in danger of getting kicked out of his after-school program due to aggression. Family relationships have suffered.

Ronald lives under conditions of chronic toxic stress: He lives in poverty, his father is incarcerated, and his mother is struggling with depression and anxiety.

Ronald's pediatrician reports no concerns about Ronald's physical health.

Problems:

1. Behavioral: aggression, impulsivity, lack of focus (trouble with work completion), hyperactivity
2. Emotional: impulsive anger, relational difficulties
3. Cognitive: inability to reflect

Note that the list does not encompass all of Ronald's problems, but rather focuses on what is most important. We would want to focus on the behavioral components of treatment first: If Ronald could learn in school and get along with family and friends, his life would be much better and his mother could breathe a sigh of relief.

You have completed your case conceptualization. This is a good time to check with your client.

Ask:

- *Did I get this right?*
- *Is there anything I left out?*
- *Is there anything I need to add?*

Make sure that you are working collaboratively with your client on identifying problems and treatment goals. Behavioral skill building can be more directive than other forms of mental health treatment, and collaboration ensures that a therapeutic alliance and a "joint ownership" are built (Dobson and Dobson, 2017, p. 53). A solid therapeutic alliance, client and therapist ownership of the case formulation, problem identification, and treatment planning are the bases for treatment success.

When you are working with Ronald's teacher you will have to be especially diplomatic. Remember, you are a guest in the school building. Listen first before talking. Teachers are often a valuable source of information. They know what has not worked. Additionally, respect the process for putting classroom-based interventions in place. Understand that 504 intervention plans and IEPs (individual education programs) have specific processes attached to them. As mental health providers, we can help parents advocate for the educational needs of their children, but we do not control the process because that is based in the educational system. Collaboration with parents and school personnel is of the utmost importance.

If you don't work collaboratively, treatment success is jeopardized from the start. You may think that you understand your client's basic problems. You may have a great case conceptualization in your mind, and you may even be correct. However, if your client or the client's parent disagree with you, the child may never fully participate in treatment, and the likelihood of treatment success diminishes.

How can you ensure that you are working collaboratively with your client and the client's parent?

- Ask frequently: *Did I get this right? Is there anything you want to add? What part of what I am saying does not sit right with you?*

- If your client is not ready for the kind of change you have in mind, go back to basics. Ask the miracle question: If you had one wish and it would come true tomorrow morning, what would your wish be? What would your life be like? Ask your client to describe, in detail, what life would be like. Build collaboration based on that wish. If you are working with a child (or a very materialistic adult) you may have to explore the differences between material things your client wants vs. the life they want.

- Acknowledge reluctance and ambivalence before and while you encourage your client to move into change processes. Voice understanding that change is hard.

- Understand that collaboration and trust are built and that it is your responsibility to create the foundation. You will have to model collaboration and trust.

Once problems have been identified collaboratively, the treatment plan can be completed.

Here is a visual representation of the assessment process:

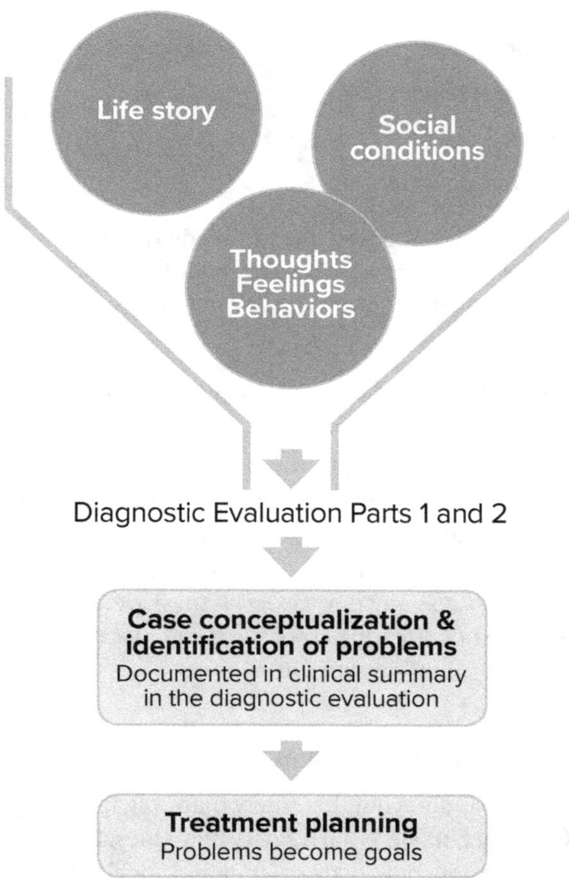

Figure 19

Suicidal Ideation and Safety Planning

Clients with ADHD are, by definition, impulsive. Children and adolescents who are verbally and behaviorally impulsive may threaten suicide or engage in suicidal gestures because they are having a difficult feeling, which results in an impulsive response. If your client discloses thoughts of suicide, complete a formalized suicide risk assessment. Do so in a caring and compassionate manner, stating that you are asking your client these questions because you want him or her to be well. Document completion of a formal suicide risk assessment in your case notes and ensure that it is scanned into the client's electronic record. When children and adolescents talk about suicide, you should always take notice (whether the child has ADHD or not) and ask:

- *What do you mean by that?*
- *What made you upset/angry/sad?*
- *What would you do?*
- *What keeps you from doing this?*

Once you have completed the formalized suicide risk assessment, you will need to complete a safety plan. Any safety concerns about a client must also be reported and discussed with your supervisor on the day that they occur.

What If I Conclude that My Client Is Not Actually Suicidal?

If you conclude that your client is not actually suicidal, you must discuss this conclusion with your supervisor. You must document how you arrived at this conclusion (formalized risk assessment and clinical judgment combined). You must then explore what drove the client to make a suicidal statement. Did the client not understand what he was saying? Was he feeling emotionally out of control and needed assistance? Be sure to address any new issues. If these problems are not identified as client problems and are not already part of the client's treatment plan, they need to be incorporated into the client's treatment.

What Is the Function of a Safety Plan?

Tolin (2016) rightfully points out that safety planning in no way guarantees that your client will not harm herself. What a safety plan does, however, is denote to both you and the client the seriousness of the matter and specifically the importance of taking action.

By collaboratively creating a safety plan with your client you are:

- expressing genuine concern and compassion for your client. You are expressing that you value your client as a human being and you want her to stay alive so she can create "a life worth living" (Dimeff & Linehan, 2001, p. 2).

- you are modeling immediately the importance of taking positive and life-affirming action. Sometimes all kinds of feelings can become so intense, so unbearable, that they "flip" into depressive feelings. If this happens, pay close attention to your client's level of depression and hopelessness by asking clear questions about suicidal thoughts and behaviors. When children with ADHD express suicidal thoughts, you must assess for other mental health conditions such as depression and anxiety.

What Should Be Included in a Safety Plan?

Use the OGS Safety Planning Form to create your safety plan. This form will identify:

- concerning thoughts;
- concerning behaviors;
- things the client can do (behavioral activation to shift attention);
- people the client can talk to (behavioral activation aimed at changing attentional focus to supportive and caring relationships); and
- triggers and removal of triggers from the environment. If medications are a trigger, they should be secured. No person with suicidal thoughts should have access to firearms in the home or elsewhere. Even if they are locked away, the risk of gaining access is there, and a plan should be made to temporarily remove them from the home.

Can a Safety Plan Guarantee the Safety of Your Client?

A safety plan cannot guarantee the safety of your client. It does, however, indicate that you and your client have adequately addressed the issue of suicidal thoughts and behaviors and that you, the clinician, have actively taken all appropriate steps to help your client stay safe and alive.

What About Children?

When creating a safety plan with a child, the parent must always be involved. If a child discloses a safety issue and the parent is not present, you must contact the parent immediately (and notify your supervisor). A meeting must be scheduled on the same day to create a safety plan. Remember, safety planning is a collaborative process. A meaningful safety plan involves addressing the concerns of both the parent and the child.

If you have determined that your client is struggling with suicidal thoughts and takes medication for ADHD (or anyone else in the home takes any kind of medications), you must ensure that those medications are secured. In most cases this will mean that all medications are in a locked box with only the parent having a key and the key staying with the parent at all times.

What Will Not Work:

- Meeting the client and parent with a ready-made safety plan that does not take into account the specific family circumstances.

- Creating a vague safety plan, including statements such as, "will call a friend" or, "parent will put away all medications."

- Things that are impossible, such as "parent will supervise client at all times" when the parent works full time.

What Will Work:

- Being compassionate and inquisitive about the client's and family's circumstances. Learn as much as you can to collaboratively create a workable safety plan.

- Being specific. Outline where the client will go, who the client can call (include phone numbers), and what the client will do. An example of this would be: "Client will build a Lego tower in the kitchen while guardian . . ."

- Things that are possible, such as: "Parent will ensure appropriate supervision of client. Aunt (insert name) will play Legos with client/go for a walk with client . . ."

- Being specific about what helps your client. If your client has ADHD and physical activity helps him decrease feelings of depression and hopelessness, include in the safety plan specific activities your client loves and can actually engage in.

What If Nothing Works?

Sometimes nothing seems to work. When this is the case, it is important to consider the following factors:

- Is there anything reinforcing the client's need to be hospitalized? Will the client receive more attention and perhaps compassion if she is so ill that she requires hospitalization? Is attention what the client actually needs? If so, how can your client receive more? Is a partial hospitalization program needed? Some form of respite? Keep in mind that your client may express an actual need. This is not manipulation on the client's part. Your client may not be able to tell you (yet) what she needs. This in itself is a clinical issue that requires attention.

- If your client is a child: Is the parent simply exhausted from caring for a mentally ill child? Is a more intensive level of services needed? Is respite needed? Does the parent need his or her own services?

- Is the client's family in a very dysregulated state? Can you assist with calming emotions? Can you instill hope that things will get better?

Sometimes hospitalization is needed to stabilize a client. This does not mean that you or the client missed something. It does mean that a better plan is needed. It is important to begin with planning for discharge right away. What will be different? What can you do? What can your client do? How can the environment change?

Treatment Planning

Safety always comes first. Client behaviors such as suicidal gestures or actions or severe self-harm (that may not be intended but could result in death) need to be addressed first. Here are some ways to respond to suicidal thoughts and behaviors:

- Making the environment safe by identifying and removing triggers.
- Changing client behavioral responses to triggers.
- Increasing skills to manage triggers and resulting emotional states (skill building).
- Examining and changing automatic thoughts leading to suicidal behaviors.
- Building and strengthening relationships.

Is it necessary to address all three elements of the cognitive triad in the treatment plan? What about behavioral interventions for those who struggle with thinking things through (a factor very much inherent in ADHD)?

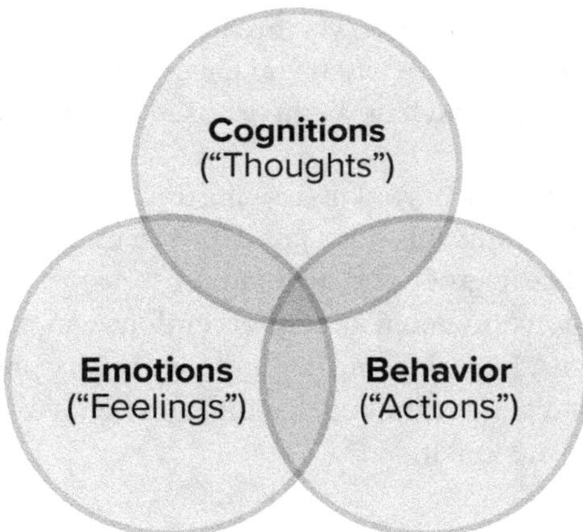

Figure 20: The cognitive triad

It is not necessary to address all three elements of the cognitive triad equally and right away. In fact, Tolin (2016), referring to behavioral interventions, recommends that "you should strongly consider using these strategies as the 'main course' in your CBT" (p. 161).

Behavioral skill building works mostly in the area of behavioral interventions. It also uses psychoeducation to modify parent responses to child behavior which, in turn, will affect how the client thinks (cognitive element).

Why Start with Behavioral Interventions?

Generally speaking, interventions targeting behaviors may be more accessible to clients. In addition, when it comes to the treatment of ADHD, we are looking to move the client into thoughtful and calm action—away from impulsive actions and hyperactivity and into meaningful and planful activity.

Frantic action is not likely to be effective in managing life. If that can be changed and your client can learn to take calm and realistic action, she is likely to develop a greater sense of control and mastery.

Community Mental Health Practice Alert

Our clients often struggle with basic skills for many reasons. Remember those therapy interfering conditions?

Lack of resources related to poverty can make our clients anxious and frantic. It makes sense that our clients are anxious when they think about losing their housing or food stamps.

Therapy interfering conditions can lead to skill deficits in people who are otherwise competent. Poverty may lead to an educational impairment. It is difficult to learn when you are hungry or worried about housing. It is difficult to learn when you have to move a lot. If you grew up in an old house and you have been exposed to lead, learning can become a real challenge.

While our clients may have skill deficits, this does not mean that they are incapable of learning. It is not a good idea to underestimate our clients' ability to learn, grow, and overcome.

Psychoeducation and behavioral interventions can be very empowering for our clients. Experiencing competence is very powerful and can lead to further changes in thinking, feeling, and behavior—just the kind of ripple effect we are looking for.

How to Build a Treatment Plan:

1. Address safety issues first. This includes creating a safety plan right away if necessary. If you are unsure if one is needed, consult with your supervisor.
2. Start with behavioral interventions, such as creating a schedule of activities, developing real-world skills, building relationships, and getting active, all with the goal of increasing your client's sense of control over his life.
3. Address cognitive elements such as automatic thoughts as they occur. Help your client and her parent change negative automatic talk. If your client has had some success using behavioral interventions, this will be a natural step as

you now have evidence that your client is competent and that things can go well. Help your client and parent use the evidence!

4.	Address faulty thinking such as, "Things need to go well all the time."

5.	Be on the lookout for core beliefs, and use Socratic questioning to address faulty core beliefs.

Building a Treatment Plan for Ronald:

Ronald's treatment plan will need to address the following problems as identified in the diagnostic evaluation and case conceptualization:

1.	Behavioral: aggression, impulsivity, lack of focus (trouble with work completion), hyperactivity.

2.	Emotional: impulsive anger, relational difficulties.

3.	Cognitive: inability to reflect.

Once again, working collaboratively is paramount. If identification of goals is a problem, ask: *If you woke up tomorrow morning and all your problems were gone, what would life be like? How would you notice that all of your problems are gone?*

Ronald's treatment plan for the time being may look like this:

Goal 1: Ronald will accept support/structure in day-to-day life.

Method 1: Client and family will receive education regarding the client's mental health symptoms.

How are you going to know that Ronald and his mother understand how symptoms impact Ronald's functioning in all areas?

Listen for Ronald's self-talk. What does he tell himself about his behavior and his symptoms?

Listen to Ronald's mother when she talks to him about his behavior.

Method 2: Client will accept alternative parent intervention to promote attention and decrease impulsivity.

This is where behavioral skill building happens.

Method 3: Client will accept and practice co-regulation techniques.

This is where relational joy experiences and co-regulation happen.

Note that you can begin treatment with just Goal 1. A treatment plan is a work in progress and should be adjusted as necessary. Ongoing collaboration is the key to successful treatment planning and successful treatment. Work on the treatment plan with the client. Say things like:

- *This is your plan.*

- *Is there anything on your plan that we should change?*

- *What is working for you? What is not working?*

What Are Socratic Questions?

Tolin (2016) defines Socratic questioning as "a way of helping the client arrive at a conclusion by asking carefully worded questions" (p. 159).

Here are some examples of Socratic questions:

- *What does having ADHD mean to you?*
- *How did you come to think about it this way?*
- *Is there another possible way of thinking about it?*
- *How do you know that what you are thinking is true?*

What Socratic questioning is not:

- Getting the client to agree with you ("lip service").
- Here is an example of lip service: "Don't you agree with the fact that . . .?" This is a yes/no question. It does not invite thinking and exploration.
- Manipulating the client to agree with you.
- Getting the client to think exactly like you.

What Socratic questioning is:

Socratic questioning is a process of asking open-ended questions that point your client in the direction of alternative and more realistic ways of thinking about a problem. Socratic questions point in the direction of evidence. It is up to your client to discover the answers to your Socratic questions and the impact that the newly discovered evidence can have on thinking, feelings, and being.

Socratic questioning is not trying to get the client to agree with you. "Don't you agree that . . . ?" is a yes or no question. It does not invite thinking and exploration.

There is no evidence that telling a client or parent what to think and feel is effective. Think about yourself. Most of us want a say. We feel that we are right and, if we are not, it may take us some time to adjust the way we think about something. We consider the evidence, sometimes reluctantly, and we adjust our thinking because we are in conversation with someone who cares about us. Our clients make changes to their ways of thinking and doing things because they discover new meanings and interpretations in conversation with someone who cares about them.

The Golden Rule of Behavioral Skill Building

Listen compassionately. Then ask questions that point the client and parent in the direction of evidence that can change the way they think, feel, and act.

What is the Role of the Worker/Parent/Client Relationship in the Treatment of ADHD?

Beck et al. (1979, p. 27) clearly states that attention must be paid to the therapeutic relationship. CBT is more than a set of techniques. Dobson and Dobson (2017, p. 67) compare the therapeutic relationship to the "vehicle" that drives change. Tolin (2016, p. 11) references Carl Rogers in calling for empathy, genuineness, and unconditional positive regard. However, Tolin (2016) also makes it clear "that the therapeutic relationship is *necessary*, but not *sufficient*" (p. 138).

CBT is focused on what is happening in the here and now. In order to help your client, you have to attend to that. You have to attend to the relationship because it drives the change process. If something is wrong in the relationship between the provider, the parent, and the client (i.e., let's say that the relationship is not collaborative and the client does not trust the therapist), then change is unlikely to take place.

Here is a visual representation of the role of the provider relationship in CBT:

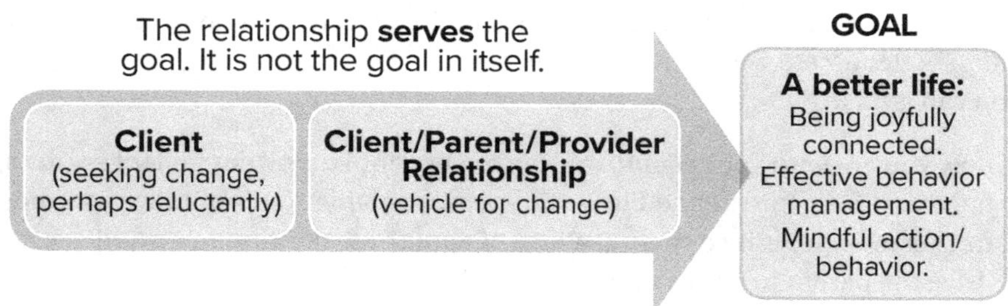

Figure 21

Being Attuned: Building Affect Regulation in the Therapeutic Relationship

Being attuned to your client's emotional state is just as important in CBT as it is in any other form of therapy. Attunement builds the therapeutic relationship.

If your client and his parent feel that you are attuned, then they are much more likely to trust you. But attunement alone is not enough in CBT. Let's look at the cognitive triad again and how attunement plays a role:

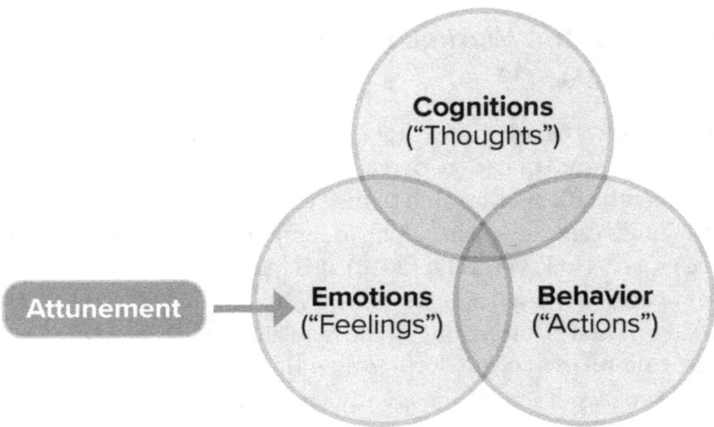

Figure 22

Attunement puts you in touch with your client's emotional state. Attunement also puts the caregiver in touch with the child's emotional state. You (and/or the parent) can then better assess what drives behavior.

You can adjust:

- how you are with your client: You can lower your voice if your client seems agitated and feels threatened but is still unaware of this. You can move your body further away to reduce client feelings of panic or fear. Attunement will also drive the parent to adjust their way of being with the client;

- what you do with your client: You can turn on soft music to help your client increase mindful decision making and problem solving. The parent can do the same; and

- what you say to your client and how you say it: You can ask your client if she is feeling threatened or accepted, and the parent can do the same.

When you are attuning, you are working with the emotional component of the cognitive triad.

Attunement by itself does not "fix" anything. It helps your client and the parent feel more comfortable. If they feel more comfortable and trust that you are attuned with them and can handle the complex and intense emotions they are feeling, then they are much more willing and able to move into work within the cognitive and behavioral components of the cognitive triad. Attunement is an important part of the helping relationship. It is also an important part of the relationship between parents and children.

Children and adolescents with ADHD can be difficult to attune with. And once we, or parents, attune with them, we may not like what we feel with them. It is important that providers and parents are or become able to recognize and sit with the complex emotional states children are in.

What About Co-Regulation?

Co-regulation is a term coined by Allan Schore (2008), the founder of Modern Attachment Theory. Co-regulation is not a CBT term or technique, but understanding it can be helpful when using CBT.

Co-regulation happens when you, the provider, attune with your client. This attunement is initially a right-brain-to-right-brain process, meaning that it happens naturally. Once you are attuned with your client and sense that he is emotionally dysregulated and may need help with affect regulation, you can help him regulate.

Co-regulation is not a verbal process, but it involves a decision on your part, namely to help your client regulate. You may want to breathe slower, relax your body, shift your gaze, or change the tone of your voice. Your state of mind (and body) can have an impact on your client's state of mind and body. You can help your client down-regulate an intense affective state using co-regulation.

Co-regulation can be especially helpful when working with children and adolescents with ADHD. These children are biologically driven to physical or inner restlessness. Co-regulation can help these children experience a different way of being. They can, for a moment, experience stillness. The parent (or you) can, for a moment, experience being in motion.

Co-regulatory processes happen in therapeutic and other relationships all the time. You may want to use co-regulation when your client is not ready or able to use words to regulate intense affective states (perhaps because no one has modeled this effectively for him).

How does co-regulation fit into the cognitive triad of CBT?

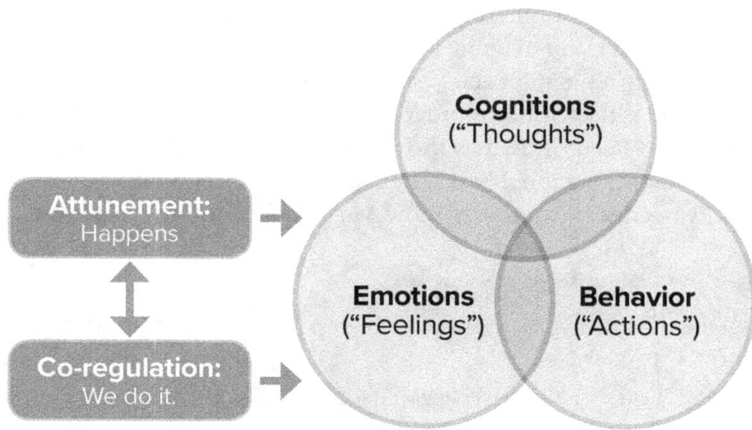

Figure 23

Co-regulation can be helpful when your client is stuck in an unregulated and intense affective state and is unable to reflect on his emotions.

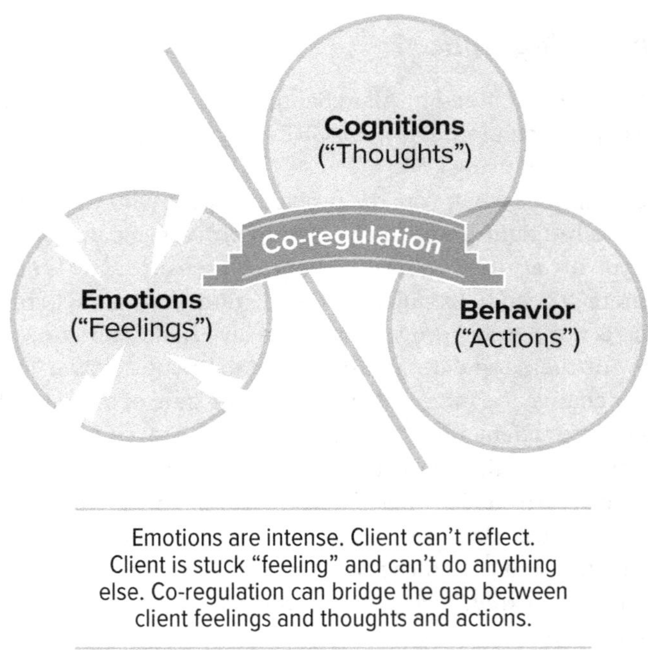

Emotions are intense. Client can't reflect.
Client is stuck "feeling" and can't do anything
else. Co-regulation can bridge the gap between
client feelings and thoughts and actions.

Figure 24

Co-regulation builds the bridge from the emotional component of the cognitive triad to the cognitive and behavioral components. When your client is stuck in an emotional state, unable to reflect on it in any way, co-regulation helps him build a connection by moving the emotional part of the cognitive triad back into the triad: You can now do CBT instead of being stuck on work related to feelings only. You could also say that co-regulation gets your client ready to do CBT.

Once your client is back into a more regulated and balanced affective state, she can think, act, and reflect. Ultimately the experience of co-regulation is meant to implicitly teach self-regulation. If your client already self-regulates well, co-regulation is not really needed. Attunement, however, should continue to happen.

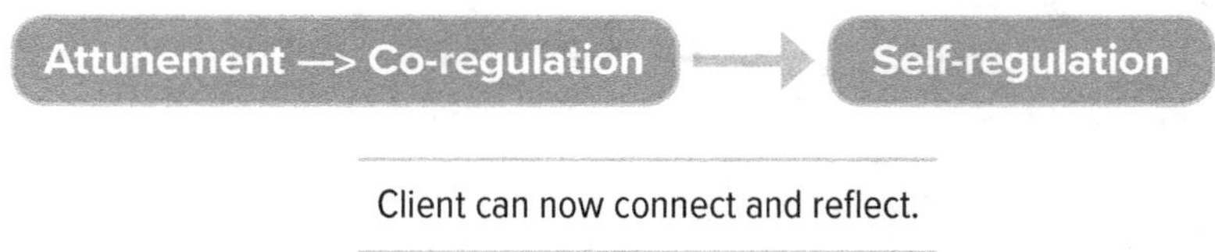

Client can now connect and reflect.

Figure 25

Just like attunement, co-regulation is used in the service of accessing the full cognitive triad with your client. When you are doing CBT, co-regulation is not enough. It is a vehicle for change.

You can use co-regulation with your client and his parents. Once the parent "gets" it, you can provide psychoeducation about the process of co-regulation. The parent can then use co-regulation with their child. This makes sense. You are only with the client for a limited amount of time weekly, perhaps an hour or two. If the parent can master co-regulation, your client can learn that emotional states can be regulated much quicker because the parent is there much of the time. Teachers can also be helpful.

Children and adolescents with ADHD are often overwhelmed by their feelings. They struggle with problem solving and make impulsive decisions, leading to difficult situations with peers and adults. When these children get in trouble, parents can become emotionally reactive and make things worse, or they can help the child regulate by using co-regulation. Parents will have an impact on their children's emotions either way. It's best to go with positive co-regulation!

Behavioral Training, CBT Techniques, and CBT Structure

Sometimes CBT can seem a bit formulaic to a therapist. This can happen when you think of it as a set of rules and techniques. You may think that you have to use an automatic thought record if you are doing CBT with a client. Or you may rigidly stick to an established structure for a session when what is needed is some flexibility and attunement.

Tolin (2016, p. 9) uses the analogy of being a chef vs. being a cook. When you are doing behavioral training, be a chef. Add your own flavor. Serve what the client is likely going to eat. But also serve something that stretches the client's palate. This is how your client grows.

Keep in mind that you can use many kinds of techniques when doing behavioral skill building—as long as you are working with your client on changing cognitions, emotions, and behavior to better fit the reality your client is facing.

Still, there are ways in which CBT and behavioral skill building are different from other forms of therapy. CBT and behavioral skill building are more directive and structured than other forms of treatment (such as interpersonal psychotherapy). Treatment has a structure. There are things to be learned. Every session has a structure. You can be flexible. But when you are being flexible, you are very much aware that you are doing this and why you are doing this. To stick with the culinary analogy: There is a menu. The menu can vary, but there is always a menu.

CBT creates a structure and a plan for your client. The message is: *There is a way out of the chaos ADHD can bring. I can teach you the steps you need to take.*

Creating Structure

Treatment has a structure: As Tolin (2016) puts it: "CBT tends to not be a forever, Woody Allen–style treatment" (p. 8). The same is true for behavioral parent training.

Treatment is focused on the collaboratively established goals, not on other things that come up in the course of treatment/the course of a session. This does not mean that treatment goals can't be revised if necessary. If a client develops suicidal ideation while in treatment, clearly the treatment plan needs to be revisited and revised.

As client problems vary, so does length of treatment. Dobson and Dobson (2017) reference a 12–16 session length.

Community Mental Health Practice Alert

Clients in a Community Mental Health setting often present with a multiplicity of symptoms and problems. Our clients are often dually diagnosed. And they are often also physically ill. They may have ADHD and anxiety. They may have lifelong exposure to toxic stress. At OhioGuidestone, more than 55% of our clients have an ACEs score of 4 or more, putting them at much higher risk for a variety of physical and mental health problems. What this means is that your client may have ADHD and asthma. They may also struggle with an addiction that is diagnosed or undiagnosed.

If your client struggles with more than one mental health problem and additional physical and environmental issues, it unlikely that treatment duration will fall within in 12- to 16-week range.

It is important, however, to keep in mind and to discuss with your client and the parent that treatment has a course: There is a beginning and an end. The goal of treatment is to resolve the mental health issues that brought your client into treatment. You, the parent, and your client should be aware where you are in the treatment. Are you just beginning? Are you in the midst of it? Or are you almost done? You should frequently discuss this.

Once again, creating structure is important. When using CBT, length of treatment can vary depending on the complexity of symptoms and problems. Structure, however, is a constant.

Creating Structure When Discussing Course and Length of Treatment

You can use a simple visual aid like the figure below to discuss the course and possible length of treatment with your client.

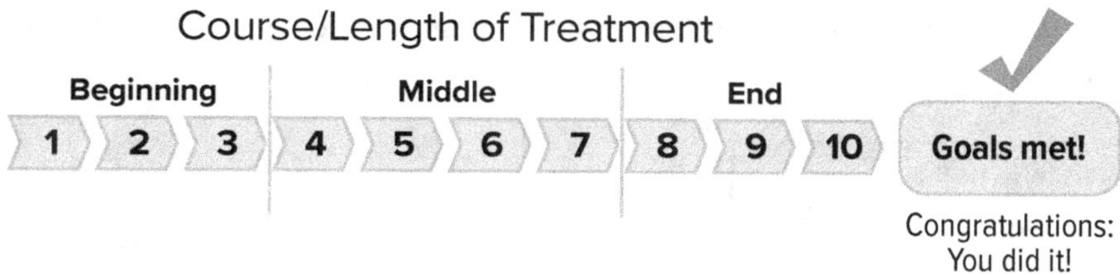

Figure 26

Creating Structure for Each Session

Here is an example of how you can structure a session with your client:

- **Check-In:** This is brief, perhaps five minutes. Is there anything new that is relevant to treatment? Have ADHD symptoms gotten better, worse, or remained the same?

- **Identify Today's Tasks:** Again, this is brief. Identify what needs to be done today. Be collaborative about this. If your client is unfocused and wants to add things that are not relevant to treatment, it is OK to be directive and refer to treatment goals. If new things have come up, help the client evaluate how they fit into treatment and rate how important it is to address them right now. Will they detour treatment or move the client forward?

- **Homework Review:** Homework is an integral component of CBT. Homework brings the content of therapy into the real world. This is where skills will need to be practiced and new ways of thinking, feeling, and acting can be tried. Celebrate successes, even the small ones, and problem-solve about things that did not work.

- **Work on Today's Tasks:** This is the "meat" of your session. Be sure to anchor your work in the treatment plan and the cognitive triad. This is where your behavioral, emotional, or cognitive work takes place.

- **Summarize the Work:** You are the "guide" through treatment and through each session. Summarize periodically what you are talking about and how it fits into treatment progress.

- **Identify New Homework:** New homework can originate from the homework review at the beginning of the session and/or today's tasks. You and the client can identify what needs practice. Be sure that homework can realistically be accomplished.

- **Closing:** Summarize session takeaways. Clarification of questions. Feedback about session.

Adapted from Persons, Davidson and Tompkins (2001), Essential Components of Cognitive Behavioral Therapy for Depression. Washington, DC: APA.

Here is a simplified version to keep handy for your client as you travel through each session:

Session Structure
1. Check-In
2. Identify Today's Tasks
3. Homework Review
4. Work on Today's Tasks
5. Summarize the Work
6. Identify New Homework
7. Closing

Figure 27

Essential Techniques

Remember, behavioral skill building in the context of CBT can borrow techniques from a variety of evidence-based forms of therapy, such as dialectical behavior therapy (DBT) or acceptance and commitment therapy (ACT). There are, however, a few essential intervention components you should use.

Psychoeducation

Dobson and Dobson (2017) define psychoeducation as "the provision of information about relevant psychological principles and knowledge" (p. 96). Psychoeducation takes place throughout the course of treatment. At the beginning of treatment, you should provide your client with appropriate information about:

- ADHD: Symptoms and evidence-based treatment
- Behavioral skill building 101: Go over the cognitive triad (but don't call it that). It is important that the parent understand that he or she will be the major change agent in the child's life. You will be giving the parent tools to use. The client will be working on thoughts, feelings, and behaviors and understanding that these are connected. You can also determine together where the client is most willing and able to start work. For many of our clients, behavioral work is the most accessible.

- Explain that treatment is collaborative, structured, focused, and present-oriented.

- Explain that other areas of the client's life may need attention, such as the school environment and peer relationships. Explain that treatment will be designed to address all areas of need.

- Resources: Periodically assess what your client needs. Does he need access to an advocacy or support group? Legal assistance? Job training? Resource-building is an important aspect of CBT because increased access to resources gives your client opportunities to act. As ADHD can lead to frantic and ineffective action or inaction, helping your client build a roadmap can be life-changing.

- Explain that a community mental health worker will be working on the behavior skill-building component with the parent, child, and school, and a therapist will work with the child and parent on emotional and relational problems related to the client's ADHD symptoms.

Socratic Questioning

Socratic questioning is a process of asking open-ended questions that point your client in the direction of alternative and more realistic ways of thinking about a problem. Socratic questions point in the direction of evidence. It is up to your client to discover the answers to your Socratic questions and the impact that the newly discovered evidence can have on thinking, feeling, and acting. Remember telling your client the answers to the questions you are asking is not effective. When using behavioral skill building, you should be asking a lot of Socratic questions. As tempting as it may be to give the parent and the client answers, they would be your answers, not theirs.

Homework

Tolin (2016, p. 154) identifies the following kinds of homework:

- **Reading assignments** tailored to the client's and parent's specific needs and abilities.

  - This can be tricky for our clients. Assess your client's ability to take in written information. Keep it simple. Use handouts that contain visual representations of the information you want him to review. Reading assignments are, of course, a form of psychoeducation. They are also designed to empower and change the way your client thinks about himself, others, and the world.

- **Monitoring**

  - You can create simple checklists to help your client and parent monitor problematic behaviors and thoughts. Be sure to explain that monitoring is designed to establish a baseline and determine treatment needs. Parents of young children should help them make the check marks on the monitoring chart. Here is what a simple monitoring chart could look like:

	Mon	Tue	Wed	Thu	Fri	Sat	Sun
Complete 30 minutes of home-work							
Hours of TV							

Figure 28

- You can use this chart over the course of several weeks to monitor decreased time video gaming (if this is a goal). Honesty, of course, is key to monitoring. Be sure that you collaborate with your client and parent on a realistic goal and a charting system that feels right. Be sure to explain to the parent that the monitoring chart cannot be used in a punitive way. There should be no threats like: "If you don't do this for me, I will not give you a check mark."

Learning and Practicing New Behaviors

Skill Building

New skills will have to be learned together in session, then practiced in the real world. In other words: It is easier to talk about a new skill/new behavior than to engage in it. You should explain that there is no such thing as failure when practicing a new skill or behavior. Each "mistake" will guide both of you to make changes and refine the work, and to examine negative automatic thoughts. Each perceived mistake is a new learning opportunity and guides the way you create behavioral change together.

Behavior Changes

Your client with ADHD may need specific behavior changes. You may want to assign a specific behavior that you want your client to increase. It is a good idea to use a self-monitoring chart to track the new behavior. Be sure to keep it simple and set realistic goals. Instead of asking your client to always respond to questions in a polite way, ask him to practice taking three deep breaths before answering a question three times per day. Here is a simple chart to monitor behavior change:

	Mon	Tue	Wed	Thu	Fri	Sat	Sun
Took 3 deep breaths before acting X							

Figure 29

By setting a realistic goal, you are making sure your client can be successful now. This is especially important because your client may have become used to failure or may perceive himself as a failure. Celebrate the small successes, then raise the bar.

If you set the bar too high you run the risk of increasing his anxiety and perhaps even having him drop out of treatment. If you set the bar too low, your client is not learning anything. The key is to collaborate with your client and parent on defining just the right amount of behavior change.

Behavioral Changes

Because ADHD drives your client to impulsively act, she will have to learn a new way of acting: deliberate and planful action.

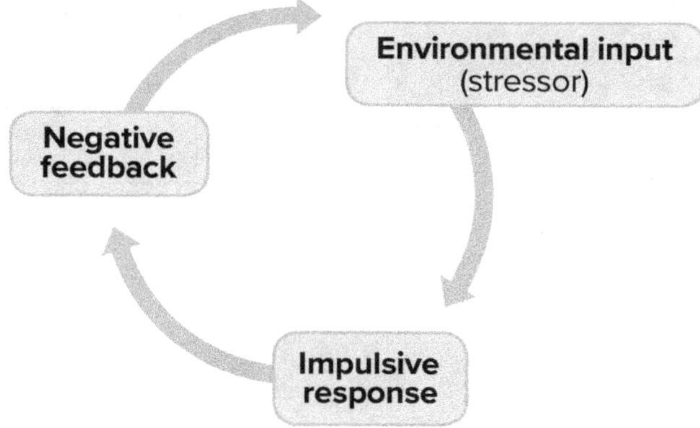

Figure 30

Provide psychoeducation to your client and parent about this cycle. Explain that just by changing one part, the whole cycle can begin to change. Learning to take time with problem solving and decision making can really make a difference!

The following figure shows what the cycle of behavioral change will look like:

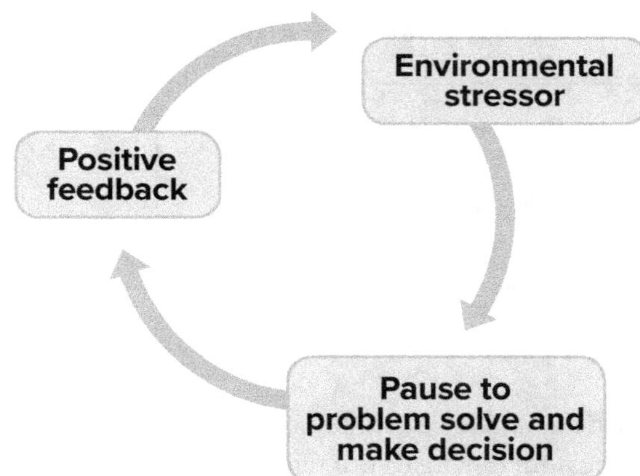

Figure 31: The cycle of behavioral change.

Tolin (2016, pp. 224-226) outlines the benefits of activity scheduling and explains that it goes hand-in-hand with self-monitoring. While it is good to be ambitious about behavioral changes and activity scheduling, it is equally important to be realistic. You are teaching your client and parent to create achievable and realistic behavioral goals.

Here is a simple activity schedule you can use with clients. You may have to help the parent and client be realistic about what can be scheduled. Because children with ADHD may have lots of plans, they may need to be taught to understand that things take time. They also need to understand that parents may not have the same amount of energy they have.

	Mon	Tue	Wed	Thu	Fri	Sat	Sun
Morning							
Afternoon							
Evening							

Figure 32

Cognitive Restructuring

Let's take another look at the role of thoughts:

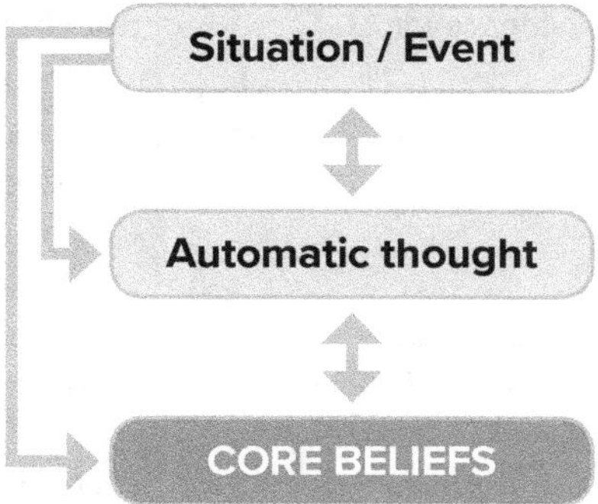

Figure 33: Note that core beliefs are much harder to identify than automatic thoughts (AT's). AT's just appear, we do not have to ask for them. Because they appear so often, they are easier to bring into conscious awareness.

Negative and faulty core beliefs can create a negative feedback loop in your client's life. But they can be difficult to uncover. Core beliefs are triggered by a situation or event. Once a core belief is triggered, it sends out its "messengers"—those pesky negative automatic thoughts.

Negative automatic thoughts are much easier to address because they show up all the time. They may even "bug" your client.

Here are some examples of automatic thoughts:

- "I always mess everything up."

- "No matter what, I will be in trouble."

- "No use trying."

- "My teacher hates me."

- "My mom hates me."

Automatic thoughts can be examined. In CBT, you and your client are looking for evidence for and against the truth of the automatic thought.

Here is what this would look like:

A situation or event triggers a negative automatic thought, which in turn affects the way your client feels. But what if the thought is just the brain letting off some steam? When you have ADHD, your brain may let off a lot of steam. You may have a lot of thoughts, a lot more than most people, and it may be difficult to understand which thought is relevant and important at the moment. Parents can help their children with this sorting process. It's good to be systematic about this. Parents can ask:

- "How does this thought fit into what is happening and important right now?"

- "How can this thought be useful with making good decisions right now?"

- "What kind of thought is this?"

- "What thoughts do I need to put aside?"
- "What thoughts are just there, but not important?"

Automatic Thought (AT)	Evidence for AT	Evidence against AT
I mess everything up.	Argument with teacher.	• I went to school today. • Passed spelling test. • Great recess! • . . .
She hates me.	She is mad at me about the thing I said.	• We talked. • We make each other laugh. • She gave me a hug. • . . .
I am failing.	Failed spelling test.	• Just got into district art show. • Passing grades, even in spelling. • . . .

Figure 34

Notice that if left unchecked, each of the automatic thoughts outlined above has the potential to deteriorate emotions and behavior even further.

A blank version for you to use with your clients can be found in the appendix.

Keep in mind that automatic thoughts can be relentless. Once you have examined them with your client, it is OK to use humor when one shows up. You can talk to an automatic thought! Here is an example:

> *Hello there. There you are again, trying to trick me. Not going to happen. You, my uninvited friend, are just a brain fart. Stinky and unpleasant. I am going to leave you now and think better thoughts. Goodbye!*

Talking to the automatic thought in this way creates distance from it. It is far easier to examine a faulty thought from a distance!

Why do you want your client to examine automatic thoughts?

Automatic thoughts create feelings. If your client can dismiss those faulty automatic thoughts, then he can begin to let go of the feelings based on those thoughts.

If you and your client run into a set of automatic thoughts with a similar theme, you are probably onto a core belief. Core beliefs, too, can be examined for their truthfulness.

Interventions

Psychoeducation and Behavioral Interventions (TBS and PSR)

The following interventions are designed to be delivered in the form of therapeutic behavioral services (TBS) and psychosocial rehabilitation (PSR) by nonlicensed, qualified mental health providers.

INTERVENTION 1

Setting the Stage

This intervention is designed to facilitate your initial connection with the client and the caretaker. When you arrive at the home, the parent will likely have a number of urgent issues or complaints. The child is likely to feel afraid about what will happen in the meeting, believing that he is in trouble. And the parent may think that you are judging her parenting skills and blaming her for the child's behavior problems. Keep in mind that because there is a child with ADHD in the home, the parent is likely stressed and exhausted. Additionally, there may be many disruptions related to symptoms in the session. You will have to be patient.

Target skill: Accept support and structure.

Method: Client and the family will receive education regarding the client's mental health symptoms.

What you will need: ADHD fact sheet. Marker. Fidget items. Small ball to throw back and forth. Jenga blocks. Paper and drawing tools. Index card.

1. Begin with empathy. Thank the parent and the child for inviting you into their home. Explain that even though an assessment has already been completed, you would like to hear from them what is going well in the home and what is not.

2. Introduce today's task: understanding how symptoms and behaviors relate.

3. Work on today's task: Ask the parent:

   - *What does your child do that you love?*

   - *What do you love about the way your child is? What is just wonderful about your child?*

   - *What is your child doing that is tough for the both of you?*

   It's best to use the name of the child when asking about him. Be sure to make eye contact with both parent and child while the parent is talking.

4. Ask the child:

   - *What does your mom/dad/caretaker do that you love?*

   - *What do you love about the way your mom/dad/caretaker is? What is just wonderful about them?*

   - *What is your mom/dad/caretaker doing that is tough for the both of you?*

5. When the child struggles with fidgeting, simply hand the child an item to use for fidgeting. Say:

   - *I understand that you just need to move. Here, take this.*

   - *You can move this item around in your hands.*

   - *We can pass this item back and forth.*

   - *Only one rule: No throwing!*

6. Listen and validate parent and client feelings of frustration. You can simply say:

   - *I understand that . . .*

   - *It seems like . . .*

   - *It's OK to be frustrated with each other.*

7. Explain that there is hope and help. You can say:

   - *ADHD is very treatable.*

   - *It's not your fault.*

   - *It's biology. It's the brain.*

   - *We can make this better.*

8. Also explain that there is no miracle cure. A child with ADHD will continue to be a more active child. The key will be to help the child manage ADHD-related behaviors. Be sure to explain that ADHD-related behaviors are an expression of symptoms. You can say:

   - *It's biology.*

   - *You are not causing this.*

   - *Your child is not doing this on purpose or doing this do you.*

9. You can give parents the Centers for Disease Control and Prevention ADHD fact sheet (see References for URL).

10. Check in with the child. Make sure she understands that you are not here to blame, but rather to help.

11. Take out the Jenga blocks. Ask the child to build a tower any way he wants. Ask the parent to just sit and observe, not to intervene. When the child is done, compliment him on the work. Brainstorm together:

    - *What went well during the building process?*

    - *Was there frustration? If there was, how did the child handle it?*

    - *How did the child make decisions? Were some made too quickly?*

    If the child clearly demonstrated symptoms of ADHD during the building process, name them. Validate the child's and parent's symptoms of frustration. Relate difficulties to ADHD symptoms and reframe these difficulties as expressions of symptoms. Here is an example of what you could say:

    > *I noticed that you got really frustrated when the tower fell over again, that you just did not know what to do with that feeling and that it was difficult to start over. Many children with ADHD have these same kinds of difficulties. It's just a part of having ADHD. We can work with this!*

12. Summarize what you have done so far: You have learned what parent and child appreciate about each other and how ADHD symptoms can make life difficult. You have provided psychoeducation about ADHD—specifically,

ADHD is a biological illness, not a personal fault. You have used Jenga blocks to demonstrate how symptoms can impact everyday functioning.

13. Assign homework: Give the child and the parent each the following index card:

Figure 36

Ask them to carry this card and take it out when they notice an ADHD-related behavior. Ask the parent to make a note of the behavior on the back of the card. Be sure to explain that the purpose of the homework is to notice symptoms, not to be punitive about them! Ask the parent to bring the index card back to the next session.

14. Closing. Be encouraging when you leave. You can say this:

- *We can tackle this together.*
- *These are symptoms.*
- *Symptoms don't have to boss you around.*
- *You can take charge!*

INTERVENTION 2

Understanding Treatment

This intervention is designed to help the parent and the client understand treatment choices. You are providing psychoeducation about evidence-based treatments for ADHD. Specifically, you will help the parent understand the need to use effective behavior management and skill building. You will also explain that medication management has been found to be effective for the treatment of ADHD in children, especially when used in combination with behavior management. It is important, however, to emphasize that you are not *recommending that the child take medication.* Only a medical provider can do so. You can, however, help the parent determine whether to make an appointment with the child's medical provider and discuss medication.

If the child is younger, it is not necessary for her to be present during this session. If she is present, adapt the content to include her.

Target skill: Reduce hyperactivity, inattention, and impulsivity.

Method: Client and her family will receive education regarding her mental health symptoms.

What you will need: Poster board and marker. Paper. Symptom-intensity scale.

1. Begin with empathy. Welcome the parent and the client (if present).

2. Identify today's task: learning about ADHD symptoms, related behaviors, and treatment.

   - *Today we are going to talk about what works for managing ADHD symptoms.*

   - *Think of this as choosing from a menu of options.*

   - *What you choose is your decision.*

   - *I can tell you what works.*

3. Review last week's homework. Ask the parent (and the client, if present) to take out their lightbulb index cards. Help them review how they used the cards. Ask:

   - *Did you take your index card out last week?*

   - *What kinds of "aha" moments did you have?*

   - *Which behaviors were you able to recognize as symptoms?*

   - *How did your feelings about those behaviors change once you thought of them as symptoms?*

   - *Did you react differently toward your child/parent once you identified a behavior as ADHD-related?*

Provide positive feedback for every behavior the parent/child accurately identifies as ADHD-related. You are modeling an important component of behavior management: positive reinforcement.

4. Work on today's task. Begin by asking how "big" or disruptive the symptoms are. If the child's parent is present, you can use the symptom intensity scale to gauge the intensity of the child's symptoms:

Figure 37

In essence, you want to find out how intense the child's problem behaviors are and how much disruption they cause. If the parent gets daily calls from school about the child's behavior, or if the child often uses physical aggression, you are most certainly at 8 or above.

If the parent is stressed out by the child's behavior but feels some understanding of how to help the child manage, then you are looking at the middle range.

If the child is present, you can ask: *How big are your symptoms?* Then hold a hand close to the floor (just a few things are bothersome, but it's not much of a problem); then hold your hand at about hip height (things are quite bothersome and cause quite a few problems); then hold your hand above your head (things are out of control, the child gets in trouble all the time).

5. Lay out the treatment options. Use a poster board. It could look like this:

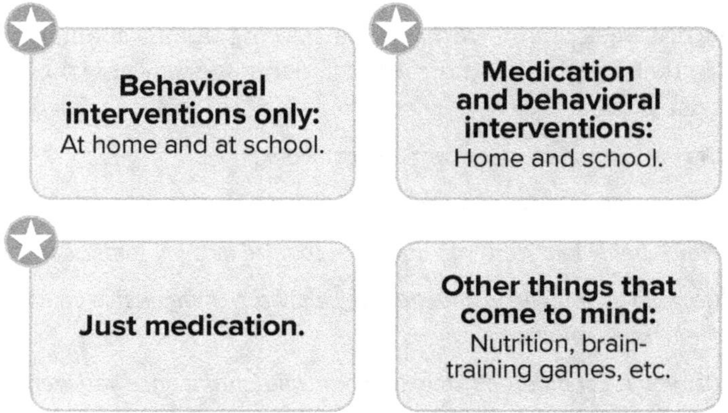

Figure 38

Explain that evidence-based treatment options are marked by a star. You can also explain that what is right for a child varies case by case. When it comes to "treatments" that are not proven, you can say:

- *There is nothing wrong with eating right. In fact, eating right is helpful for all of us.*

- *It is unlikely that cutting out sugar will cure the child's ADHD.*

Advise the parent to discuss any nutritional changes with the child's pediatrician.

Explain that brain-training programs can be fun and that children and adults can often improve their scores, but that better scores are not proven to translate into improved behavior and better functioning in the real world.

Explain that lifestyle changes, such as more outdoor playtime, can be helpful, especially if the parent participates and thus builds a better relationship with the child.

If the parent and/or the child indicate that the behaviors are out of control and unmanageable, recommend a referral to a medical provider for a medication assessment. If the child is also suffering from other mental health issues, recommend that the child is seen by a child psychiatrist.

6. Acknowledge that decisions about treatment can be difficult and may take some time. Encourage the parent to look at the whole picture. Ask:

    - *If nothing changes, what could happen?*

    - *What changes do you want to see?*

    - *What has to change quickly?*

    - *What role do you think you need to and want to play?*

7. Summarize what you have done so far: You have gauged the child's level of symptoms and looked at treatment options.

8. Assign homework: Ask the parent to think things over and make a treatment choice decision. Also explain that the parent can change her mind about treatment option. Here is an example:

    - *After initially agreeing to a psychiatric evaluation for the child, the parent decides that she wants to try behavior therapy only.*

    - *After a couple of weeks, the parent changes her mind again and wants to add medication to treat ADHD symptoms.*

    - *Of course, this is OK! It simply reflects the parent's process of coming to grips with the child's symptoms and the need for treatment.*

9. Closing. Conclude the session by saying:

    - *There are options for you and your child.*

    - *Pick what you are comfortable with.*

    - *Change is possible!*

INTERVENTION 3

Beginning Treatment

This intervention is designed to jump into the nitty-gritty of behavior management. If your client's parent chose medication management only, then you have already stepped back, explaining that the child can return to treatment should further treatment needs arise.

Target skill: Accept support and structure in day-to-day life.

Method: Client will accept immediate feedback and consequences for their behavior.

What you will need: Markers. Poster board.

1. Begin with empathy. Welcome your client and the parent. Ask: *How was your week? What went well? What did not go well?*

   Be sure to provide positive feedback and model enthusiasm for all the little things that went well. Give positive feedback equally to the client and to the parent. You can say:

   - *Wow.*

   - *That's great.*

   - *Amazing job.*

2. Identify today's task: building support and structure for the client.

3. Review last week's homework: In this case, briefly review the treatment decision the parent has made. As you are providing TBS or PSR in the form of Child Regulatory Skill Development, you will need to explain what this is and how it works. You can say:

   - *Using behavior management is a great decision.*

   - *Behavior management works.*

   - *You, the parent, are here all the time.*

   - *What works best for behavior management is positive reinforcement. This is what we will talk about today.*

4. Work on today's task. Provide psychoeducation about behavior management. Here is what you can say:

   You, the parent, know your child best. And you are also here a lot more than I am. Behavior management teaches you the skills to help your child manage his behavior. You are your child's coach.

   ADHD is a biological, brain-based disorder. But this does not mean that your child can't learn to manage behaviors related to symptoms. You are your child's coach and teacher. Behavior management is very much about cheering your child on when he does the right thing.

5. Take out the poster board and help parent and child create a list of ways in which the parent can provide positive reinforcement for appropriate behaviors. Be sure to include lots of things the child is interested in. Keep "rewards" for positive behavior relational. Material rewards often cause problems later on, such as the child demanding a reward they have not earned.

Here is a form you can use for the poster board:

<table>
<tr><td>A job well done deserves a:</td></tr>
<tr><td>Hug
Wow!
Amazing!
High Five
To the park with mom . . .
. . .</td></tr>
</table>

Figure 39

Keep filling the poster board with ideas, and simultaneously practice how to use positive reinforcement. Give high-fives every time the child comes up with an idea! If the child is interested, he can decorate or illustrate the chart.

6. Respond to objections to the idea of positive reinforcement by saying:

- *We all do better when we are praised for what we do right.*

- *Research tells us that we need to support behaviors we want to see more.*

- *Positive reinforcement supports positive behaviors. It also builds positive relationships.*

- *When your child has a positive relationship with you, he is more likely to behave well. It's a win/win.*

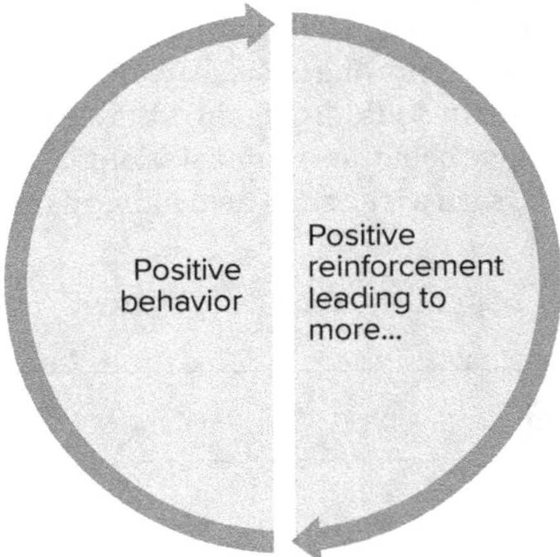

Figure 40

7. Frequently, the parent will ask what to do if the child misbehaves. Coach the parent to do the following.

   - *If your child misbehaves, ignore the behavior. It is not necessary to address every mistake your child makes. We all make mistakes.*

   - *As soon as your child does something right, no matter how little, provide positive reinforcement. This changes the tone of the conversation.*

   - *If the child continues to misbehave, ask: What do you need? Find out if the misbehavior is an expression of need to connect with the parent. If it is, respond to the need if you can. If you can't respond right there and then, tell the child when you can. Keep in mind that children with ADHD struggle with impatience.*

   - *If the behavior is dangerous, assist the child with stopping the behavior. Here are some examples of dangerous behaviors:*

     - *Running into the road.*

     - *Waving a knife at someone.*

     - *Pushing a sibling down the stairs.*

   Here are some examples of behaviors that seem dangerous to adults but are not actually dangerous: refusing to wear a coat when it is cold (coat can be carried); saying a bad word; sticking out tongue; eating sweets after dinner; refusing to brush teeth. Reiterate the importance of ignoring behaviors that are not actually dangerous in order to avoid power struggles.

8. Review what you have done so far: You have explained how positive reinforcement works. You have created a list of positive reinforcers with input from the parent and client. You have explained the type of behaviors that can be ignored in order to avoid a power struggle.

9. Assign homework: Ask the parent and client to keep the poster board in a prominent place at home. Ask them to provide positive reinforcement to each other when they do something good and right, no matter how small.

10. Closing. Provide positive reinforcement about today's interactions. Say:

    - *You did great.*

    - *I loved your questions. They were great questions.*

    - *You also had great ideas.*

    Give the parent and the child a high-five to model positive reinforcement.

INTERVENTION 4

Bumps in the Road

This intervention is designed to address the real-life bumps in the road and to help the parent understand and manage the balance between positive reinforcement, ignoring behaviors that are annoying but not dangerous, and the careful use of consequences and punishment. Negative consequences and punishment often become meaningless and ineffective through overuse.

Target skill: Accept support and structure in daily life.

Method: Client will accept immediate feedback and consequences for behavior.

What you will need: Poster board and markers. Index cards.

1. Begin with empathy. Welcome your client and the parent with a smile. Tell them how proud you are of them for returning to treatment.

2. Identify today's task: working with ADHD-related behavior problems as they happen.

3. Review last week's homework. Ask:

    - *Where is the poster board right now?*

    - *How often did you look at it?*

    - *Which reinforcers did you use a lot? And why?*

    - *Which reinforcers did you not use? And how come?*

    - *Should we add some reinforcers? What should we add? If there is something to add, write it on an index card, then give it to the parent to add to the poster board.*

    Encourage the parent and child to celebrate each day that includes positive reinforcers. Offer some ideas for celebrating:

    - *Read a book together.*

    - *Do a happy dance.*

    - *Make an announcement to the entire family about the great day. Or call other family members to announce how well the day went.*

    - *Blow a kiss to each other.*

4. Work on today's task: dealing with the bumps in the road. You can say this:

    Nobody is perfect. Every once in a while you will do something that hurts someone else. Perhaps you are having a very bad day. Let's find out what should happen then.

5. Show the parent how behavior management works best, using the following image:

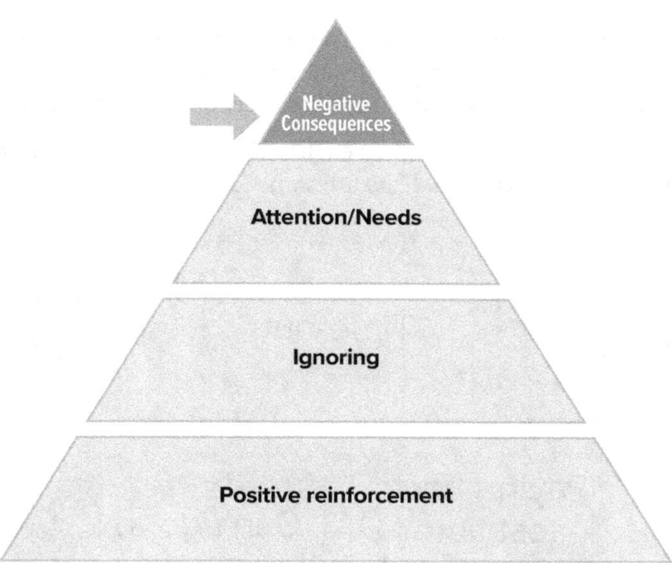

Figure 41

Point out to the parent that negative consequences are a very small component of discipline, the last resort for behaviors that are dangerous or extremely hurtful.

6. Brainstorm with parent and client: What falls in this category? Create a list of behaviors that warrant negative consequences. Listen for behaviors that do not really belong on the list, as many parents struggle with differentiating between annoying and disrespectful behaviors and dangerous ones. Use the pyramid to help the parent sort. Ask:

   - *Who is getting hurt?*

   - *What kind of hurt is it?*

7. Be sure to connect the need for negative consequences with the family value system. You can say:

   - *Hurting others is not acceptable because they are people, just like you and me.*

   - *In this house we love and treasure each other. That's why we can't hurt each other.*

   - *Hurting only creates more hurting. This is easy to explain. When a child hits another child, the other child may hit back. More and more people get hurt.*

   - *In this family we stop the hurt.*

   - *We do get angry.*

   - *But we don't hurt each other.*

8. Once you have determined what warrants a negative consequence, create a list of five that would work for this family. Be sure that the child has input. If the child has input, she is more likely to accept the consequence.

9. Take out five index cards and on each, write one negative consequence that parent and child agree on. Here are some ideas:

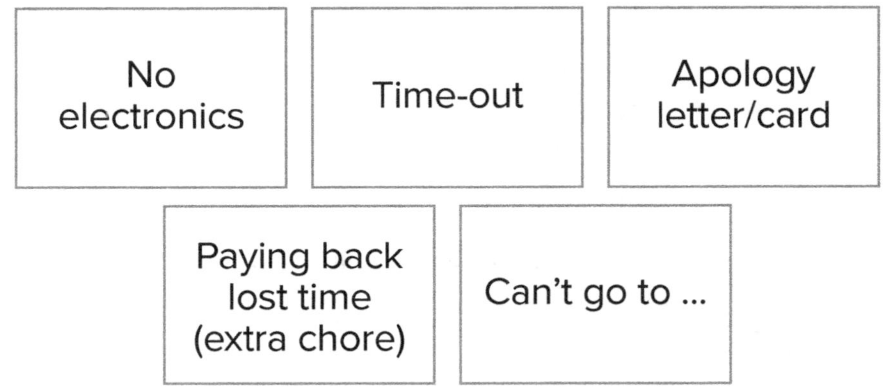

Figure 42

Every family will have to choose their own consequences. Generic consequences often do not work. Additionally, educate the parent about the need for the consequence to follow the dangerous behavior as closely as possible. You can explain it like this:

> *Your child with **ADHD** already struggles with making some connections. If you give the child a time-out on Sunday for something he did on Thursday, he is not going to be able to make the connection. Too much time has passed.*

10. Role model, then role play how to hand out a consequence. Role model a calm voice when giving and accepting a consequence, then ask parent and client to role play giving and accepting a consequence. Immediately provide positive feedback for any aspect of the role play that went well.

11. Summarize what you have done so far: You have explained that positive reinforcement should be used often and with enthusiasm. You have explained that negative consequences should be used sparingly and only when dangerous or hurtful behavior is involved. You have identified what those behaviors are, and the family has agreed upon a set of consequences.

12. Assign homework. Ask the parent to:

   - *continue to use positive reinforcement often and enthusiastically throughout the day;*

   - *continue to ignore misbehavior that is not dangerous;*

- *provide attention to the client when possible. Perhaps the client needs an activity to distract him; and*

- *use a negative consequence only when hurtful or dangerous behavior is used (send the list of such behaviors home with the parent). Give the parent an index card to log the use of negative consequences. Ask the parent to bring the index card to the next meeting.*

13. Closing. Say:

Keep using those hugs and high-fives. They keep you connected and reinforce good behavior. Now let's also practice how to give and accept a consequence.

You can even say:

Let's see if a consequence is even needed this week. If it is, this is perfectly fine. If no consequence is needed, great!

INTERVENTION 5

The Distraction Box

This intervention is designed to further drive understanding of the behavior management pyramid. There may be times when positive reinforcement does not work, but negative consequences are not warranted. This intervention spells out how to use ignoring.

Target skill: Accept support and structure in daily life.

Method: Client will accept immediate feedback and consequences for behavior.

What you will need: Strips of paper and pencil. Image of behavior management pyramid. Small box.

1. Begin with empathy. Welcome your client and the parent with a smile. Tell them how proud you are of them for coming back and working on managing ADHD-related behaviors. You can say:

    - *I know you did not choose to have ADHD.*

    - *I know it can be difficult to live with ADHD.*

    - *You are doing a great job helping each other.*

    - *When you help each other like this, both of you benefit!*

2. Introduce today's task: using tools to manage ADHD-related behavior.

3. Review last week's homework. Ask:

    - *How did the last week feel?*

    - *How much positive reinforcement happened?*

    - *How often did you have to use negative consequences?*

    - *What was the impact of focusing on positive reinforcement?*

    - *Did this work? Or did you find yourself stuck in old ways of doing things?*

    If the parent had a difficult time moving away from too much punishment, focus on providing him or her with positive reinforcement for small changes. You can say:

    - *Practice makes perfect.*

    - *This may take some time.*

    Ask the parent to show you the negative consequences index card. Take a look together. Make sure that negative consequences were only imposed for dangerous and hurtful behaviors, and that the consequences "fit" the situation and were not excessive or disconnected from the event. Review with the parent and client:

    Here is how negative consequences (used very sparingly) can work:

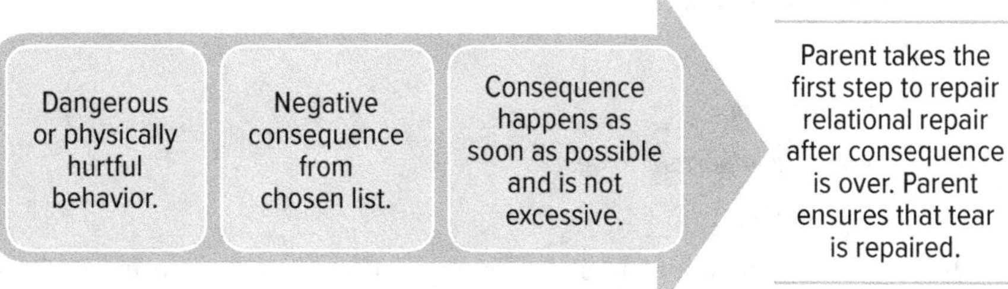

Figure 43

4. Work on today's task: Working on ignoring behaviors that do not warrant negative consequences.

5. Take a look at the behavior management pyramid together:

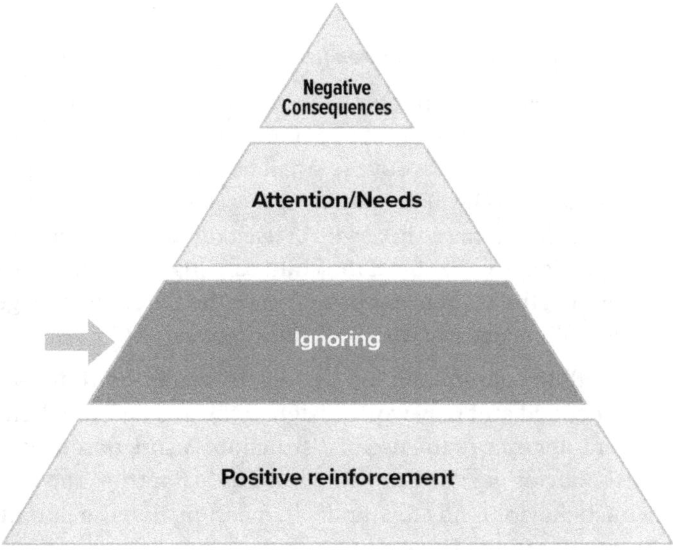

Figure 44

6. Ask the parent to give an example of a behavior that can be ignored. Then help the parent understand what conscious ignoring signals:

- *The behavior is not severe.*
- *The parent believes the behavior will pass, if ignored.*
- *The parent believes the client can figure this out and stop the behavior.*
- *The parent believes everyone makes mistakes.*

If the parent struggles with the last point, you may want to ask what it would feel like if someone called attention to every mistake she made. Here are some examples of common adult "misbehavior."

- *eye rolling at work*

- *swearing*

- *procrastinating*

- *forgetting important things*

- *overreacting*

7. If the client is present in session, you could now provide examples of ignoring that the parent has already practiced without noticing. Many parents will ignore sibling arguments if they feel that no one is likely to get hurt.

8. Next, explain the concept and purpose of distraction. You can say:

    - *Children often misbehave when they are bored.*

    - *Children with ADHD get bored more easily. Their brains call for constant action. If there is nothing going on, they get bored. When kids get bored, they do things to attract their parent's attention. Often, this is some sort of misbehavior.*

    - *A bored child that acts out often just needs something to do.*

9. If the child is present, ask her for a list of things she really likes to do. If she can write, give her little strips of paper and ask her to write each suggestion on one of those strips. Take out the small box. Read each suggestion to the parent and ask if it's OK. If the parent agrees, it goes into the distraction box. When you are done, there should be at least ten workable suggestions in the box. A suggestion is workable if the child can engage in the activity without parental help. If the child is not present, ask the parent to engage in the distraction box-filling activity with the child at home.

10. Now, ask both the parent and the client to think of situations in which distraction is needed and may work. Listen to the answers and help the parent expand her tolerance of the use of distraction. Again, parents often feel that every misbehavior needs correction, but this is not true. Too much attention on misbehavior tends to amplify it, meaning that the parent will get the opposite result of what is needed.

11. Review what you have done so far: You have reviewed the behavior management pyramid. You have explained how distraction can be used to manage ADHD-related behavior problems. You have created a distraction box to use at home (or parent will do this at home with the client).

12. Assign homework: If the client was not present in session, ask the parent to work on creating a distraction box with the client. The distraction box should sit in a prominent place in the home, within reach of both child and parent. When the client engages in an ADHD-related misbehavior, the parent should first:

    - *try positive reinforcement for positive behaviors also occurring;*

    - *try ignoring the behavior if it is not dangerous or harmful; and*

- *assist the client in a kind manner with pulling a distraction from the box. This should be done playfully, not punitively. When the child has pulled a distraction, the parent should clap or provide some other positive reinforcement and send the child off to the activity.*

If the child is present, say this:

When you feel bored, you can go to the distraction box. You don't have to wait for your parent to tell you to pull a distraction! You can just do this.

Instruct the parent to provide positive feedback every time the child uses the distraction box. A quick high-five and smile will work wonders!

13. Closing. Provide positive feedback and encouragement. You can say:

    - *You are learning so much.*

    - *This will be great for the both of you.*

    - *You can be proud for learning new ways of doing things!*

INTERVENTION 6

Choosing Connection

This intervention picks up where the last one leaves off. What is a parent to do if positive reinforcement and distraction do not work?

Target skill: Accept support and structure in day-to-day life.

Method: Client will accept immediate feedback and consequences for behavior.

What you will need: Willingness to engage mindfully. Index cards and pen. Markers or pencils. Cookie.

1. Begin with empathy. Welcome your client and the parent with a smile. Provide positive feedback for making it this far. You can say:

   - *Learning new ways of managing behavior can be tricky.*

   - *But you are sticking with it. Great job.*

   - *I can see how much you care about each other even when things are tough.*

   - *You are learning more every day!*

2. Introduce today's task: building relational connections when things are tough.

3. Review last week's homework. Ask:

   - *When did you use the distraction box?*

   - *What worked about using the box?*

   - *When did this not work?*

   - *Did your child ever use the box without prompting? (If he did, ask him to tell you all about this and then give him a big smile for a job well done.)*

   If the distraction box was not used, find out what the barrier was. You can ask:

   - *Did you lose the box? Let's make a new one!*

   - *No need to use it? No problem!*

   - *It felt silly? Tell me about that.*

   If the child is older, he may feel silly about using the box. Try a distraction list. What matters is that the client and parent work with the idea of distraction.

4. Work on today's task: choosing connection in the face of poor behavior. Explain that poor behavior can be connection-seeking. Parents often struggle with this idea. You can say:

   - *Children with ADHD often need attention and connection.*

   - *If they do not get this quickly, they may do something to get your attention.*

   - *Sometimes that something is expressed in poor behavior.*

   - *The child does not do this on purpose.*

- *But the child in some way understands that if he acts out, you are more likely to pay attention. (This might also be a good time to reiterate the importance of positive reinforcement.)*

5. Review the behavior management pyramid:

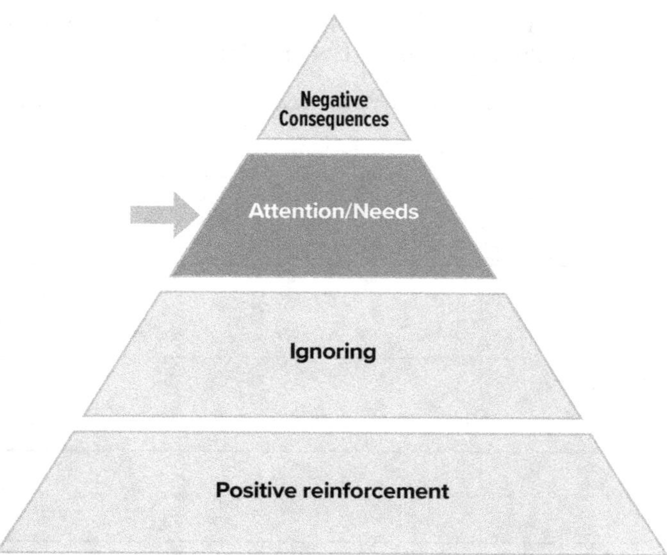

Figure 45

6. Tell the following story:

    Ella is a child who cannot wait. And today her mother is asking her to be quiet. Ella's mom has to finish a work project and needs Ella to play quietly. Ella plays quietly for a few minutes, then calls for her mother. Her mother ignores her. Ella calls again, but louder. Again, her mother ignores her. Ella gets up angrily and knocks over a vase. Water spills all over the floor and there are shards everywhere.

    Ask:

    - *What could Ella have done differently?*

    - *What about her mother?*

7. Introduce the idea of focused parental connection seeking to manage behavior. Give the following example:

    Ella is a child who cannot wait. Ella has ADHD and her mother knows that waiting is difficult for Ella. Today Ella's mom has to finish a work project and needs Ella to play quietly. But because Ella has a hard time with waiting, her mom promises to play a quick game with her every 20 minutes. Mom sets a timer for 20 minutes and works. Ella watches the timer. She is still impatient, but knows that when the buzzer sounds, she gets to play with her mom for five minutes. Ella's mom finishes her project!

8. Ask: *What is different this time?* Introduce the idea that children will do well when their needs are met. Explain that children with ADHD struggle with waiting. They can be impatient. It's just a brain thing.

9. Ask the client and parent to identify ways in which the client's needs can be met when he is seeking connection at an inconvenient time. Create a list of those ideas. Be sure to explain that the connection ideas have to be practical and cannot involve a lot of time. Here is a form you can use:

Connection Ideas
Hug
Quick story time
Playtime with a friend
Nap
Snack together

Figure 46

Of course, the list can be as long as you need it to be. Alternatively, use index cards to create the list. Your client may also enjoy illustrating them.

10. Be sure to reiterate to the parent that the child may not always know what his needs are. This is where having a list can be helpful. If he is already upset, he can simply point to something on the list or grab the appropriate index card.

11. Give the parent the following advice: When in doubt about what the child needs, offer a hug. A hug can often defuse a difficult situation. You can explain to the parent and the child that hugs make the body and the brain feel good. It's a biological thing!

12. Summarize what you have done so far: You have reviewed the behavior management pyramid. You have explained that children with ADHD may

use misbehavior to get parental attention. You have identified ways in which the parent can provide attention to the child in order to prevent or stop poor behavior.

13. Engage parent and child in connection practice. Provide a cookie, but be sure to ask about food allergies first. (Have the package ready for the parent in case he needs to check). Ask the parent to break off a small piece and feed it to the child. Then ask the child to do the same for the parent. Explain that pieces of the cookie should be as small as possible. Watch for smiles and laughter. When these happen, point out that these are moments of connection that do not take much time and are fun for everyone.

14. Assign homework: Send the list of connection ideas or index cards home and ask the parent to follow the following steps when helping the child manage behaviors:

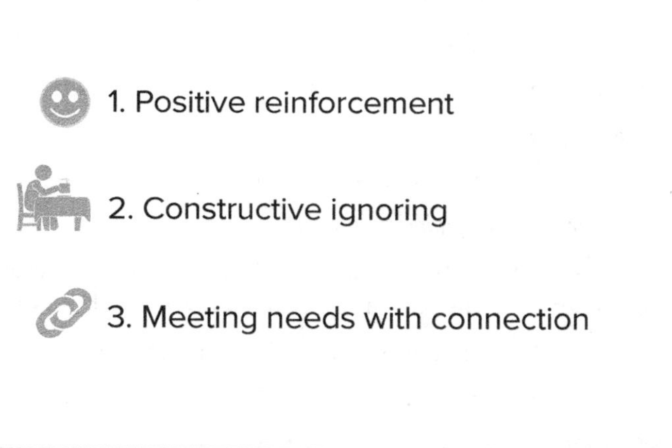

Figure 47

15. Closing. Leave your client and parent with words of encouragement:

- *Positive reinforcement is the way to go!*

- *Sometimes your child just needs to connect with you.*

- *There are simple and quick ways of connecting with your child.*

- *When in doubt, use a hug to connect. A hug can often interrupt a process that could make things worse.*

INTERVENTION 7

Choosing Joy

This intervention addresses the child's basic need to connect with the caretaker through a joyful and carefree experience. Learning is implicit rather than explicit. What your client will learn, implicitly, is that her adult caretaker wants to spend time together, that time together can be joyful, and that he is unconditionally loved and accepted. This is communicated first through attunement, then co-regulation. Joyful moments serve as a counterbalance to the demand and necessity that the child make changes, which by itself will make the child feel deficient.

Target skill: Reduce impact of mental health symptoms.

Method: Client will accept, practice, and utilize co-regulation techniques with a support person or caregiver.

What you will need: Index cards and pen. Small box. Colored pencils. Access to small toys or other items that can be used to create moments of joy.

1. Welcome your client. Ask:

   - *How was the last week?*

   - *What went well?*

   - *How are you using positive reinforcement?*

   - *Where are you struggling together?*

   Listen and reflect back. Be sure to provide positive reinforcement about steps your client and his parent have taken, no matter how small.

2. Introduce today's task: building joy in times of conflict.

3. Review last week's homework. Ask:

   - *When did you use attention to manage behavior?*

   - *How did you use attention to manage behavior?*

   - *In what way did this work?*

   - *What were the bumps in the road?*

   Review any problems with attention-giving to manage behavior. Children with ADHD often struggle with waiting for attention. If the child struggled, what changes can be made? Do distraction and attention need to be combined?

   If the child cannot let go of attention when time is up, how can this be managed? What transitional object can be given to the client to help him?

4. Work on today's task: choosing joy to manage behavior. You can explain by saying:

   - *Joy is necessary for everyone, including you and your child.*

   - *Children with ADHD are often disciplined a lot more than other children because of behaviors related to ADHD symptoms.*

- *This is why your child with ADHD needs moments of joy every day.*

- *It helps the child reconnect with you.*

- *It helps you reconnect with your child.*

- *Joy makes life worth living.*

The best way to demonstrate this is to introduce moments of joy into the session. Here are some ideas of tasks you can ask the parent and child to engage in (keeping in mind that tasks are dependent on the child's developmental level).

- *Itsy Bitsy Spider: Ask the child and parent to place their hands on opposite sides of the table, sing the "Itsy Bitsy Spider" song, and walk the hands towards each other, using the fingers as legs. Then, when the hands meet, they run off together, perhaps off the table. Watch for moments of joy (when the eyes light up).*

- *Gummi Bear Hide-and-Seek: Ask the parent and the child to look away. Hide two gummi bears close by. Where you hide them should be dependent on the developmental level of the child. Then ask parent and child to look for the gummi bears together. Once they find the gummi bears, ask them to each eat one gummi bear on the count of ready-set-go while looking at each other. Watch for moments of joy.*

5. Take out ten index cards and a pencil. Ask the parent and child to create a list of everyday joy activities. These activities need to be:

   - *simple (not requiring lots of stuff);*

   - *quick; and*

   - *relational (must involve parent and child eye contact).*

6. Write each joy activity on a list, then place it in the Joy Box. Parent and child can now decorate either the Joy Box or the index cards to increase a sense of ownership for the joy activities.

7. Summarize the work: Today you have created a box to contain a list of joyful activities that client and caretaker can engage in when they struggle with each other.

8. Assign homework: Send the Joy Box home and ask the parent to initiate at least one joy activity every day. More is better! The parent should present the Joy Box to the child and ask him to draw one activity for them to engage in. Send a chart like this home to track homework completion and ask the parent to bring the chart to the next session. A simple check mark or a pretty sticker indicates completion of the activity.

Joy Box Activity
Monday
Tuesday
Wednesday
Thursday
Friday
Saturday
Sunday

Figure 48

9. Closing. Send your client and parent home with words of encouragement:

- *Have joy together.*
- *Joy helps you connect.*
- *Joy makes life better.*
- *Enjoy each other!*

Repeat the Choosing Joy intervention whenever child and parent seem to be getting frustrated with each other and overly focused on behavioral compliance for its own sake. Reintroduce the idea that joy connects people, and connection is what makes life meaningful.

Remember: How you are with the client and parent is very important. Model joy during your sessions. Greet the client and parent with enthusiasm. Let them know how much you value the connection you have with them. Be playful while coaching them. There really is only one way to teach joy: Being joyful!

INTERVENTION 8

The Basics

Children with ADHD often struggle with recognizing some basic things, such as when they are hungry, thirsty, tired, or have to go to the bathroom. Their attention is simply busy attending to all those other things that pop into their minds unannounced. Because of this, children with ADHD may be cranky due to hunger, thirst, and bathroom emergencies. Parents often struggle with the sense of urgency that children with ADHD can display. Parents may ask themselves: Why now? Could the child not have eaten when we all ate together? Or a teacher may wonder: Why did the child not go to the bathroom at recess? Why now when I am teaching a math lesson? Adults need to help children with ADHD attend to their basic needs. If the child is cranky, perhaps she has not eaten anything or was unable to sleep the prior night.

Target skill: Accept support and structure in day-to-day life.

Method: Client will accept support and structure to decrease impulsive, inattentive, and hyperactive behaviors.

What you will need: Poster board. Markers

1. Welcome your client and the parent. Ask:

    - *How was the last week?*

    - *What was different in the last week?*

    - *What went well and what did not?*

2. Introduce today's task: paying attention to basic needs and meeting them.

3. Review last week's homework. Ask the parent to take out the Joy Box Activity Chart. Take a look together. Ask:

    - *What was it like to schedule joy every day?*

    - *Which activity did you enjoy the most and how come? (Listen for moments of joy and help parent and child recall these moments. Provide positive reinforcement in the form of verbal praise/high-fives.)*

    - *What were the barriers? What did not go well? If there is an activity that did not work, it can replaced with a new one. Here are some possible additions: Dancing together. Singing a favorite song out loud together. Jumping together holding hands.*

    Sometimes parents take away joy activities as a negative consequence. You should explain that this is not a good idea. You can say: *The more you take away joyful moments, the less likely the child is to behave well. Joyful moments are like medicine. Once prescribed, they must be given.*

4. Work on today's task: attending to the basics. Explain that children with ADHD often struggle with paying attention to important things like hunger, thirst, exhaustion, and the need to use the bathroom. Explain that this lack

of attention is a symptom. You may want to hand out the lightbulb index card again for use at home:

Figure 49

Tell the following story:

> *Devon began his day with a bang. He jumped out of bed and landed on a Lego castle. He was excited about the new day and began playing, putting the Lego castle back together. A bit later he heard his mother yell, "Breakfast is ready!" But Devon did not pay attention. He was playing. And Devon's mother was busy getting the other children ready. Suddenly it was time to get on the school bus.*
>
> *Devon's mother realized that he had not eaten and gave him a granola bar with strict instructions to eat the bar while waiting at the bus stop. He forgot. He arrived at school and went to class. At lunchtime Devon was so excited to see his friends that he only ate a bite. By afternoon Devon was cranky and irritable. His teacher noted this on his daily chart. When Devon got home, things got worse. He and his mother got into an argument. Devon called his mother a name, and she sent him to his room. From the kitchen his mother could hear him stomping around in his room. When dinner was ready, she went to get him, but he was asleep on his bed.*

5. Ask the parent and child to be detectives. Ask: *What went wrong? What is the first thing that went wrong? What went wrong throughout the day?*

6. Once the mystery of Devon's bad day has been resolved, explain the need to check for the basics when the child is struggling.

7. Provide three index cards and ask the child to decorate those cards with the basic needs of hunger and thirst, sleep, and bathroom time. When the child is done, ask the parent to write those needs on each index card. If there are other basic and urgent needs the child or parent wants to add, this is OK.

8. Summarize the work: Today your client has learned to name basic needs that can go unmet and lead to behavior problems. He has created index cards to remind him of those needs, and the parent has labeled the cards.

9. Assign homework: Send the "needs" index cards home with the parent. Ask the parent to check with the child about basic needs when he is cranky. Tell the parent to simply ask:

   - *Are you hungry? (If yes, provide food/snack. If the child says he is not hungry but has not eaten enough, offer food.)*

   - *Are you thirsty? (Always offer water!)*

   - *Do you need a nap? Power naps are OK!*

   - *Is it bathroom time? Just go!*

   Ask the parent to make a quick note on the back of the index card whenever there was a basic need.

10. Closing. Give words of encouragement. You can say this:

   - *You can support each other.*

   - *Everyone needs to eat and sleep.*

   - *Sometimes we forget.*

   - *It's OK, that's what parents are for. It's good to be reminded.*

INTERVENTION 9

Ready, Set, Chart!

This intervention is designed to help your client and caretaker thoughtfully use behavior charts. Charts provide an opportunity for positive reinforcement, not a justification for punishing the child for missing the mark. This is important to understand. Behavior charts should:

- create opportunities for success;
- remind the child and parent what tasks lie ahead;
- be simple to understand, preferably visual for younger children;
- be created in collaboration with the child and parent;
- be used thoughtfully, not mechanically;
- prompt the parent to provide positive reinforcement for a job well done, no matter how small;
- help the child recognize and celebrate what she can do; and
- provide relational rewards for a job well done.

Behavior charts should not:

- be used as an opportunity to scold the child;
- be too complex for the child's developmental level and related skills;
- be tedious to use;
- focus on material rewards;
- micromanage the child's life. There is more to life than charts; and
- be used to diminish joy in the child's life.

A chart is fun to use when both the child and the parent view it as a challenge to do well. It will be "dead on arrival," however, if it reflects the parent's need for perfection. Charts should be used in the context of a loving and nurturing relationship.

Target skill: Develop planning and goal-setting skills

Method: Client will accept parenting interventions to promote positive attention.

What you will need: Paper and markers. Stickers. Anything to decorate the chart. Glue. Scissors.

1. Welcome your client and the parent. Ask:

    - *How was your week?*

    - *What did you enjoy together this week? What was it about the activity that you enjoyed? Did it make you smile?*

    When you notice moments of joy, amplify them. Ask the client to tell you more about those moments and encourage the parent to chime in. Joy connects them, and when they are connected, everything becomes easier.

2. Introduce today's task: using charts to increase positive behaviors.

3. Review last week's homework. Ask:

   - *In what way did you use the Needs index cards?*

   - *What need came up most often?*

   - *How did you address this need together?*

   - *What went well about addressing needs? What still needs tweaked?*

   Explain that if a specific need came up a lot, it should be addressed preemptively from now on. Here is an example:

   > Devon always forgets to eat and is cranky a lot because of this. He is simply too busy to recognize when he is hungry. Whenever possible, Devon's mom sits with him during mealtime, and they connect about something fun while they eat. She also keeps a jar of attractive and healthy snacks ready. During snack time mom (or another adult) sits with Devon and just has fun with him. Devon's mom also made his teacher aware that he often forgets to eat. He is allowed to take one extra snack break as needed and keeps a healthy and attractive snack in his desk.

   Here is another example:

   > Sherize has trouble falling asleep at night and often wakes up and wanders around the house. When she can't fall asleep she turns on the TV in her room and watches crime shows. She reports that she really enjoys them. In the morning Sherize has trouble getting out of bed and often falls asleep at school.
   >
   > Sherize's mom removed the TV from the bedroom. Sherize is not happy about this, but her mother replaced the TV with a machine that makes soothing sounds. She has also added story time before bedtime. Sherize really enjoys this time with her mother.
   >
   > When Sherize continued to struggle with falling and staying asleep, her mother took her to the pediatrician, and they came up with a plan to address this issue medically. Sherize's mother is conflicted about this, but she and Sherize have gotten a full night's sleep for the first time in months.
   >
   > Sherize's mental health provider addressed the issue by teaching her relaxation exercises. Her mother practices these exercises with Sherize every night and provides positive reinforcement for participation. The relaxation exercises are imaginative and fun, and Sherize enjoys them. Bedtime routines are still a work in progress, but things are better: Sherize no longer falls asleep at school.

4. Work on today's task: Using charts to reinforce planning, goal setting, and task completion. You can explain like this:

    - *Planning is more difficult for children with ADHD.*

    - *They are often distracted and just forget about tasks.*

    - *The chart is a reminder.*

    - *The reminder should be simple.*

    - *The reminder should be fun to look at.*

    Ask what simple tasks the client struggles with. Be sure to check in with both the client and the parent. Create a list of no more than five simple tasks that need to be addressed. Organize the list by importance. Here is a chart to use:

Simple Things That Need to Be Done
Most important:
Least important, but still important:

Figure 50

Explain again the need to keep it simple. Here are some simple task examples:

- *Brush teeth.*

- *Put book by the door.*

- *Put socks in clothes hamper.*

Here are some examples of tasks that are complex. Complex tasks will need to be broken down into smaller sections.

- *Be a good kid.*
- *Do the homework.*
- *Get ready for school.*

"Get ready for school" is really many tasks summarized in one phrase. Your child with ADHD is unlikely to know all the steps involved and successfully complete them without support.

5. Begin working on a chart for the most important simple thing. Use the child's language. This will ensure that she understands what the task is. Here is an example of a task in adult language:

> Child will follow household rules about laundry.

Here is the same task described in child language:

"I will put my dirty clothes in my clothes hamper before I go to bed."

Here is an image that can be used to reinforce the task:

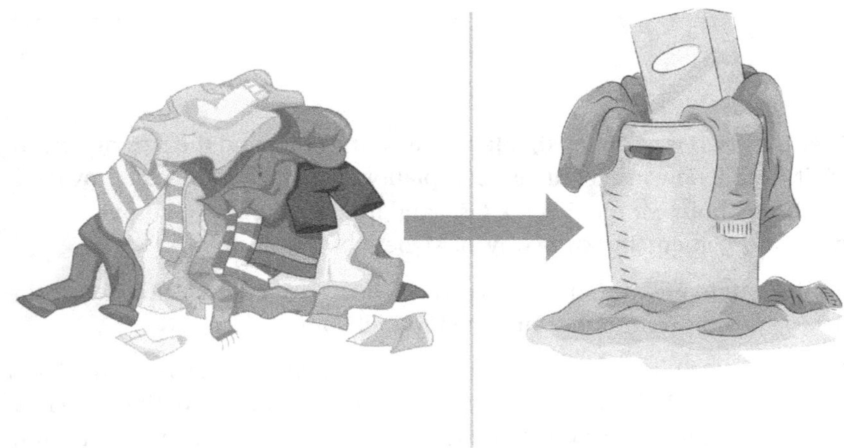

Figure 51

These are just sample images. Keep it simple. If the child wants to illustrate the chart, this is a great way to take ownership.

Here is a sample chart to use:

<table>
<tr><td>The Thing That Needs to Be Done</td></tr>
<tr><td>The thing that needs to be done is:</td></tr>
<tr><td>Here is what the job well done looks like (draw or insert picture):</td></tr>
<tr><td>When the job is done we will (insert relational positive reinforcement):</td></tr>
</table>

Figure 52

6. Once the chart is completed, role play with the child and the parent how to use it. Model how to act out task completion, how the parent can provide support without completing the task, and how the parent can provide positive reinforcement along the way and when the task is done.

7. Ask the parent and the child to role play. Make corrections as needed and provide positive reinforcement for a job well done.

8. Review what you have done so far: You have explained how behavior charts work within the behavior management system. You have identified the five most important simple tasks that the client needs to learn to complete. You have then chosen the most important one and created a simple behavior chart for this task. You have used role play to coach the parent and child on how to use the chart.

9. Assign homework. Send the task chart home with client and parent and ask them to post it in a prominent place. Ask the parent to coach the child once per day to complete the task, provide appropriate task support without completing the task, and then provide positive and relational feedback for task completion. If the child does not complete the task, the parent should increase support and take notes about potential barriers. Once the task is completed, the parent should draw or place a star on the chart. Ask the parent to bring the chart back to the next meeting.

10. Closing. Leave with words of encouragement:

    - *(To the parent) You are a great coach for your child.*

    - *(To the child) You can learn to do this, and it can be fun.*

    - *Look at the two of you. You are a great team!*

Once the child has learned to complete the first task, you can move on to the next task and create a chart for it. The intervention should be repeated at least five times to address all the simple tasks that need completion.

Alternate Chart Completion sessions with Choosing Joy sessions. Your client should never feel like her life is just about completing tasks. Simply help the parent and child identify another way in which they can choose joy. You may want to refer to Kearney et al., *Using Joyful Activity to Build Resiliency in Children in Response to Toxic Stress* (2017).

Remind the parent not to micromanage. Client and parent should only work on one chart at a time. Otherwise things can become overwhelming. If there is a need to go back to a prior chart, this can always be done.

Remind the parent that the key to behavior management is positive reinforcement. This also means that the parent will need to maintain a cheerful attitude. Failure is always a learning opportunity for child and parent!

INTERVENTION 10

Piecing It Together: Using Behavior Charts and Positive Reinforcement to Manage More Complex Tasks

This intervention builds on the prior one teaching the use of behavior charts. Child and parent now understand how to use behavior charts for important and simple tasks. It is now time to help them learn how to address more complex tasks.

Target skill: Develop planning and goal-setting skills.

Method: Client will accept external modeling of multistep problem-solving routines.

What you will need: Paper and markers. Stickers. Anything to decorate the chart. Glue. Scissors.

1. Welcome client and parent. Ask:

    - *How was the last week?*

    - *What did you do together that made you happy?*

    - *How did you make meals more joyful?*

    - *How about bedtime?*

2. Introduce today's task: using behavior charts to manage more complex behaviors and tasks.

3. Review last week's homework. Ask the parent to take out last week's chart. Take a look together. Ask:

    - *How many stars/stickers are there?*

    - *Parent: How do you feel when your child earns a star/sticker?*

    - *Child: How do you feel when you earn a star/sticker?*

    - *How do you feel about each other in those moments when you work together to get the task done?*

Help parent and child celebrate the child's behavioral successes, no matter how small. If there is one sticker on the chart, consider this a success and work from there. If chart completion was a struggle, ask about the struggle. Ask:

    - *What got in the way?*

    - *In what way are you making this a joyful task? In what way are you not?*

    - *Parent: Are you able to celebrate the small successes?*

Are there relational tears that need repair before parent and child can successfully engage in managing behavior through charts? If there are, they must be addressed in order for behavior management strategies to be successful. When there is a significant relational tear, this puts both parent and child into a different affective state: Sadness can turn into anger; anger can turn into rage. Sadness can also turn into withdrawal. In these cases, the primary tasks become building connections between parent and child.

Collaborate with the child's therapist. The child's therapist will help parent and child explore and understand relational hurt and means of reconnecting.

You can help parent and child engage in joy activities. These activities can also begin to rebuild a connection.

Simple tear-and-repair happens in relationships every day. But when the parent refuses to talk to the child, or if the child feels completely unloved, behavior management is difficult.

4. Work on today's task: You can explain that more complex tasks are tasks that contain multiple steps, such as getting ready for bed or for school, or doing homework. You can also explain that complex tasks can be especially difficult for children with ADHD. They may simply get distracted after the first step and move on to another activity. You can remind parent and child that getting distracted in such a manner is a symptom, not a personal fault.

5. Ask parent and child to identify three important and complex tasks that are difficult for the child to complete. Ask: *If these were no longer a problem and got done on a regular basis, would your life be better? If the answer is yes, you have found your tasks.*

6. Then ask the child and parent to pick the most important one.

    Introduce the idea of "chunking a task." Explain that complex tasks can be broken down into smaller steps. You can give the following example. In order to get ready for bed you have to:

    - *stop what you are doing.*
    - *wash up or take a bath.*
    - *brush your teeth.*
    - *put on pajamas.*
    - *get into bed.*
    - *say goodnight to each other.*

    For a child with ADHD, it's easy to forget a step or two.

7. Ask the parent and child to break down the task they have chosen into the necessary steps and write them down.

8. Identify each step on a separate behavior chart. (See the following chart.) If there are five steps, you will need to complete five separate mini-charts.

The Thing That Needs to Be Done
The thing that needs to be done is:
Here is what the job well done looks like (draw or insert picture):
When the job is done we will (insert relational positive reinforcement):

Figure 53

9. Ask the child and parent to complete each mini-chart. Remember to use language chosen by the child, and let him decorate each chart to increase a sense of ownership with the task.

10. Line up the charts in order on a larger piece of paper. Your final product will look something like this:

The Big Thing That Needs to Be Done
Step 1
The thing that needs to be done is:
Here is what the job well done looks like (draw/insert picture):
When the job is done we will (insert relational positive reinforcement):
Step 2
The thing that needs to be done is:
Here is what the job well done looks like (draw/insert picture)"
When the job is done we will (insert relational positive reinforcement):

Figure 54

You get the idea. This more complex chart will give your client and the care-taker a roadmap for task completion. You can say:

- *This is your roadmap.*
- *Just complete one step at a time.*
- *Your job as a parent is to coach your child, not to do things for your child.*
- *Be sure to provide positive reinforcement after every step.*
- *Be patient. You may not make it through the entire list on your first try. This is a new way of doing things. It will take time.*
- *You are not just coaching your child how to complete this task. When you use a chart like this you are helping your child learn how any task is completed— by working on each step, one at a time. This is a life skill that is especially important for children with ADHD.*

11. Review what you have done so far: You have explained the need to break larger tasks down into smaller chunks. You have identified three important and complex tasks and chosen one to work on first. You have created a task completion roadmap.

12. Assign homework. Send the task completion roadmap home with the parent. Ask parent and child to give this task a try once every day. Ask the parent to place stars or stickers on the roadmap for each chunk that is completed and to provide a relational reward at the end of each step. Explain again that it is not important to make it all the way through on the first try, but that positive feedback about the small steps is vital. Ask the parent to bring the roadmap back to your next meeting.

13. Closing. Provide words of encouragement. You can say:

- *This is a great step in the right direction.*
- *Working together really pays off.*
- *Just take one step at a time.*

All by Myself: Fading Support

This intervention is designed to help the client become more independent. The parent will learn to *fade* emotional support, meaning the parent will provide less and less support for task completion over time until the child can successfully complete the tasks independently. The key, of course, is to pace the withdrawal of support in a way that the child is able to tolerate. When you withdraw too much support at once, the child is likely to fail. If you strategically fade support for components of the task that the child has mastered, the child will eventually be able to complete the task alone.

Target skill: Improve executive functioning.

Method: Client will accept the use of modeling by caregiver to learn and use scaffolding and encouragement during her attempt to solve problems.

What you will need: Paper squares for origami (pre-cut). At least one (better to have two) fidget items. Water.

1. Welcome client and parent. Ask:

   - *How was the last week?*

   - *How did you create joy for yourself?*

   - *How did you create joy for each other?*

   As always, highlight areas in which client and parent connect and create joy in each other's lives. Enthusiastically praise success in those areas.

2. Introduce today's task: Learning to be self-sufficient when completing a task.

3. Review last week's homework. Ask the parent to take out the task-completion roadmap. Take a look together. Say to the client:

   - *Show me how far you got.*

   - *How many steps did you accomplish?*

   - *In what way was it helpful to have a roadmap of what to do?*

   - *When did you get frustrated?*

   - *When were you happy about how you did?*

   - *What changes would you like to make?*

   Ask the parent:

   - *How helpful was it for you to have this roadmap for coaching?*

   - *When did you get frustrated?*

   - *When were you happy about how things went?*

   - *In what way can the roadmap be improved?*

If there is a need, create changes to the roadmap together. Then ask the client and parent to continue to use the roadmap until the client has mastered the task as evidenced by full completion of all components.

Repeat this intervention at least two more times until the client has mastered the two most important complex tasks. Be sure to intersperse chart- and task-oriented interventions with interventions building joy and connection. Repeat the intervention as needed.

Remind the parent:

- *Use positive reinforcement as your primary behavior-management tool.*

- *When things don't go well, ignore poor behavior that is not dangerous.*

- *If things are still difficult, check to see if your child needs attention.*

- *If there is dangerous or hurtful behavior, use negative consequences sparingly and be sure to reconnect with your child after the consequence is over.*

4. Work on today's task: fading behavioral support to foster independent completion of a task. You can explain:

    - *The goal of behavior modification is to help your child eventually internalize all the steps to completing tasks and solving problems.*

    - *Children with ADHD often need more support with this.*

    - *Children with ADHD can learn to use charts to coach themselves to complete tasks and solve problems.*

    - *Fading support means stepping back and letting the child try on her own.*

    - *Fade support slowly, step-by-step.*

5. Provide the parent and the client with a paper square. Explain that they will learn to fold a paper cup out of the square and that, at first, you will give them a lot of support. Walk parent and child through the step of folding a paper cup. You can find instructions online at:

    web-japan.org/kidsweb/virtual/origami2/exploring01_02.html

    Just for the fun of it, demonstrate that these cups actually hold water and you can drink out of them. Of course, they only work once.

6. Repeat the activity but with less support. Re-teach folds as needed.

7. Repeat the activity again. Ask your client and the parent to guess which step comes next.

8. Many children are able to fold the paper cup by themselves on their fifth try. The exact number is dependent on the child's skill and developmental level.

9. Explain what you just went through. You slowly faded support but jumped in to help as needed.

10. It is helpful to ask the parent about how much she wants to jump in and help when the child does not need help. Explain that task completion is not about perfection, but rather about learning to do things independently.

11. Ask the parent and child to complete a simple task that the client has practiced before without parental support.

12. Review what you have done so far. You have explained how support for a task can be gradually withdrawn to foster independence. You have demonstrated how to fade support using an origami activity, and your client and the parent have agreed on a task that the child will attempt to complete without support.

13. Assign homework. Provide a task completion chart:

The Thing That Needs to Be Done
The thing that needs to be done is:
Here is what the job well done looks like (draw or insert picture):
When the job is done we will (insert relational positive reinforcement):

Figure 55

Ask the client and parent to complete this chart together outside of session. The client should then attempt to complete the task every day. The parent should prompt the client but remain in the background if not needed. Explain to the parent that it is OK for the client to make mistakes while practicing.

When the child asks for support, the parent should help her think things through, but not give answers.

The parent should provide positive reinforcement if the child tries to take steps but does not complete the task. Ask the parent to provide a star on the chart for every time the client has attempted to complete the task, and to bring the chart to your next meeting.

14. Closing. Send the client and parent home with words of encouragement:

- *You are ready to step it up.*
- *One step at a time.*
- *It takes courage to try something new.*
- *Just support each other.*

Behavioral Interventions: Skills Training (TBS and PSR)

So far interventions have focused on helping the child regulate ADHD-related behaviors with support from the parent. The CDC recommends those kinds of interventions for children who are 12 and under. For further information regarding treatment recommendation for children of different ages you should follow these CDC guidelines: Behavior therapy for children with ADHD. (2016).

You should also keep in mind that the chronological age of the child can differ from developmental age. Many of the children we serve present with emotional and behavioral developmental challenges. They may be 12 years old but may not be ready emotionally and behaviorally to engage like others their age. Many of our clients were or are exposed to environments of toxic stress, which can drive them and their parents into a kind of survival mode. When this happens, emotional and behavioral learning takes a backseat.

When you are wondering about your client's developmental age, always consult with your supervisor.

All of the following interventions will work best when they are used with both the client and the parent present. If the parent understands and learns the interventions, he or she can then use them in everyday life with the client. Additionally, the parent will then have increased opportunities to provide positive reinforcement.

When you are working with a teenager, intensive skills practice becomes even more important as the parent role in the teen's life changes. As teens become more independent, they still need parental support and positive reinforcement, but they also need more intensive practice to put them in the "driver's seat." Behavior changes will need to be internalized as the parent will not always be there to reinforce them.

INTERVENTION 12

Stop and Go

This intervention is designed to help your client learn, in a playful manner, how to listen carefully.

Target skill: Maintain attention over distractibility.

Method: Client will learn and practice delay response techniques.

Materials: Mainly space. It is good to have a space that is at least 10 feet long. You can do this activity outside, weather permitting.

1. Welcome your client and the parent. Ask:

   - *How was the last week?*

   - *What went well?*

   - *Where were the struggles?*

   - *What kind of quality time did you spend together?*

2. Introduce today's task: learning to listen with care. Explain to parent and child that attending with care can be difficult for children with ADHD, but it can be learned and practiced in a playful manner.

3. Work on today's task: Ask your client to stand at the opposite end of the room, facing you. Ideally that would be at least 8–10 feet away. Ask the parent to observe with care and explain that he or she will be engaging in this activity with the client shortly.

4. Explain to your client that the key to this exercise is listening. Explain that when you say "go," you want him to walk (not run) toward you one step at a time. Explain that when you say "stop," you want him to stop right away and not take another step.

5. Start the exercise. Make it simple at first. Say "go" and "stop" at regular intervals until your client reaches you.

6. Praise your client for doing well. Laugh with your client if he struggles with stopping. Say, "Practice makes perfect."

7. Send your client back to the other side of the room. Begin the exercise again, but this time make it more difficult—vary the intervals between saying "go" and "stop." Once again congratulate your client when he reaches you.

8. Next: Your client becomes the "teacher," in charge of making you go and stop. Make mistakes. Don't listen. Have your client correct you until you "get" it.

9. Now introduce the parent into the activity. Your client gets to teach his parent how to practice "go" and "stop." Make sure that this is not taken too seriously. It should be fun.

10. Have the parent instruct the client to "go" and "stop." Encourage playfulness.

11. If all goes well, you can introduce another level of complexity. Give the parent and client the printout of a stop sign. Ask them to use the stop sign instead of words to say stop and go.

Figure 56

When this part of the activity is concluded, ask:

> ***What is easier for you: Following directions using words, or following directions using the picture?***

12. Summarize what you have done so far: You have explained that focused attention can be difficult for a child with ADHD. You have demonstrated how to practice focused attention in a playful manner. You have helped parent and child practice focused attention using words and a stop-sign picture.

13. Assign homework: Ask parent and child to practice focused attention in a playful manner at least once per day at home. Send the picture of the stop sign home with them. You can explain that they can practice using words or the image; either one is OK. Send the following homework chart home:

Time:	Mon	Tue	Wed	Thu	Fri	Sat	Sun
Completed Stop and Go Activity							

Figure 57

Explain that a sticker or star should be given for every attempt, not just when the client and the parent are listening well to each other. Instruct the parent to provide positive reinforcement for the client every little step along the way. Also explain that it is best to pick a specific time of day to complete the activity. Of course, if the activity is so much fun that the client wants to complete it before the set time and the parent has the time to do so, this is fine.

Make sure that this exercise does not become about the parent controlling the client or vice versa. This is not a parenting exercise, but rather a skill-building exercise.

14. Closing. Send parent and client home with words of encouragement:

- *Paying attention can be fun!*
- *It's OK to laugh when you are learning.*
- *Have fun with this! It's like playing together.*

INTERVENTION 13

Back to the Blocks

This intervention is designed to help your client practice shifting attention. Many children with ADHD find it difficult to shift from one task to another. This can be especially difficult when the child shifts from a nonpreferred task to a preferred task and is then asked to shift back.

Target skill: Maintain attention over distractibility.

Method: Client will practice attention skills through the use of games requiring focus, planning, organization, attentiveness, and problem solving.

Materials: Jenga blocks or similar building blocks. Small pieces of candy or chips on a plate. (If client is a child, ask the parent for permission. If client is diabetic, substitute another tasty item that does not contain sugar.)

1. Welcome the client and the parent. Ask:

    - *How was the last week?*

    - *What was the best time you had together in the last week?*

    - *What was the most difficult time you had together in the last week?*

    Listen for moments of connection. Amplify those moments. Help parent and child understand that it is possible to connect even when they are having a difficult time together. Reiterate the importance of repairing relational hurt.

2. Introduce today's task: learning attention skills, thinking things through, shifting focus.

3. Review last week's homework. Ask the parent to take out the homework chart. Take a look together. Ask:

    - *What part of this was fun?*

    - *How much did you laugh?*

    - *Did you notice any changes after a few days of practice?*

    Explain the need to keep practicing focused attention. You can say:

    - *It just takes a minute to practice.*

    - *And you get to have fun together.*

    - *It's a win/win situation!*

    If client and parent did not practice, find out what got in the way. Identify barriers and help remove them. A common barrier for not completing homework can be the lack of time. This activity, however, can be completed in five minutes or less! Additionally, parents can be anxious about doing things right. Help alleviate this anxiety. As long as the client practices stop and go following verbal or visual prompts, the activity is done right. There is no need for perfection.

4. Work on today's task: learning to shift attention when there is a pleasant distraction. You can explain that distractions are tricky for children with ADHD, and they may need prompts when they have to return to a task.

5. Ask your client to begin building a tower with the blocks. Praise her for building a nice tower. Remind her that this exercise is not about building a perfect tower, that she should just enjoy the process of building.

6. If the parent intervenes because she feels that the tower is not right, ask the parent to let the client build the tower without interruption even if the parent feels the tower is not good enough.

7. Once the client is absorbed in the process of building the tower, say: "Look over there. There is candy on the plate in the corner. You can go and have one piece."

8. Most kids (and adults) will get up at this point and walk to the plate. Let the client take a piece of candy (don't put too many on the plate) and then say, "Let's get back to the blocks."

9. Take the plate with the candy and put it out of sight. If the client becomes upset, you can say: "It's a game. Don't worry. There will be more."

10. Encourage the client to start building again. Help her immerse herself again in the process of building.

11. Begin talking with the client about how tempting the candy is and how easy it is to walk away from the blocks when there is candy. Blocks are fun, but candy trumps blocks most of the time.

12. Ask: "When there is candy in sight, right over there, how hard is it for you to stay seated and build a tower?"

13. Comment on the client's tower. Point out a special feature of the tower so your client knows that you appreciate it.

14. Now: Get the plate out again and say: "Would you like another piece of candy?"

15. Most kids and adults will take another piece and abandon the blocks.

16. Once again, talk with your client about how easy it is to leave the blocks and focus on the candy.

17. Once again say: "Let's get back to the blocks." Put the plate of candy away again.

18. If the client whines about wanting more candy, use this as an opportunity to talk about how hard it is to focus on something when a more tempting thing is present. If the parent is embarrassed about the way the client is behaving, you can say:

   - *If there is candy, we all want it. That's just human nature.*

   - *Can you give your child a hug? This is difficult for her, and she may need your support.*

19. Now include the parent in the activity. Ask the parent to practice the back and forth between the tower and the candy. Explain the importance of humor when practicing. Make sure that this exercise remains playful and does not become about control.

20. Review what you have done so far. You have explained how difficult it can be for children to shift attention from one task to another, especially when the shift is from a task the child really enjoys to one she does not enjoy as much. You have practiced with the client how to shift attention using a prompt. You have given the parent and the client opportunity to practice together.

21. Assign homework: Ask the parent and client to practice the activity at home. Once again: Humor is important. No need to get upset when attention "floats." Instruct the parent to say: "Let's just get back to the blocks." Give the parent the following homework chart to complete. The parent should mark each daily attempt to practice with a star or sticker. Ask the parent to bring the chart to the next meeting.

    Remember: The use of homework charts is essentially a prompt. Charts increase accountability.

	Mon	Tue	Wed	Thu	Fri	Sat	Sun
Practiced shifting attention							

Figure 58

22. Closing. Leave your client with words of encouragement:

    - *It's a fun way to practice shifting attention.*
    - *You get to have snacks while doing so.*

INTERVENTION 14

Listen and Repeat

This intervention is designed to help your client practice focused attention as well as expanding capacity for working memory. Your client will have to pay attention to words and remember them. Again, this activity should be fun. Be sure to introduce an element of laughter. Allow the client to use drawing as a memory aid.

Target skill: Improve executive functioning.

Method: Client will engage in activities to improve inhibition of responses, working memory and processing speed in complex situations; and to build emotional control.

Materials: Playfulness, paper, pencil.

1. Welcome your client and the parent. Ask:

    - *How was the last week?*

    - *What new thing did you learn?*

    - *What new thing did you learn about each other?*

    Highlight areas of joy about learning new things.

2. Introduce today's task: learning to focus attention.

3. Review last week's homework. Ask the parent to take out the Shifting Attention homework chart. Take a look together. Ask:

    - *How easy or difficult was it to practice?*

    - *What part of practice was fun? Did you laugh while practicing?*

    - *What part was difficult? Did you argue? If you did, what was the argument about?*

    - *Are there any changes you would like to make? If yes, what are they?*

    Explain that shifting attention can be practiced every day in playful ways. Help the client and parent identify situations in which this can happen, such as shifting from play to homework.

4. Work on today's task: focused attention and memory. Explain that it can be difficult for children with ADHD to pay attention and even more difficult to remember things from one moment to the next. If it is helpful, you can take out the "It's a symptom" card to reiterate that the child is not intentionally disregarding what is being said.

Figure 59

5. Invite your client to play "listen and repeat" with you. This exercise can be adapted for all ages and developmental levels. Ask the parent to initially listen to the first round. The key to this exercise is to keep it simple, at least at first. We want the practice of focus to be playful and fun, not frustrating.

6. Invite your client to say a word and explain that it is your job to say it back. It can be any appropriate word. It is best if it is a fun word. You could go with a theme, such as favorite foods, animals, or people.

7. Let your client lead you. He will say a word, and you will say it back.

8. Now, ask your client to say two words and go through the same thing. When you repeat the words back you may want to pause and think after the first. This is to keep your client at ease.

9. Now, ask your client to say three words. Again, when you say the three words back, think after each word. Don't make it look too easy.

10. Without knowing it, your client has already practiced focused attention. He has thought of three words and put them in order. He has challenged you to repeat the words. Say: *You did great choosing words to remember for me. I liked those words*.

11. Now challenge your client to play the game with you. This time you will choose the words. Adjust your words depending on age and developmental level. For a first-grader you may want to choose words like *dog, cat,* and *mouse.* The key here is to keep it simple so that the client can succeed.

12. Give your client a piece of paper and a pen. Tell him that it is OK to draw the word you just said (to avoid the embarrassment of forgetting). If your client draws what he hears, once again, he is practicing focused attention.

13. Go through the exercise up to three words. Help if needed. Say: "You did great remembering" after each word or set of words. You can add more words as appropriate. The key is to stop when frustration emerges. This exercise is about playful practice, not competition.

14. If a client struggles with remembering words, you can make up a song to help him remember. Use a well-known melody and put the chosen words to the song. Something like "Twinkle, Twinkle Little Star." Sing the song together to help your client remember.

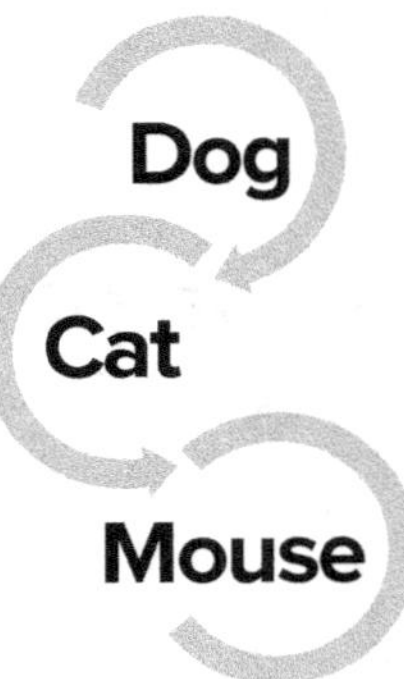

Figure 60

Tip: If you want to, you can add movement. This can be effective when trying to keep a child engaged. You and your client could jump just a little when saying the words back. This adds another element of fun.

15. Now: Ask the parent to participate. First, the client gets to say the three words and the parent has to remember them.

16. Then it is time to switch. The parent gets to choose the words and the client says them back. Coach the parent to make this fun for the client, to choose words that engage him. Remind the parent to be playful. Children learn best when they have fun. Again, the parent can create a song or rhyme to help the child remember, and it is OK to add movement if this helps.

17. Review what you have done so far: You have explained how ADHD can affect focus and memory. You have introduced the idea that focus and memory can be practiced, and you have demonstrated how to do so. Lastly, the parent has helped the client practice focus and memory skills.

18. Assign homework: Ask the parent to practice the focus/memory exercise at least once per day. Remind the parent to keep it fun and explain that it is best to keep practice short—just a couple of minutes per day will do. Give the parent the following homework chart to track completion, and ask her to bring the chart back to the next meeting.

	Mon	Tue	Wed	Thu	Fri	Sat	Sun
Practice focus and memory							

Figure 61

19. Closing. Encourage your client to practice. You can say:

- *This is fun.*
- *You get to play with [mother/father/grandmother/grandfather, etc. as appropriate].*
- *And you get to learn at the same time.*

Remind the parent to end each practice with a hug or high-five.

INTERVENTION 15

Story Time

This intervention is designed to help your client create a sense of sequence and order when telling a story. Children with ADHD can struggle with telling a story in a sequential way. They may rattle off elements of the story out of sequence, which makes it difficult for others to keep up. This intervention uses the prompts: Who? What? Where? When? How? These prompts can help your client communicate better.

Target skill: Improve executive functioning.
Method: Client will learn and use communication skills.
Materials: Just your ability to tell a good story, paper, pencil.

1. Welcome your client and the parent. Ask:

   - *What was your best day at school and why?*

   - *What was your best day at work and why?*

   Highlight moments of interpersonal connection and joy.

2. Introduce today's task: organizing a story to tell. Explain that it can be difficult for children to create order when they are telling a story.

3. Review last week's homework. Ask the parent to take out the homework chart. Take a look together. Ask:

   - *How often were you able to practice?*

   - *What went well? What was fun?*

   Ask the parent to recall the best practice moment and describe it to the child. Watch for and highlight moments of joy, and reinforce the idea that growing together can be fun.

4. Work on today's task: Invite your client to participate in a story-telling exercise. Ask the parent to initially listen and watch. Explain that the child will create the story by telling you the "who, what, where, when, and how" of the story. Ask him to choose fun components and use his imagination. This exercise is about maintaining attention, which is easier when joy is involved. Give the client a few minutes to think about the elements of the story. During this time, the parent can function as a consultant for the child and help identify story elements. The story, however, must be the child's, not the parent's.

5. Ask: *Who is the story about?* Make a note of it, write it down, or draw it. You are modeling focused attention.

6. Ask: *Where does the story take place?* Again, make a note of it on your piece of paper.

7. And so forth. When you have all the elements of the story identified, it is time to tell the story as you understand it. Ask your client to listen.

8. Tell the story. Use your notes/drawings to model how to stay on task. If your client interrupts, this is OK. Explain that he will get to tell the story also, as soon as you're done.

9. Ask your client for feedback about how you did.

10. Now: Invite your client to tell the story in his way, using the prompts "who, what where, when, and how." Listen attentively, make a note of what is different (draw or write). While the client is telling the story, the parent serves as a consultant and coach. If the child forgets to address a prompt, the consultant can remind him.

11. When the child is done, provide positive feedback. Make a note of any differences. Say something like: "I like how you focused on the way the dog came running back to you," or something of that sort.

12. Praise your client for being able to tell a story. Say: "It was so much fun listening to you. You are a great storyteller."

13. What if your client gets stuck? Can't choose topics? Can't tell the story? Make sure the components are simple. Work together on creating the story. Explain how much fun it is for you to create a story together. Remember: Learning is relational. You want to create an experience of success. It's OK for the parent to coach the child along the way.

14. Summarize what you have done so far: You have explained that telling a story in sequence can be difficult for children with ADHD. You have introduced a way of practicing bringing order into communication using a self-created story and the prompts "who, what, where, when, and how." Your client has created a story with the parent serving as a coach/consultant. Your client has practiced telling the story in order.

15. Assign homework: Ask the client to create a story at home using the prompts. Ask the parent to serve as a coach and consultant. Also explain the need not to take over. It should be the client's story, not the parent's. The story should be fun for the client to tell. Ask the parent to help the client with documenting the story. A younger child can create a sequence of drawings; an older child may write it down. If writing is a barrier, the parent can serve as a scribe. Ask them to bring the story to your next meeting.

16. Closing. Send the client and parent home with words of encouragement. You can say:

    - *We all have stories to tell.*

    - *Telling stories connects us.*

    - *And it is great practice for organizing your thoughts!*

Here and Now and Over There

This intervention introduces working with the Premack principle. This principle tells us that we are willing to do something we don't particularly enjoy if we know that after that activity or task, we will be able to do something we really do enjoy. Here are a few examples:

- doing 45 minutes of homework, then playing a round of Candy Crush;
- cleaning her room, then watching TV;
- preparing taxes, then going to see friends.

Most parents intuitively use the Premack principle already. When using the Premack principle with children with ADHD, it is important to keep in mind that they have a difficult time waiting for things. Rewards—in the form of doing desirable things—need to be interspersed more frequently.

It is not important that parents know the name of the principle. They just have to understand the sequence:

Figure 62

As with any kind of behavioral intervention, the Premack principle has to be applied consistently to a specific situation. Here is an example:

> When 8-year-old Jason gets home, he picks up his tablet and plays video games. His mother decides to use the Premack principle for homework. She explains that from now on Jason has to complete 30 minutes of homework before being allowed to use the tablet for 30 minutes.
>
> The first few days are tricky, but after a while Jason understands that he can't use the tablet until he has completed 30 minutes of homework. Jason now does his homework every day. His mother helps him when he needs it.
>
> One day, Jason's mother is upset and distracted. When Jason gets home from school he seizes the opportunity (and the tablet) and starts playing video games. Jason's mother is too upset to address the issue, and the next day Jason immediately grabs his tablet when he gets home. Later, homework completion is a struggle.
>
> Jason's mother decides to address the issue right away. She explains to Jason that they will return to the sequence of work first, then reward the following day and that she will hold his tablet until he has completed the 30

minutes of homework. Jason is not happy about this but recognizes that his mother is determined. It takes a few more days to get back to the routine.

This principle should not be applied to eliminate all love and joy from a child's life. Children should not have to behave well to receive parental love. Hugs can be used as quick positive reinforcement, but they should also be given freely at other times. Children should receive hugs for just being themselves.

There should always be playtime. The Premack principle could be misused if applied like this: "You can't ever play until you have completed all of your homework and all of your chores." For many children with ADHD, this would mean they would simply never be allowed to play. This kind of punishment could then make a bad situation much worse. If a child knows that she can't possibly complete all of the work, she is less likely to even try. Children need to experience love and joy every day.

Target skill: Maintain attention over distractibility.

Method: Client will accept structure and support to decrease impulsive, hyperactive, and inattentive behaviors.

Materials: Two poster boards or large pieces of paper, writing/drawing tools, collage materials: newspapers, scissors, glue, glitter, etc.

1. Welcome your client. Ask:

   - *How was the last week?*

   - *What did you say to each other in the morning to connect?*

   - *How did you connect at night to end the day well?*

   Be sure to help client and family identify at least one way in which they can connect at the beginning and end of every day.

2. Introduce today's task: moving from things that have to get done to things you want to do and vice versa. You can say:

   Moving from one task to another can be difficult for children with ADHD. This is especially true when they have to move from a task they love to a task they don't really love. We can make this move easier by rewarding time spent on the task that is not so much fun with time to be spent on a task that is fun.

3. Review last week's homework: Ask the parent to take out the story the client has created (with "who, what, where, when, how" prompts). Ask the client to read the story or recount it from memory.

   Provide positive feedback for telling the story with all of the elements. If your client forgot an element, ask about it.

   You can then tell the parent to use the prompts whenever the child comes home with a story that is difficult to follow. Using the prompts will make it easier to remember components. The prompts can be used to understand how a situation on the playground played out or which friends argued!

4. Work on today's task: Invite your client and the parent to create the "Land of Here and Now" and the "Land of Distractions."

5. Lay out the poster boards labeled with the two different titles.

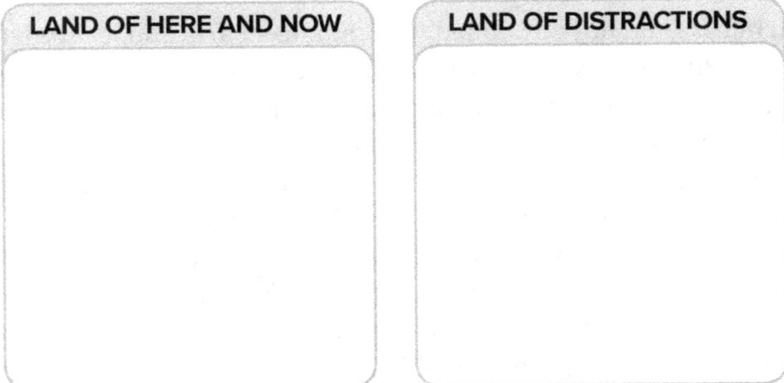

Figure 63

Now: Instruct your client to "fill" the land of distractions first. It should contain everything that she finds "shiny" and "exciting" and keeps her from doing what she needs to do. Let the parent contribute. Just be sure that the parent does not scold the child. You can say: "It is normal to want to do fun things and to not want to do things that are not so fun."

Explain that shiny and exciting things are not bad. They can, in fact, be wonderful and should be enjoyed when the time is right.

This exercise can be adapted for all ages and developmental levels. We all have shiny things that distract us. You can ask the parent: "Have you ever found yourself watching television when you should have been folding laundry? Getting distracted from a not-so-fun task is really easy."

Now, invite your client to fill the "Land of Here and Now." The parent can help. What are the things that the child really struggles with? Think of things that have to get done, like homework, chores, meeting with boring relatives.

When both "Lands" are populated, talk with your client about which place seems more fun. Ask her to show her favorite things from the "Land of Distractions."

Explain that it is possible to move things from the "Land of Distractions" over to the "Land of Here and Now."

Explain the idea of rewarding oneself with a fun thing once demands are completed. For example: "You can play with your toy car (or drive your real car) once you have completed your homework/cleaned the house." Explain that things don't have to be so separate. You are now beginning to coach the parent to use the Premack principle!

Ask your client to move one item from the "Land of Distractions" over to the "Here and Now." Help her define how she can use this item appropriately to stay focused on what needs to be done. Perhaps your client likes to dance. She can dance for five minutes for every fifteen minutes of homework completed. Of course, the parent should set a timer and help the child return to task!

You can play "hopscotch" and ask the child to jump from the "Here and Now" to "Distractions" and back.

6. Summarize what you have done so far: You have explained how to alternate between fun things to do and things that have to get done. You have used the metaphors of "the land of here and now" and "the land of over there" to illustrate how easy it is to get distracted. You have introduced the idea of using the fun things as rewards for completing tasks. You have also explained the need to keep love, joy, and play within reach at all times. They are a child's birthright!

7. Assign homework: Ask client and parent to pick a task that is hard for the child to complete. Then choose the reward item. Find a balance between what needs to get done and fun. You will have to negotiate how much time is spent with the reward and how much is spent on the task. This depends on the child and the level of ADHD. Some children may have to switch more than others. It is important to set things up so that the child can be successful. Here is a sample chart to use:

Homework: 30 minutes	Dance together: 10 minutes

Figure 64

Remind the parent that the child will need help with transitioning back to the less-desired activity. The parent should assist with the transition and help the child regulate difficult emotions such as anger and frustration.

8. Closing. Send client and parent home with words of encouragement:

- *Rewards are always fun.*

- *All you have to do is get the one thing done.*

- *Then you get to do the thing you want to do.*

- *It's easy as one, two, three!*

INTERVENTION 17

Going Fishing

The following intervention addresses emotional issues that may arise. Children with ADHD can find it difficult to respond to and manage their frustration, and it can turn into anger. Additionally, the intervention addresses the need to plan ahead, to have ready the things needed to complete an activity. In other words: If you are going fishing, you should pack a fishing pole or at least a net.

Target skill: Improve executive functioning.

Method: Client will learn and practice ways to manage strong emotions and impulse control.

Materials: Fishing game, the one with the fishing pole with the magnet and little fish to catch. You can buy it or make it. To make the game you need a small stick, string, and a magnet. You can draw little fish, laminate them, and then put paper clips on them so that they will "stick" to the magnet. Shallow bowl (pond).

1. Welcome your client and the parent. Ask:

    - *How was the last week?*

    - *What special thing did you do together?*

    - *What good thing did you do for each other?*

    Reiterate the importance of helping each other and connecting. If your client and the parent struggle with this, you can suggest:

    - *drawing hearts for each other;*

    - *saying something nice for no reason, or giving a compliment;*

    - *doing the chicken dance together.*

2. Introduce today's task: going fishing! You can explain that, in order to engage in this activity, you will need to prepare (have a fishing pole) and manage your emotions (be patient, curb frustration).

3. Review last week's homework. Ask:

    - *In what way did you follow through with switching between things the child wants to do and things he has to do?*

    - *When did this work well?*

    - *What went wrong?*

    - *Did you argue? And if you did, how did you resolve the argument?*

Help client and parent correct any mistakes made while using the Premack principle. Perhaps the parent is using it in a punitive way. Or perhaps the parent or child is getting angry while using it. Perhaps the wait for the reward is too long (or too short). Make corrections as needed. Help the parent understand the need to be supportively unemotional about the task-reward sequence. You can also show the following image again to help client and parent refocus and understand.

Figure 65

4. Work on today's task: Invite your client and the parent to "go fishing" with you. Put the fish in a shallow bowl. Spread them out. Some should be difficult to catch, some should be easy.

5. Give your client the fishing pole but without the magnet. Ask him to go fishing. You may hear some protest at this point. Praise your client for pointing out that you need the right tools to get the job done. Give him the fishing pole with the magnet.

6. Let your client go fishing. Observe: How hard is it for him to say calm enough to catch fish? How frustrated does he get when he does not get a fish? Provide support as needed. Prompt your client to take a break and breathe when he gets frustrated. Explain that it is hard to say focused when frustration gets in the way. Model calm breathing (belly breathing) and help your client practice. Then get back to fishing.

7. When the client is done, ask how this felt. Ask the parent to give the client compassionate feedback about fishing.

8. When your client has caught all the fish, provide praise for staying focused, overcoming frustration, and getting the job done.

9. Invite the parent to go fishing and the child to give compassionate feedback. Be sure to also practice belly breathing with the parent.

10. If you think your client can handle it, make it harder to catch fish by using a longer rod and moving farther away from the pond. Once again, provide support, help manage frustration, offer praise when the task is completed.

11. If your client is a child, give your client a laminated paper fish to keep as a reminder of his ability to get the job done!

12. If your client is an adult, ask: "What fish do you need to catch this week?" In other words: What needs to get done? Help identify the tasks and ways to complete them. Remind your client to use calm breathing to decrease frustration.

13. Review what you have done so far: You have introduced the idea that some tasks can be emotionally frustrating and will require preparation. You have provided an opportunity for client and parent to go fishing. You have provided feedback and helped them regulate strong feelings by using belly breathing.

14. Assign homework: Send the fishing game home with the client. If the family is crafty you can ask parent and child to make their own fishing game. Ask parent and child to fish together once per day, with each taking a turn. Ask

them to use belly breathing to manage frustration and anger as needed. Ask the parent to complete the following homework chart and bring it back to the next meeting:

	Mon	Tue	Wed	Thu	Fri	Sat	Sun
Played fishing?							
Managed frustration?							

Figure 66

15. Closing. Encourage client and parent.

- *You get to do this together.*
- *You get to help each other manage feelings.*
- *And it is fun to go fishing!*

INTERVENTION 18

Let's Hop

This intervention will help your client with ADHD carefully follow directions, one step at a time. Children with ADHD often want to jump ahead and do things quickly. If a child does this when doing origami, they will quickly find out that the item they have folded does not look or work the way it is supposed to. This intervention uses origami to help your client learn to listen, follow directions step-by-step, and manage frustration along the way. The parent can serve as a coach in this process.

You should be proficient in making a paper frog before you work with your client on this. You can find a tutorial on the website OrigamiClub.com (or you can search for similar resources online).

Target skill: Improve impulse control.

Method: Client will accept external modeling of multistep problem-solving (executive) routines.

Materials: Paper squares. Origami paper is expensive; you can use printer paper and cut it into squares. Use the rectangular leftover pieces of paper to make more, smaller squares. Scissors, pencils, colored pencils, crayons.

1. Welcome your client and the parent. Ask:

    - *How are you feeling today?*

    - *What makes this a good day?*

    - *What makes this a tough day?*

    Reinforce the idea that most days will have components of fun and frustration and that this is just normal. You can say:

    - *It's great to have fun together.*

    - *It's normal to get frustrated with each other.*

    - *Every day can have a little of both.*

2. Introduce today's task: learning patience and following multistep directions by folding paper into a frog. You can explain:

    - *Paper folding is fun.*

    - *But it takes patience.*

    - *We need to do this step-by-step or it won't work."*

3. Review last week's homework. Ask the parent to take out the homework chart and look at it together. Ask:

    - *Was this fun to do?*

    - *How easy or difficult was it to go fishing?*

    - *When did you laugh?*

    - *When did you get frustrated?*

    - *How did you use belly breathing?*

You may want to show the following video to reinforce the idea of belly breathing to manage frustrations:

Sesame Street (2012, October 19). Sesame street: common and colbie caillat— "Belly breathe" with elmo [Video File]. Retrieved from https://youtu.be/_mZbzDOpylA

You can then practice together.

4. Work on today's task: Invite your client to do some paper-folding with you. Have a folded frog ready and demonstrate how to make it jump, then ask both the client and the parent give it a try.

5. Give your client and the parent a square piece of paper each. Have your own piece ready. Explain that you will be folding your frogs together. Explain that it is important to go step-by-step and take the time to make great folds. Otherwise the frog will not hop as nicely.

6. Now begin folding. Show the first fold and prompt your client and the parent to do the same. Help them with making an accurate fold if needed. You want the frog to hop. Be sure to instill faith that they can do the job as long as they take time with every fold.

7. After each fold you should check each other's folds. You may want to make a "sloppy" fold once and have your client correct it. If there is a need to correct a fold, help your client and the parent with this.

8. Now just proceed step-by-step with the folds. Explain and demonstrate each fold before your client executes it. If your client struggles with listening and wants to jump ahead, help her take a short break by putting the paper down and taking a calm breath. Then return to folding.

9. Sometimes it is a good idea to help with creasing. Children often have a hard time with this.

10. Once your frogs are done, demonstrate how to make the frog hop. Finding the right spot may take a minute. Children tend to press too hard, and you may have to demonstrate that less pressure will probably work better.

11. Now let's make those frogs hop. It is amazing to see how far they can hop. Some hop really high. Generally speaking, smaller frogs hop better, but there is a limit to how small they can be.

12. Clients may want to fold more than one frog. This is OK. Some fold entire frog families. This is a great opportunity to talk about family.

13. Younger clients often want to color their frogs. Be prepared for some interesting patterns!

14. Now: Talk with your client and the parent about how the exercise went. Ask:

   - *Was it hard to do things one step at a time?*

   - *Did you become frustrated when a fold was difficult?*

   - *Did you want to race ahead and get the frog done?*

<ul>
<li>*Were you able to listen to instructions?*</li>
<li>*What helped you slow down?*</li>
</ul>

15. Point out the benefits of following directions one step at a time and look at the result of doing so: a pretty frog that actually hops.

16. Review what you have done: You have used paper folding to demonstrate the need to take time and follow directions carefully. You have used belly breathing to regulate feelings of impatience and frustration. You have folded frogs, made them hop, and decorated them.

17. Assign homework: Ask your client and the parent to each fold one frog per day together. You can say: *You will have a whole army of frogs!*

    Be sure to print instructions for frog folding for the parent. Be sure that the parent understands not to scold the child for making mistakes, but rather praise her for finishing and be helpful in the process. Ask the parent to snap a picture of all the frogs they have folded together.

18. You can substitute the frog with any other developmentally appropriate folding pattern. Let your client choose a pattern within her ability range!

19. Closing. Send your client home with the following words: *I wonder if you and your parent will be able to show me how to make a frog all by yourselves next time? I can't wait to see!*

INTERVENTION 19

Tower Time

Building something, even something very little such as a tower out of blocks requires planning skills and the ability to manage frustration. Because building is also a form of play for children, it is a perfect setting for children with ADHD to practice and improve on their planning skills and their ability to manage feelings. The parent can serve as a collaborator and coach. The key to this intervention is not to take it too seriously. In life and in play, the things we build will occasionally fall over. This is just another opportunity to start over and practice.

Target skill: Develop planning and goal-setting skills.

Method: Client will accept the use of modeling by caregiver to learn to use scaffolding and encouragement during the child's attempt to solve problems.

Materials: Jenga or other building blocks. Patience. Humor.

1. Welcome your client. Ask:

   - *What did you do outside in the past week?*

   - *Where did you go together?*

   - *What is the best thing you did together?*

   Help the parent and client truly listen to each other. What was the best thing for the parent? What about the client? Those things do not have to be the same!

2. Introduce today's task: building a tower to practice planning and patience. You can explain that this is another opportunity to practice thinking before acting and dealing with frustration.

3. Review last week's homework. Ask to see a photo of all the frogs parent and child folded together. Then ask the client: *Do you think you and your parent together could show me how to fold a frog?*

   Ask parent and child to demonstrate the newly acquired skill. Then explain that the other skills they learned and practiced were planning and patience. You can say:

   > *These are skills you need every day, when you are packing your book bag or doing your homework or getting ready for dinner! These skills come in handy all the time!*

4. Work on today's task: Invite your client to build a tower. The task is to build a tower as high as possible. Resist the temptation to help, and ask the parent to simply sit back and watch.

5. If the tower falls quickly, ask the parent to step in, coach the client to use belly breathing to calm, and then provide one helpful tip, such as: "If the bottom of the tower is not big enough, the tower will fall over much easier."

6. Let the client build another tower. This time ask the parent to coach the child to take time placing blocks. They can ask: "If you put a block here, what do you think is going to happen? Is the tower going to stand or fall?"

7. If the tower falls, let the parent coach the child to manage frustration. The parent can say: "This is just a game. This is how we learn. Sometimes the tower stands, sometimes it falls."

8. Switch roles. Have your client coach the parent. The parent may want to build a "funky" tower, small at the bottom, and see what the child says. The parent can ask: "Should I put this block here?" The parent may want to let the tower topple and model how to manage frustration. Ask the child to coach the parent how to make careful choices and manage frustration. Be playful. Explain that in real life it is often helpful to slow down when making choices.

9. Review what you have done so far: You have introduced an activity that requires planning and emotion-regulation skills and practiced them by building a tower. The parent and child have coached each other to reinforce those skills.

10. Assign homework. Ask the parent to build a tower with the client every day. If there are no Jenga blocks at home, this is OK. You can build a tower out of pots from the kitchen or even pillows. Be sure to explain that the exercise is not about building a perfect tower, but rather about thinking ahead, weighing options, and managing frustration when the tower falls. Explain clearly that if the tower falls, it is the parent's job to help the child manage frustration. The parent should not lecture the child about how to build a perfect tower or frustrate the client by building a perfect tower herself. The parent should model playful learning and frustration tolerance. You can explain that the best way to do so may be to make some planned mistakes. Ask the parent to snap pictures of the finished towers.

11. Closing: Send your client home with words of encouragement like these:

    - *You can build great towers.*

    - *This can be lots of fun.*

    - *If you take time to think, your towers will become better!*

INTERVENTION 20

Window Shopping

This intervention helps both client and parent to recognize issues of impulsivity. We all know that when we go shopping we may suddenly want something we see. We may suddenly want ice cream if we walk past an ice cream store. Or we may suddenly want a dog because we see a cute puppy in a pet store. Of course, we can't just impulsively get all the things we want. This is clear to most adults. But for children with ADHD, resisting impulsivity and sticking with a plan is more difficult. Remember, this is a symptom, not a personal fault.

Target skill: Improve impulse control.

Method: Client will engage in activities to improve inhibition of responses, working memory and processing speed in complex situations; and to build emotional control.

Materials: You can do this exercise using a catalogue or a shopping website (with appropriate content). Paper. Pencils. Calculator (you can use the one on your phone).

1. Welcome your client and the parent. Ask:

   - *Who in your family did you see in the last week?*

   - *Who was the most fun or interesting to talk to and why?*

   - *How did you feel after talking with that person?*

   Help client and parent recognize the need to make each other feel special by pointing out how others in the family make them feel special and appreciated.

2. Introduce today's task: going shopping. You can say: *We are going pretend shopping. There will be lots of things to look at. Let's see what it is like to choose.*

3. Review last week's homework. Ask:

   - *What kinds of towers did you build?*

   - *Tell me about the most spectacular collapse!*

   - *When did you laugh together during the building process?*

   - *When did you get upset or sad?*

   - *How did you help each other with your feelings?*

   Reinforce the idea that feelings can be intense, but they can also be managed, especially with the help of family and friends.

4. Work on today's task: Ask your client to create a list of five items she really wants, perhaps for herself, perhaps for someone else. Ask the parent to do the same. You may want to reiterate that this is pretend shopping, just for fun.

5. Provide your client and the parent with a catalogue or with access to a website (best to stay on one site to keep it simple). Ask them to pick the five items that best match the lists they made.

6. Help your client and the parent acknowledge when they make changes to their lists because they see something they suddenly want. Help your client recognize impulsivity when "shopping."

7. Many clients may find it difficult to choose only five items. Simply help your client recognize the difficulty of making choices. You can say: *Choosing is difficult. Sometimes we can't have it all. We may feel sad or angry about this, but that feeling will pass.*

8. Now: Introduce a budget. Something realistic, based on the kind of site you are on. Ask your client and the parent to choose again, but this time they must stick with the budget. Provide a calculator if needed.

9. Help your client recognize frustration and label it as such when the budget limits choices. Help her understand that tension can build up when we make choices. Help her calm tension using calm breathing, relaxation music, or distraction. Encourage the parent to model, honestly, how she talked herself through frustration over having to choose.

10. You and your client should look at the items she has chosen. Praise her for staying within the budget and acknowledge how hard it can be to make choices. Prompt the parent to also provide positive feedback for the client.

11. Review what you have done so far: You have coached the client to make choices in a difficult situation using pretend shopping. You have helped the client recognize impulsivity and frustration, and you have coached the parent to model for the client how to manage frustration.

12. Assign homework: Ask the parent to set up a mini "store" in the child's room. The store can be made up of things that are already there (and that the child really likes). The parent should ask the child to "buy" three items and coach her to think the purchases through. If there is a need, the parent should coach managing frustration. Then parent and child should change roles. Ask the parent to snap a picture of the store.

13. You can say to the client: *Making choices can be tricky. Sometimes it is good to make quick choices. Sometimes it's good to take time.*

INTERVENTION 21

Tough Times

This intervention addresses the problem of impulsive aggression and helps your client take time to stop and think.

Target skill: Improve impulse control.

Method: Client will improve problem solving by identifying the problem, evaluating all possible solutions, choosing a strategy or behavior, and evaluating the outcome.

Materials: Just your ability to tell a story and role play. Paper. Pencil. Index card.

1. Welcome your client and the parent. Ask:

   - *What do you see people around you doing?*

   - *Do they always think before they act?*

   - *Is there a person who often does this well?*

   - *Who is this person, and what can you learn from him or her?*

   Be sure to also ask the parent who sets an example for her. This will help the client recognize that adults, too, make mistakes and look to others for help.

2. Introduce today's task: learning about anger and stepping back from it. You can say:

   > *Children with ADHD often experience intense anger more quickly. And they can have a difficult time stopping themselves from acting on that anger. This is a symptom of ADHD. It's a symptom that needs addressed because it gets kids in trouble when others get hurt. And we do not want you (the child) in trouble. We don't want you to hurt someone.*

3. Review last week's homework: Ask the parent to show you the picture of the store she set up at home. Ask the client:

   - *What was it like to have a pretend store?*

   - *Was it difficult to make choices?*

   - *What did you buy and why?*

   - *What did your parent buy?*

   - *Do you think it was difficult for your parent to make choices? Did she take time to think about her choices?*

   Reiterate that it can be helpful to stop and think when making decisions. You can say: *When we take time to think about things, they often work out better.*

4. Work on today's task: Invite your client and the parent to listen to a story about aggression (if the client is younger, use the word "anger").

5. Tell this story:

Imagine yourself on a nice day just walking down the road. It is warm, and you are enjoying yourself. You are on a break. Suddenly, out of nowhere, someone bumps into you. You did not see this person coming. You are immediately angry and so is he. He calls you an idiot for not seeing him. You can't believe this. You yell at him. He gets louder, so you get louder. All of this happens within seconds. No time to think. Things get worse: He raises his fist. You raise your fist. Fists are about to fly.

This story can easily be adapted to reflect a playground situation for your younger clients. Just use your imagination.

6. Now pause. Take a deep breath and invite your client and the parent to take a deep breath, too.

7. Help your client connect to the story by asking questions like:

    - *Has this ever happened to you?*

    - *What makes you instantly angry?*

    - *Have you ever hit/punched someone without thinking?*

    - *How does it feel to be called a name?*

    - *What do you think happens to your ability to think things through when you feel attacked with words or fists?*

8. Ask the parent to reflect on this, too, in an honest manner. It is important for the child to hear that anger is a natural emotion.

9. Ask your client and the parent to identify their personal values. Ask:

    - *What is really important to you?*

    - *How do you want to be treated?*

    - *What could happen as a consequence if a fight broke out?*

10. For a moment, help your client think about a life and world without hurt and with a deep commitment to recognizing the connections we all have with each other, whether we see them or not.

11. Refer back to the story: Ask if it is possible that the entire situation was an accident and that the client misheard what was said. Ask if perhaps the other person was just having a bad day. Ask your client if he has ever made choices he regretted when having a bad day. Ask the parent to chime in with an appropriate example. Have they ever had to step back in a tricky situation?

12. Invite your client to re-tell the story you told, this time with a better ending in which no one gets hurt. The parent should only help if needed. Take notes as the client is telling the story.

13. Ask the parent to re-tell the story as the child told it.

14. Once your client and the parent have recreated and re-told the story, help your client identify steps he could have taken to avoid a confrontation. If this is difficult, give examples. Ask:

    Could you have walked away? Could you have taken a step back? Could you have smiled and apologized, even if this was not your fault, just to make the world a better place?

15. Review what you have done so far: You have introduced the idea that it is possible to step back and make good choices even in difficult situations. You have told the story of a difficult situation, and the client has re-told the story in a way that produces a better outcome.

16. Create an index card outlining the steps your client has taken to create a better outcome. Perhaps something like this:

1. Take a breath.

2. Take a few steps back.

3. Walk away.

4. _______________________________

5. _______________________________

6. _______________________________

Figure 67

17. Assign homework: Send the index card home with the parent and the child. Ask the parent to carry the card and use it when the parent gets angry or upset and then to model use of the card for three days. After the three days, the parent should help the child use the card when there is a difficult situation. You should explain that the most important step to prevent harm is almost always to take a breath and step away! When the client is able to step away from a difficult situation, the parent should provide instant positive feedback about this. Stepping away when angry is not easy! Even adults struggle with this.

18. Closing. Provide encouragement. You can say: *Anger can be very powerful. I don't want it to be the boss of you. I want you to be the boss of it! You can do that by stepping away!*

INTERVENTION 22

Applying the Brakes

This intervention extends the previous idea of stepping back and uses the metaphor of "applying the brakes." It also introduces several more ideas about stepping back. Many clients will find that they cannot just step back, that they will need some sort of distraction in the form of sensory input to change their mind.

Target skill: Improve impulse control.

Method: Client will engage in activities to improve inhibition of responses, working memory, and processing speed in complex situations; and to build emotional control.

This exercise can follow the prior exercise (Tough Times), or it can stand alone.

Materials: Your ability to tell a story. Props, such as an orange, perfume, music, a beautiful or very funny image, piece of soft cloth, etc.

1. Welcome your client and the parent. Ask:

    - *What did you do for yourself this week?*

    - *What did you enjoy?*

    - *How do you think doing something nice for yourself affected how you treated each other?*

    Help both client and parent identify at least one nice thing they can do for themselves every day, like listen to music, read or write a poem, or learn something new.

2. Introduce today's task: applying the brakes on impulsive expressions of anger. You can say:

    We all have anger. Anger is just a feeling. We need to recognize our anger and then manage it in ways that keeps everyone safe. It's not the anger that is dangerous. It's what we choose to do with the anger that matters.

3. Review last week's homework. Ask:

    - *In what way did the two of you use your Step-Away index card?*

    - *Can you give me an example of when the index card was helpful?*

    - *When was the index card not helpful? Do you know why it was not?*

    Reiterate that emotions can be strong in the moment and that it is best to have a plan for dealing with them. You can say: *When you don't have a plan, strong feelings just take over. When that happens, we sometimes hurt others. This can be especially true for children with ADHD. Impulsivity is a just a part of it. That's why it's best to have a plan and follow it*

4. Work on today's task: Invite your client and the parent to listen to a story he may already know. Tell the story:

    Imagine yourself on a nice day just walking down the road. It is warm, and you are enjoying yourself. You are on a break. Suddenly, out of nowhere,

> *someone bumps into you. You did not see this person coming. You are immediately angry and so is he. He calls you an idiot for not seeing him. You can't believe this. You yell at him. He gets louder, so you get louder. All of this happens within seconds. No time to think. Things get worse: He raises his fist. You raise your fist. Fists are about to fly.*

5. Pause and invite your client and the parent to take a deep breath with you. Say something like: *That is quite a story. It can make us feel instantly wronged and angry.* By doing so you are modeling how to create some distance between the story and the feelings it provokes.

6. Invite your client to learn and practice several ways of applying the brakes. Summarize the story again like this: "So there you are, both with your fists raised. What can you do now to apply the brakes?" Pay attention to the parent also. How is the parent responding to the story? You can ask the parent how tense he or she is in response to the story. Normalize the angry feelings that may come up without endorsing behavioral anger outbursts. Sometimes parents want to retaliate for real or perceived insults. This can be especially true when the parent has been exposed to traumatic experiences of toxic stress. Normalize the angry feelings that may come up without endorsing anger outbursts. You should explain:

    - *Your fight-or-flight response has kicked in. You are ready to defend yourself. This is a normal human response to danger. But the response is meant to help us get ready to defend our lives. It's not meant for situations in which our lives are not in danger. The response can be calmed. It's a matter of practice.*

7. Explain that the first step is often to slow down and step back, and this can be done by breathing calmly. Explain that rage can trigger a fight response in the body that can be countered by breathing more calmly.

8. Model calm breathing: In through the nose, count to four, and out through the mouth, count to six. Practice together. Explain that breathing more calmly in a stressful situation can decrease impulsivity and make the situation more manageable. You can explain this to children by saying "smell the soup" (inhalation) and "blow on the soup" (exhalation). It's good to add some imagery. This makes it more fun. Just be sure that your client and the parent learn to breathe calmly, not rapidly, and that they breathe out longer than they breathe in.

9. You can explain to the parent that taking a breath like this can also be helpful when she feels herself getting angry at the child.

10. Offer other options for calming. Explain that some people like to carry a tissue with a bit of their favorite perfume sprayed on it to smell when they need to calm themselves. Take out some beautiful pictures and ask your client to look at them. Ask: "How do you feel after looking at this picture?" Suggest that your client carry a picture of his favorite person, pet or place; a small stuffed animal; or something scented. Be sure that the method he chooses to calm himself down fit him.

11. If your client has talked with you about his spirituality, you can say: *You have told me that you use prayer/meditation to feel more grounded. Do you think that this could work in a situation like this?* Discuss what it would be like to use prayer or meditation. Ask your client specifically what prayer or meditation he would use.

12. Explain that practice makes perfect. **Explain the need to choose more than one method to apply the brakes. Not every method works in every situation.**

13. Create an index card for the client, listing three ways of applying the brakes. Be sure that you only use things that would really work for him. Sometimes parents have great ideas, but they are ideas that would work for them, not the child.

14. Summarize what you have done so far: You have reviewed how anger can be instant and impulsive. You have explained how and why the anger response may kick in. You have come up with ideas for calming the anger response and created an index card for the client to take home.

15. Assign homework: Send the index card home with the client. Ask him and the parent to practice each of the methods chosen once every day, even if there is no anger trigger. You can explain that practice makes perfect. You can say: *I want you to be ready when anger actually happens. If you practice managing anger, it becomes natural. If you practice, it won't be so hard.*

    Give your client and parent the following chart to record homework completion. Charts increase compliance! Ask the parent to bring the chart back to your next meeting.

	Mon	Tue	Wed	Thu	Fri	Sat	Sun
Practiced anger management skills							

Figure 68

16. Leave your client with words of encouragement like these: *It's OK to feel anger. Anger can be calmed. You can step back and be in control.*

INTERVENTION 23

In the Eye of the Storm

This intervention teaches your client not to be a part of the storm of anger and rage, but rather to create a protected space for herself to wait out the storm.

Target skill: Improve impulse control.

Method: Client will engage in activities to improve inhibition of responses, working memory and processing speed in complex situations; and to build emotional control.

Materials: Poster board, all kinds of drawing tools, scissors, glue, old magazines and catalogs, etc.

1. Welcome your client and the parent. Ask:

   - *What kinds of big feelings did you have this week?*

   - *What happened when you had big feelings?*

2. Introduce today's task: using art to create a symbolic calming space. You can say: *Sometimes we can't really just step away. When there is trouble at school you can't just leave. For those cases it is good to have a room or a space in your mind where you can go to calm yourself.*

3. Review last week's homework. Ask the parent to take out the Anger Management homework chart. Take a look together. Ask:

   - *How often did you practice?*

   - *Did you practice together?*

   - *What felt good?*

   - *What do you think would work best for calming your anger?*

   Once the client has identified what works best, this will be her go-to skill to use. Parent and child should practice this skill together every day, and the parent should prompt herself and the child to use the skill when needed.

   You can reinforce the idea of using calming skills by saying to the client: *You are now a calming ambassador. You can show the world that you can calm your anger. This means that you are very strong. It's not easy to calm anger.*

4. Work on today's task: Invite your client to create an image of a storm. She can include anything that she wants in the storm of life: siblings, bullies at school, homework, tests. Ask the parent to assist the client with creating the image without taking over.

Figure 69

5. Explain to your client that she can be as creative as she wants to be. She can draw, write, paint, or make a collage of all that is part of the storm in her life.

6. It is OK to talk about the storm while the client is working.

7. When the storm is completed, ask your client:

   - *Where are you in this storm?*

   - *Are you swirling around in the storm?*

   - *Are you fighting the storm?*

8. Introduce the idea of creating a calm, centered space in the eye of the storm. This is a protected space in which your client is unaffected by the wind and rain. It can be a hiding space, but it can also be an open space where there is magically no storm.

9. Ask your client to include this calm space within the image of the storm she has created. This space can be anything she wants it to be, but it has to be protected. There should be a protective border around the space. It could be a house, a circle, or simply a glass dome. The important thing is that the storm cannot enter the space.

10. Ask your client to draw herself within this protected space.

11. Discuss with your client how thinking of herself in a protected space in the eye of the storm may change her actions. Ask the parent to chime in. You can ask:

    - *What is different when you are watching the storm but are not in it?*

    - *What different actions would you choose to manage the storm?*

12. Suggest that in the protected space she no longer has to fight the storm or react to it in ways that could be harmful to her or anyone else. She can watch the storm. She can wait out the storm. She can take her time and think about the storm that is raging around her and how to interact with it. The important thing is that she now has a choice, and she can think calmly.

13. Discuss the importance of being thoughtful, as opposed to impulsively reactive, in the storm of life. Help her understand how not being reactive, but rather taking time to make choices, could make her life better.

14. Summarize what you have done so far: You have helped your client create an imaginary space in which she is protected from the storm of life. You have helped her identify ways in which her actions would change based on being in this imaginary space.

15. Assign homework: Ask your client to set aside time every day to think of herself in a protected space. Ask her to think about the details of it and "decorate" it until it feels real and perfectly calm. Ask the client to tell the parent in detail about the protected space, and ask the parent to take notes and bring them back to your next meeting.

16. Closing. Say to the client and parent: *You don't have to be a part of every storm. You can step away in your mind. You can watch the storm from your protected space. If you do that, there is no need for impulsive anger.*

INTERVENTION 24

Every Times this Happens

The following intervention is designed to help your client plan ahead. Some problems are likely to occur over and over, such as problems during recess. Your client will create a workable plan for how to respond to predictable problems.

Target skill: Reduce impact of mental health symptoms on school, work, home, and community.

Method: Client will improve problem solving by identifying the problem, evaluating all possible solutions, choosing a strategy or behavior, and evaluating the outcome.

Materials: Index cards, writing tools, laminator (if you do not have one, it is easy to "laminate" an index card with transparent tape).

1. Welcome your client and the parent. Ask:

   - *How was the week?*

   - *What kinds of things got you off balance this week?*

   - *What kinds of things helped you experience joy this week?*

   Normalize the experience of difficulty. Amplify experiences of joy. Ask your client to go into detail when recounting joyful experiences and watch his face the moment he talks about joy. Ask the parent to connect with the client's joy and see if it spreads.

2. Introduce today's task: creating a framework for responding to challenges in a productive way every time. You can say:

   Certain things can happen over and over, like being teased during recess or somebody calling you a name. It's good to be prepared. It's good to know what to do based on what is important to you.

3. Review last week's homework. Ask the parent to take out the notes about the client's protected space and read them out loud. When the parent has read the notes, ask the client:

   - *What would you like to add?*

   - *Did we forget anything?*

   - *What makes this space protected?*

   - *How do you feel when you think about a protected space?*

   Reiterate that a safe, protected space can be thought about in most situations, even if he feels out of control. You can say:

   - *You can go there in your mind.*

   - *You can go there when you may hurt someone out of anger. You can step away and feel safe.*

4.   Work on today's task: Invite your client to tell you about a situation in which he acted without thinking and got in trouble. Ask the parent to chime in about this in a nonjudgmental way.

5.   Help your client acknowledge that it is difficult to talk about things he has done that he may feel shame about.

6.   Explain that mistakes are learning opportunities. You can ask the parent to share an example about learning from mistakes. In this way you are helping the parent understand that mistakes will be made.

7.   Listen to your client's story. When he has finished, acknowledge that this may have been difficult and thank him for telling the story. If the parent has shared a story about learning from a mistake, thank the parent, too. You can say: *See, even your mom/dad makes mistakes. That's OK. We just need to learn from them.*

8.   If you have questions about the story because something does not add up or you do not understand part of it, ask. Your questions may also help the client better understand the situation.

9.   If your client blames someone or something else for the mistake he made, verbalize this for him. Say something like this: *"It sounds like you blame* [name of the person your client blames] *for what happened, because he* [actions that person took that lead to the client blaming him]*."*

10. Explain that this exercise is about helping him make better choices and that you wish others would make better choices, too, but that we have no power over the choices of others. You can give an example like this:

> *Erica goes to recess. It's always been a struggle for her to not act out with impulsive anger when someone is mean to her. Today Emily calls her a name, a really mean one. In return, Erica slaps Emily and has to go to the principal's office. In the office she yells that it is not her fault.*

You can say: *Erica can only control what she does. She can't control what Emily does. If Erica controls what she does, she will be in a better situation.*

11. Explain to your client that you can help him create a roadmap that will help him make choices based on his values, as opposed to impulsive choices that cause problems for him.

12. Ask your client: *What is really important to you?* Write each of your client's answers on an index card. Ask the parent to comment on family values.

13. Help your client identify personal values represented by his answers. Here is an example: Your client may say that his dog (cat, sister, mother) is really important to him. Ask your client if he values connection. You are extracting the personal value from your client's answers.

14. Sometimes it is not possible or advisable to move into identifying abstract values. This is OK. You can just reiterate: "So I understand that your dog is really important to you."

15. Next: Explain that you are going to create a roadmap for what to do in the situation your client experienced based on the values he has told you about. Here is an example: Erica really loves playtime with her friend Sarah at school. If she hits Emily, she won't be allowed back at school for a few days.

16. Invite your client to complete the "if this happens, then I will do that" exercise.

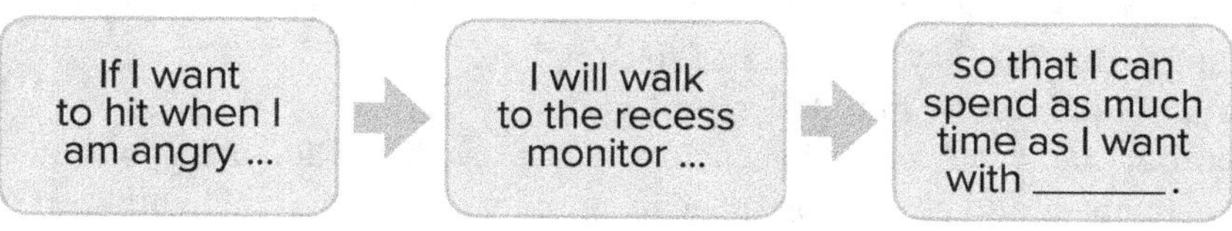

Figure 70

17. Ask your client write this roadmap down on an index card.

18. The card should be small enough so that it can easily be carried in your client's back pocket.

19. Make sure that the steps your client identifies are realistic. In this case, you want to be sure that there is a recess monitor. Choose another more workable solution if there is none.

20. Review what you have done so far: You have helped your client think about what is important to him and have identified a predictable problem. You have come up with a way of responding to the problem that is in line with the client's values. Laminate the card and give it to the parent.

21. Assign homework: Ask the parent to carry the card with him for the next week and read it to the child every morning. Explain that it is important to plan ahead so that he will remember what to do the next time he might make an impulsive mistake. Challenge your client to respond to the predictable problem as outlined on the card. When this happens, the child should tell his parent about it, and the parent should provide positive reinforcement: a big hug and high-five for a job well done.

22. Closing. Encourage your client to make great choices. You can say: *You actually win when you make better choices. You are doing the right thing. And you get to do the things that are important to you.*

INTERVENTION 25

Changing the Channel

The following intervention is designed to help your client recognize the moment of distraction and impulsive choices. We are all familiar with finding ourselves engaged in an activity we suddenly "floated" into. Children (and adults) with ADHD have this experience all the time, and they often struggle with recognizing it and returning to the task they had planned to complete.

Target skill: Improve impulse control.

Method: Client will engage in activities to improve inhibition of responses, working memory and processing speed in complex situations; and to build emotional control.

Materials: Music.

1. Welcome your client. Ask:

   - *How are you feeling today?*

   - *What did you do right before our meeting?*

   - *How do you feel about being here?*

   Help your client recognize the sequence of activities and feelings and perhaps make connections between them.

2. Introduce today's task: changing the channel by choice instead of acting impulsively. You can explain:

   Life can move fast. We often do things on a whim without thinking. Children with ADHD may find themselves doing something impulsively instead of having made a conscious decision. Making a decision is like changing the channel on TV. You press a button. It does not just happen. We can learn to make conscious choices by paying attention to what we are doing.

3. Review last week's homework. Ask:

   - *Did you review the index card every day?*

   - *What kind of discussion was there about the card?*

   - *Did you have an opportunity to use the steps outlined on the card? If there was opportunity, how did it go? Did things end well?*

   Be sure that the parent follows up with positive reinforcement about making new and better decisions.

4. Work on today's task: Ask your client to tell you about her favorite music. Then ask her if it would be OK to listen to this music together. Explain that listening together may help you better understand who she is and what she likes.

5. Listen to your client's choice of music together for a few minutes. If your client talks while the music plays, this is OK. You can respond.

6. When the music is finished, ask your client what she likes about it:

Is it the beat you like? The words? Does this music remind you of something?
Does it make you want to dance? Or does it calm you?

7. Involve the parent in this process. Help the parent recognize what music the client likes and accept the child's taste in music.

8. If your client is a child or an adolescent, you will have to make sure that the choice of music is appropriate.

9. Ask your client if she will allow you to play a piece of music she may not like. Explain that this piece will only play for as long as she will let it and that she will have the ability to "change the channel" and go back to her choice of music just by saying "change the channel" to you. If a parent is present, let the parent choose a piece of music. Most parents (unless the child is very young) will have different taste in music.

10. Play a song that you are pretty sure your client is not going to love (her prior choice of music will your guide your decision). Most children don't enjoy classical music as much as adults do.

11. When your client asks you to "change the channel," go back to your client's choice of music.

12. Now: Introduce the idea that your client has the ability to make conscious choices instead of impulse-based choices in everyday life. Explain that she can "change the channel."

13. Ask your client to identify a situation in which she impulsively made a choice. Have her describe as many details as she can to you. Involve the parent in this description of what happened. Highlight the differences between choices and things that just happen.

14. Role play the situation with your client. Involve the parent. Explain that the role play is not about scolding the child for being impulsive, but rather about teaching her to make decisions. When the moment of impulsivity arrives, say, "Let's change the channel."

15. Explain that changing the channel can be done in many ways: By removing oneself from a situation, by distracting oneself (perhaps by listening to a favorite song), by calling a friend, by doing jumping jacks, by mindfully eating something, by reminding oneself of what is important.

16. Repeat the previous role play involving impulsivity. Help your client change the channel during the exercise. If the first thing does not work, this is not a problem; just move on to the next thing. If your client struggles with changing the channel," acknowledge this. Ask her and the parent to play a game with you. Be attentive to your client. If she will allow it, use humor. Help your client immerse herself in the game, then help her recognize that she has just changed the channel.

17. Review what you have done so far: You have explained the difference between impulsive actions and conscious choices. You have introduced the

metaphor of changing the channel for making conscious choices. You role-played how to make conscious choices.

Assign homework: Ask your client to practice changing the channel. You may want to give an example: ***When you are about to impulsively buy*** [item client was about to impulsively buy], ***just change the channel by*** [action client can take to stop herself from the impulsive purchase].

Figure 71

You may want to give out a laminated index card with a visual reminder to help your client prompt herself when needed. Give the laminated card to the parent. Ask the parent to model using the card for two days. On the third day the parent should give the card to the child and provide verbal prompts about conscious choices using the "change the channel" metaphor.

18. Be sure to encourage your client to make conscious choices. You can say: ***You can learn to slow yourself down and make choices. It just takes time to learn. And practice. You can do this.***

INTERVENTION 26

Sit with It

This intervention encourages the use of mindfulness as an antidote to impulsivity. Mindfulness does not deny the existence of impulsivity, but rather slows down the mind and body. Mindfulness observes impulsivity nonjudgmentally and waits for conscious choices to emerge.

Target skill: Improve impulse control.

Method: Client will increase self-control and self-efficacy through the use of mindfulness skills, body awareness, and executive-functioning development.

Materials: A good place to sit. Attractive item such as gummi bear or toy.

1. Welcome your client/parent. Ask:

     - *What great choices did you make in the last week?*

     - *What not-so-great choices did you make?*

   Help your client recognize his ability to examine his choices. You can say:

   > *Looking back, we can sometimes recognize what was a good choice and what was not. This does not mean that we have to be sad or mad about the bad choice. It just means that we plan ahead for choices that will come up in the future.*

2. Introduce today's task: not acting impulsively even when it is very tempting. Explain that this is going to be a bit of a challenge, but a fun one.

3. Review last week's homework. Ask:

     - *In what way were you able to change the channel?*

     - *When did this work?*

     - *When was it tough?*

     - *How was your parent able to help you?*

   Highlight any success with making conscious choices. Be sure to remind the parent to provide positive feedback every time the client tried to make conscious choices.

4. Work on today's task: Invite your client and the parent to engage in an exercise of "sitting with" tough impulses without acting on them. Explain that you will be there to support him.

5. You should all be sitting comfortably. Put an appropriate, extremely desirably item between the two of you. If should be an item that almost anyone would want. For kids, a gummi bear is often a good idea. You could try a donut for an adult. Toys can work, too.

6. Give yourself, your client, and the parent the following challenge: Look at the item. Do not try to distract yourself. Acknowledge how much you want the item. If you think of something else, this is OK. Tell your client to acknowledge wanting the item using words, then to let thoughts wander

without clinging to the thought of wanting the item. Model this by saying the following out loud:

> *Well, hello there, thought of wanting the* [item client impulsively wants]. *There you are again. It is OK that you are there. Just because I am thinking about wanting* [item client impulsively wants] *does not mean I have to actually have it. This is just a thought.*

7. It is OK to talk during the exercise. If your client needs encouragement for "sitting with it," provide the support needed.

8. Depending on the age and developmental level of your client, you may want to sit with it for two minutes or the most of session. It just depends what is needed.

9. Explain intermittently that the key to this exercise is not to deny the existence of impulses but to accept them. Explain that it is possible to live with them without giving in to them.

10. When you have completed the exercise, ask the parent and client to talk about the pressure to act that can build up when seeing something you want. Ask: *How did you handle it?*

11. Review what you have done so far. You have introduced the idea that impulses can be observed nonjudgmentally. You have engaged the client and the parent in an exercise to learn the mindful observation of an impulse. You can give the desired item to the client at this point.

12. Assign homework: Challenge your client and the parent to "sit with" a very tempting item (but not a dangerous one) every day for the next week. Help the parent and the client choose the item. Be sure to only choose an item that will not cause a problem. Send home the following index card for support:

<table>
<tr><td>

I see the ________________________________.

I want to ________________________________.

It is OK that I want to ____________________.

I am just going to "sit with it."

It is OK to want, and it is OK to "sit with it."

</td></tr>
</table>

Figure 72

13. Closing. Send the client and the parent home with words of encouragement. You can say: *This is tough! Just be with the feeling that this is tough. Even tough situations pass!*

     Be sure to remind the parent not to scold the client about lack of impulse control. Remember: It's just a symptom.

INTERVENTION 27

Going On a Trip

The following intervention introduces your client to the usefulness of planning ahead and also to the need to organize the planning process using the metaphor of going on a trip. Children with ADHD often become overwhelmed and give up when trying to plan ahead. This intervention will help them learn to divide the planning into manageable steps.

Target skill: Develop planning and goal-setting skills.

Method: Client will increase capacities in daily-living skills by developing appropriate and realistic expectations and limitations for behavior, breaking down behaviors into a sequence of steps.

Materials: If you are completing this exercise with a child, it might be good to use props such as a small suitcase and toy versions of things you may need on a trip. Index cards.

1. Welcome your client and the parent. Ask:

   - *In what way did you help each other today?*

   - *In what way did you praise and appreciate each other today?*

   Remind the parent that children with ADHD often get a lot of negative feedback and that negative feedback can really impact how the child thinks of himself. Say: *As a parent you can use positive reinforcement not only to help change your child's behavior but also to help him feel better about himself.*

2. Introduce today's task: Learning to plan ahead step-by-step. You can say: *Planning can be difficult for children with ADHD. It just seems overwhelming. But you can learn to do it step-by-step.*

3. Review last week's homework. Ask:

   - *How many times did you try to "sit with it"?*

   - *What was it like to sit with the item?*

   - *How did you feel?*

   - *Were you able to recognize wanting the item but not taking it?*

   Provide positive feedback for every attempt to just sit with it. Introduce the idea that it is possible to just sit with intense feelings such as anger and rage. They can be recognized but don't have to be acted upon impulsively.

4. Work on today's task: Invite your client and the parent to plan a trip. You may want to ask where they have always wanted to go. After you determine the destination together, introduce the idea that a trip takes planning. You can show an image of suitcases to illustrate the need to plan ahead and pack. You can ask what can happen if you don't.

Figure 73

5. Ask your client what he might need to do and pack to get ready for the trip. Help him make a list of what is needed. Ask the parent: What did the client not think about? Add the missing items to the list.

6. Be sure to talk about the joy of going on a trip. Also discuss the work of planning ahead. You may want to look at some pictures on the Internet of where your client wants to go in order to build excitement.

7. Make a list with your client and the parent of all that needs to happen. If you are working with a younger child, he can draw the list or you can write. If the list is very short, be sure to add things that are needed. Your client might need a passport, for example.

8. When the list is sufficiently long, ask your client what it is like to look at it. Is he getting frustrated? Does he feel it might not be worth the work?

9. Talk about what it would be like to actually be on the trip, sunbathing on the beach, hiking in the mountains, or going on rides in Disneyland.

10. Suggest it might be easier to complete everything on the list if he divides it up. Take out a few index cards and help your client divide up the list into manageable parts. Help him determine what needs to be done first, such as applying for a passport and booking a flight. Those things go on the first index card. The list can be drawn or written depending on the child's abilities. Ask the parent to be a scribe if this is OK with the client.

11. Explain the need to complete tasks outlined on the index cards one at a time. Explain that this may help him avoid frustration and feeling overwhelmed. Say: ***Don't look at all the cards at one. Just take the first one and begin!***

12. If your client is a child, begin "packing" with him. Make it fun. If something on the client's list is missing from your selection of props, no problem. He can draw it and put the drawing in a suitcase. Involve the parent as a coach, helping the child stay focused.

13. Be sure to remind your client about the fun times ahead once all the tasks are completed.

14. Discuss with your client how many things in life can be like going on a trip. Many things call for planning ahead. Ask the parent to help the child break

down complex planning tasks into steps. If the child is younger, limit the number of steps to three. Ask the parent and client what tasks need to be broken down. Here are some examples:

- *Getting ready for school.*
- *Doing homework.*
- *Cleaning room.*

15. Review what you have done so far: You have introduced the idea that planning ahead is often needed and helpful. You have explained how to break down the planning process into manageable steps using index cards one by one. You have playfully helped your client learn to plan and divide up tasks.

16. Assign homework: Help your client and the parent identify one thing that needs to be done in the next week. Help him make a list and create index cards. Challenge him to use the cards to complete the task. Ask the parent to serve as a coach, taking out each card one by one and providing positive feedback for completing each step. Be sure that the task you choose is not too complex. You want your client to succeed.

17. Closing. Leave your client with words of encouragement like these: *Planning is fun because it helps things work out better. When things work out better, everyone has more fun!*

INTERVENTION 28

Just One Hour

Children (and adults) with ADHD often have difficulty understanding how time passes. They are simply too busy in their minds to pay attention to the passing of time and hence are often late with things. This intervention will help your client "look" at a chunk of time and organize it.

Target skill: Reduce impact of mental health symptoms on school, work, home, community.

Method: Client will accept use of a timer to help facilitate increased initiation and speed of task completion.

Materials: Index cards. Writing and drawing tools.

1. Welcome your client and the parent. Ask:

    - *Do you ever struggle with how quickly time passes?*

    - *Is it difficult to organize your time?*

    - *Does it seem like the day is suddenly gone and nothing got done?*

2. Introduce today's task: planning an hour.

3. Review last week's homework. Ask:

    - *How did that one task you were planning for go?*

    - *In what way did you use the index cards to plan? Did you follow the step-by-step, card-by-card way of getting things done?*

    - *How much of the task did you get done?*

    - *What was different about using the index cards vs. not using them?*

    Explain that many tasks can be approached in this way. Children with ADHD often have trouble with planning and execution of planned steps. You can explain that the index cards will help the child learn the specific task, as well as planning in general. Ask the parent to coach the child to use index cards for planning all kinds of things.

4. Work on today's task: Invite your client to plan for just one hour of her life. Talk about the importance of planning ahead for simple things but also of planning ahead for creating joy. If your client is a child, be sure to talk about finishing chores and homework but also about scheduling playtime. Explain that there is a way to be more mindful about time. Ask your client if she has ever wondered what happened to all the hours in his day. Listen to what she has to say.

5. Provide psychoeducation: Explain that managing and even being aware of time is more difficult for children with ADHD. You can say to the parent:

    - *Time is just not on their minds.*

    - *They are busy doing and thinking about things.*

    - *But they can be taught to step back and structure time.*

6. Explain that you are going to divide the hour into three sections. Take out three large index cards.

7. The first card will identify a task that has to be completed. It should be a task that can be completed in roughly 30 minutes.

8. The second card will identify an activity your client wants to engage in. Be sure to check in with the parent to ensure the client picks an activity that is acceptable to both. It could be riding a bike, playing a game, even taking a short nap. The important thing is that it is something your client really wants to do and can complete in roughly 15 minutes.

9. The third card will identify a connection your client wants to make. Examples of connections could be calling a friend, playing a game with the parent, even going for a walk together. This should be a task that can be completed in roughly 15 minutes. The important thing about this card is that it sends the client into meaningful engagement with others. Word of caution: This card is not meant to address a conflict, but rather create connection.

10. Help your client and the parent complete the three cards, then talk with them about the purpose of the cards. They will help them more mindfully plan just one hour. They are not meant to create a "prison" of units of time. In other words: If something takes a bit more time than planned, that is OK.

11. Review what you have done so far: You have explained how time can be difficult to perceive and plan for children with ADHD. You have completed an activity together that will help your client understand better how time works and how she can plan ahead for a specific amount of time doing things she needs to do, wants to do, and that build connection.

12. Assign homework: Use the cards to live the one hour as planned.

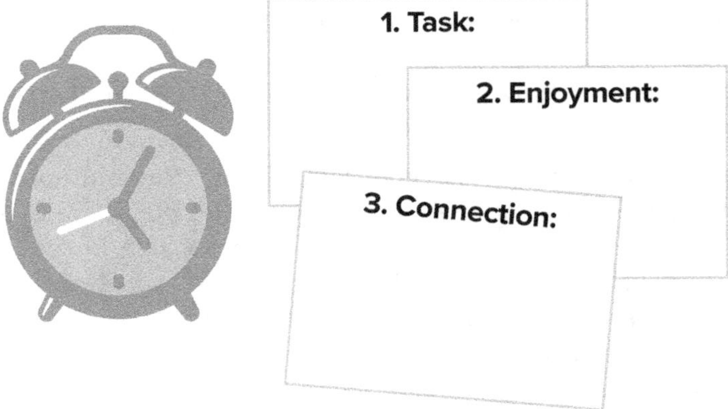

Figure 74

Ask the parent to plan ahead and pick a day and a time when this hour will be lived in the coming week. Be specific. Ask the parent to note the hour on her phone or calendar. In this way you are also helping the parent model the importance of planning and commitment.

13. Closing. Encourage your client and the parent to:

- *Plan ahead.*
- *Do what needs to be done.*
- *Do what is fun.*
- *And do what connects them.*

INTERVENTION 29

The Big Picture

Many children (and adults) with ADHD struggle to see the big picture. They may be thinking about one thing but then get caught up in runaway thoughts and find themselves thinking about or doing something completely unrelated.

This intervention teaches the skill of stepping back and taking a look at the big picture of what really needs to get done.

Target skill: Improve executive functioning.

Method: Client will accept external modeling of multistep problem-solving (i.e., executive) routines.

Materials: Poster board, writing and drawing tools. Glue or tape. Index cards. Highlighter.

1. Welcome your client and the parent. Ask:

    - *How do you like to spend your time together?*

    - *What do you enjoy doing together?*

    - *What falls by the wayside and does not get done?*

2. Introduce today's task: improving attention and focus by learning to step back and see the big picture.

3. Review last week's homework. Ask:

    - *Did you complete the task you planned for?*

    - *How did it go?*

    - *What was it like to use the index cards?*

    - *What did you do to have fun?*

    - *What did you do to connect with each other?*

    Help the parent understand that this way of structuring time can be very helpful for things like getting homework done and preparing for bedtime. There should always be time to get things done, play, and connect. If the child knows that after task completion he will get to play and then have quality time together, he is much more likely to complete the work. It's the Premack principle in action! Remember this?

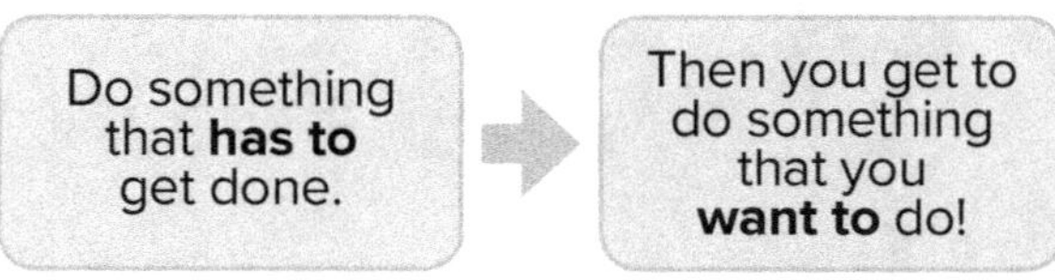

Figure 75

4. Work on today's task: Invite your client to become more mindful of all of that he is thinking. Explain that you will make a "collection" of her thoughts

about a specific subject or thing. Explain to the parent that this will help the client identify what is important, as opposed to what just pops up in the moment.

5. Be sure to explain that it is OK if the client is having a thought that does not seem to relate to the chosen subject. The thought will still be collected (written on an index card).

6. Help your client choose a topic. It could be something that she has to do. It could be related to family or relationship. It could be trouble with her friends.

7. Now: Ask your client to talk about the chosen topic. Ask: *What all are you thinking about this?*

8. Ask the parent to be a secretary and write down the client's thoughts. Be sure to ask the parent not to interpret or judge the thought, just to write it down. You can say: *This is not about whether this is a good thought. It's not about what you think about the thought. It's just about creating a record of the thought.*

9. You might need a lot of index cards! On the index cards, the parent should write what the child is saying. Here is an example: If your client has chosen the subject of an upcoming math test, write "Math Test" on an index card. If she then talks about worrying about failing, write "worried about failing" on the next index card. Next, your client might say that she is afraid of disappointment. Put this on the next index card. Perhaps now your client suddenly jumps to wanting to go to the pool. Another index card.

10. When the parent is writing things down, she should ask: "Did I get this right?" Corrections should go on a new card.

11. When you have about 20 index cards, suggest that you now examine them together.

12. Ask your client to tape all of the index cards on the big poster board one by one, reading each one to you. If your client struggles with reading, the parent should read the cards.

13. When all the cards are on the poster board, suggest it might be a good idea to create some order.

14. Ask your client to remove all the cards and glue the card with the initial topic in the center of the poster board.

15. Then ask her to glue all the cards that closely relate to the main topic close to the topic card. Cards that seem not so closely related should be glued down farther from the center. This can be a tricky task. Ask the parent to help with this.

16. Once all the cards are glued down, ask your client to draw (using a marker) the connections between thoughts. Help your client talk about which thought led to the next thought and so forth. Mark the central, core thought with a yellow highlighter.

17. Now, help your client step back and look at the whole picture. Acknowledge that there are many parts to this picture.

18. Help your client talk about how easy it is to get lost in a small part. You can explain that sometimes thoughts can run away, making it hard to see the big picture.

19. Explain that when he steps back and looks at the whole picture, it will be much easier to focus on what is important. Ask the parent to provide an example, like getting distracted from a task such as cleaning the house, then stepping back to see the whole picture. This will normalize the experience for the client.

20. Keep it simple. Stay focused on the parts/whole picture metaphor.

21. When you are all done, praise your client for being able to see the whole picture and understand that small parts can be distracting.

22. Suggest that your client often return to the main topic when thinking about things and that it might be helpful to write the main topic on an index card to aid with this. Ask the parent to be a coach for this.

23. Summarize what you have done so far: You have learned to sort thoughts and take a look at the bigger picture.

24. Assign homework: Provide the following index card to take home:

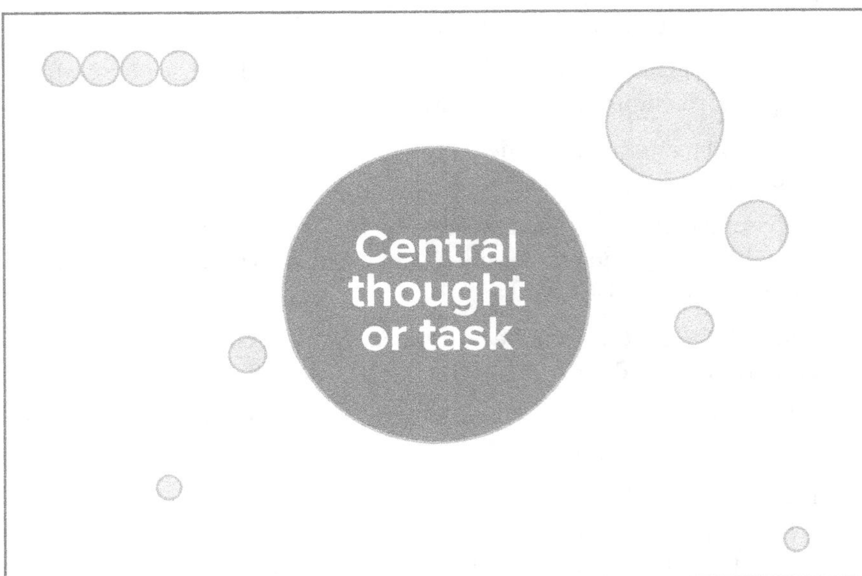

Figure 76

Help the client and parent recognize that distracting thoughts are always there, but they don't need to be attended to all the time.

Ask the parent to use the card to model returning to the central task or thought when she is distracted. The parent should model this for three days and then begin to use the card to prompt the child to return to the central thought or task.

25. Closing. You can say:

> *Understanding the big picture can be fun. You are like a detective when you use this technique. When you find the main thought or task, give each other a high-five. That's a job well done. It's easy to get distracted. But it's also not that difficult to get back on track.*

INTERVENTION 30

Taking It Slow

Many children and adults with ADHD rush through things. This is especially true when a child with ADHD is completing a task he is not interested in, such as homework. The child may claim to have completed homework, but when the parent checks, much remains to be done. The following intervention will teach the child to slow down and pay attention to detail.

Target skill: Reduce hyperactivity, inattention, and impulsivity.

Method: Client will improve self-control and self-efficacy through the use of mindfulness skills, body awareness, and executive functioning development.

Materials: Coloring pages. (Can be found on the Internet. For adults, see coloringcastle.com/mandala. For kids, see education.com/worksheets/mandalas/. Choose something age-appropriate, appealing to your client, and detailed.) Coloring pencils.

1. Welcome your client and the parent. Ask:

    - *How was the week?*

    - *Did you engage in any physical activity?*

    - *Did you play outside?*

    - *Did you go for a walk or to the playground?*

    Help the parent and client understand that the body is designed to move. Children with ADHD may need more physical activity than others. Ask the parent to build opportunities for physical activity into the child's schedule every day.

2. Introduce today's task: slowing down and giving mindful attention to a task.

3. Review last week's homework. Ask:

    - *In what way did the parent use the index card to model seeing the big picture?*

    - *How did the child react when the parent prompted the child to see the big picture by using the index card?*

    - *Was this helpful?*

    - *Can this be done without the index card?*

    - *Was there anything about it that did not go well?*

    Explain that the key to learning to see the big picture is a sense of humor and playfulness. The parent should not scold the child about getting off track, but rather, in a playful manner, model how to get back on track. When this is done with humor, the child will be better able to accept prompting about seeing the big picture.

    From now on, the parent and child should use the big picture metaphor to help keep each other on track.

4. Work on today's task: Invite your client and the parent to participate in an exercise designed to help the client become more mindful about completing work.

5. Ask your client and parent to choose a coloring page.

6. Explain that you will be coloring, too. You are doing this together. Explain that it is OK to talk and reflect while coloring. Explain that coloring can be a way to slow oneself down and become more present in the moment.

7. Talk with your client about creating something beautiful when coloring, something that he might want to hang on the wall at home. Talk about enjoying the process of coloring, taking time, not rushing through it.

8. Color together. It is perfectly fine to discuss what it is like to color. Does it feel uncomfortable? Is he worried about not doing well enough? Or does he really enjoy the process?

9. Talk with your client about paying attention to detail as opposed to "getting this done." Explain that this is not a "getting it done" exercise, but rather a "slowing down and creating beauty" exercise.

10. Ask the parent and the client to slow down by taking deep breaths together several times during the exercise.

11. Be sure to avoid any competitiveness between the client and parent. You can say: *This is not about who makes the prettiest picture. This is about making the picture.*

12. When your client has finished the picture, praise him for taking the time to create something beautiful. Be specific. Say something like: "I really like the way you took your time to color in this little detail over here. It takes a great deal of patience to pay attention to detail. You did great."

13. Then prompt the parent to do the same. Remind the parent to provide positive feedback, not criticism.

14. Then ask the client to provide positive feedback for the parent.

15. If your client struggled with this exercise, focus on the areas that are completed. And simply choose a less-detailed image next time. Now you know what baseline is!

16. Review what you have done so far: You have engaged in a coloring exercise to help your client slow down and focus on a task. You have used calm breathing as a tool to help the client slow down. You have modeled for the parent how to give positive feedback to the child.

17. Assign homework: Send home one coloring page with your client and one for the parent to complete together during the next week. Explain that coloring the is not about getting it done, but rather about mindfully creating something beautiful. No need to rush it. If needed, the image can be completed in steps. Ask the client and the parent to remind each other to take calm breaths while coloring and to bring their pictures to the next meeting.

18. Send your client home with words of encouragement. You can say:

Slowing down can be fun. You can pay attention to detail without feeling stressed out. It's just about coloring all the parts, one by one, mindfully. And suddenly it is all done!

INTERVENTION 31

Copy That

Children with ADHD often struggle with completing tasks that seem simple to others, like copying a list of vocabulary words at school. A simple distraction will get her off track and, while everybody is done with their word list, the child with ADHD may find herself being scolded for being lazy. The following intervention will outline strategies for completing a simple task to assist the child with ADHD to improve task completion. It is not that the child with ADHD cannot complete the task; it is simply that this child needs support and strategies for doing so.

Target skill: Maintain attention over distractibility.

Method: Client will be able to internalize executive routines and implement with support.

Materials: Timer. A printed list, long enough to be somewhat difficult to copy, depending on age. Here is an example:

Cat, cat, cat, mouse, cat

Mouse, mouse, mouse, cat, mouse

Cat, mouse, cat, mouse, mouse, cat

Cat, cat, cat, cat, cat

Mouse, mouse, mouse

Catmouse!

As you can see, there is no real pattern, and this is key. Your client will really have to pay attention to copy this list.

1. Welcome your client and the parent. Ask:

    - *How was your week?*

    - *In what way did you pay attention to each other?*

    - *In what way did you provide comfort to each other?*

    Reiterate the importance of touch to soothe and calm the body and mind. You can explain:

    - *It may be harder for your child to calm the body and mind.*

    - *Remember: It's a symptom. Your child is not doing this on purpose.*

    - *Providing soothing comfort such as a gentle hug or wrapping yourselves into a blanket together for reading a short story can do wonders for calming the body and mind.*

    - *Remember: You can fire up the child's central nervous system, or you can help calm it. Your child already knows how get fired up, but she needs more practice calming the system.*

2. Introduce today's task: learning to complete a simple task using strategies to maintain focus and attention.

3. Review last week's homework. Ask child and parent to show you their colored pages. Take a look together. Ask:

- *What was it like to color together?*
- *In what way did you enjoy the process?*
- *In what way did you encourage each other during the process?*
- *In what way were you able to slow down and simply enjoy the process?*
- *In what way where you not able to do so?*

Ask the parent to provide regular coloring time together to help practice mindful attention to detail and foster enjoyment in the process.

4.   Work on today's task: Invite your client to participate in a playful activity designed to help her increase attention to detail. Be sure to make it fun.

5.   Hand your client the list of words and ask her to copy it word-for-word. Explain that it is OK to ask for help. Ask the parent to copy the list twice.

6.   If your client asks for help, provide it while at the same time teaching strategies for attention to detail. Here is an example: It is easy to get confused about how many times a word has been written down. Ask your client to cross out each word on the original list after she has copied it, and to cross out each line after she has copied it. Give lots of praise. Use the word "strategy" to help your client understand that there are things she can do to complete the task (or "win the game").

7.   If your client gets frustrated, help her pause and take a brain break. Mark the point where she stopped with a red dot, and explain that this is another strategy so she will know where to start again when she is ready. You can stand up together and stretch, practice calm breathing, listen to a bit of music. Whatever works is fine. Be sure to explain that it is OK to take a break when things are tough and it is getting frustrating. If you need to, set a timer to indicate when the break is over.

8.   When the brain break is over, help your client return to copying the list. Be sure to help her find the right starting point (remember the red dot). Assist the parent as needed. You want the parent to understand the importance of using strategies and positive feedback so she can help the client use these strategies.

9.   When your client has completed the task, give her lots of positive feedback about paying attention to detail.

10.   If your client is willing, now she can create a list for the parent to copy. This is often fun for children. Tell her to make the list hard to copy.

11.   Now it is the parent's turn. The parent should try to make lots of mistakes, and the child should coach the parent to use the strategies you just taught her, including taking brain breaks. Let the child teach the parent to overcome frustration. This will help reinforce the strategies you taught.

12.   If your client is a child and is struggling with paying attention to details in school, you may want to pass on the strategies to her teacher, including the suggestion for brain breaks. Brain breaks often prevent temper tantrums.

13. You may want to create brain-break index cards to send home as reminders when things get tough!

Figure 77

14. Summarize what you have done so far: You have engaged the client and parent in an activity designed to help her learn and practice strategies for task completion and affect regulation. You have then let the client be the teacher to reinforce the learning. Here are the strategies learned and practiced:

   - *Crossing things out that are done, word by word, then line by line.*

   - *Marking the spot when taking a break.*

   - *Taking a timed brain break as needed.*

15. Assign homework: Send a fresh word list home with client and parent. Simply create a new one relating to the client's interests. Be sure to reiterate that client and parent should do this activity together, but the parent has to copy the list twice.

   Ask the parent and child to pick a date and time when they will practice together. The parent should serve as the teacher and coach first. Send the brain-break card home and instruct the client to use this card during the activity as needed but no more than twice, with each break lasting no more than five minutes. Ask the parent to bring the completed word lists to your next meeting.

16. Closing. Remind your client: *Strategies can be learned with practice. It's OK to use your parent/teacher as a coach. Brain breaks are fun for everyone.*

INTERVENTION 32

Line Them Up

Much like the prior one, this intervention teaches attention to detail, mindful task completions, strategies for task completion, and the use of brain breaks to regulate frustration. This intervention also helps your client pay attention to the body.

Target skill: Maintain attention over distractibility.

Method: Client will improve self-control and self-efficacy through the use of mindfulness skills, body awareness, and executive functioning development.

Materials: Dominoes, preferably several sets. Make sure the quality is decent; sometimes cheap dominoes are uneven and very difficult to stand up in a line. Brain-break index card.

1. Welcome your client. Ask:

    - *How was your week?*

    - *Is there something that went wrong this week? If there was, in what way could taking a brain break have helped?*

    Remind the parent that brain breaks have to be modeled. It's OK for the parent to talk about taking a brain break when she is struggling. It's also OK to vary the brain break and take conflict breaks, when client and parent are arguing and need a break from each other.

2. Introduce today's task: learning and practicing strategies for task completion and affect regulation.

3. Review last week's homework. Ask:

    - *How did your word-list task go?*

    - *Was your parent able to complete it?*

    - *What was it like to coach your parent?*

    - *Was the client able to complete it?*

    Take a look at the word lists together and provide positive feedback for completing the task. If it did not go well, ask why. Remind the parent and client to take brain breaks, separately if necessary. Make sure the parent understands that the activity is not meant as an opportunity to exert control, but rather to playfully learn strategies for task completion.

    If words are too difficult, you can substitute words with simple drawings.

4. Work on today's task: Invite your client and the parent to engage in an exercise designed to help him learn and practice attention to detail and frustration tolerance.

5. Take out the dominoes and present the challenge: Ask the client to line up the dominoes closely so that one will hit the other and cause it to fall in a chain reaction. It is important that you demonstrate how to do this. Show what can go wrong if the dominoes are too far apart or too close together. The number of dominoes you use depends on the age of your client. It might

be five for a child with very limited ability to focus, or it could be 50 for an older child or teen.

6. Ask your client to begin building the line of dominoes. If he gets frustrated, provide support and insert brain breaks (listening to music, stretching, dancing, whatever works). Then return to the task. Model for the parent how to coach in a nonintrusive way. Then ask the parent to coach the client when the client asks for help.

7. If the line of dominoes falls prematurely, help your client tolerate the frustration of this by normalizing the experience of "failure" and framing it as an opportunity to try again. If needed, reduce the number of dominoes. Remember: You want your client to succeed. Be sure the parent understands the importance of coaching the child to manage frustration if the dominoes fall too early.

8. If you notice that your client tends to work too fast, causing the dominoes to fall prematurely, introduce this strategy: Ask him to take a slow breath before putting down each domino. Demonstrate this (breathe in slowly through your nose and breathe out slowly through your mouth) and help him practice at least three times. Then ask the parent to coach the client to use the calm breaths. If the client cannot tolerate this, simply "flip" it. Ask him to coach the parent how to use calm breathing after each domino is set down. The result is the same: The client learns and uses calm breathing!

9. Check if this slows your client down enough to be calmer and more present. A calmer and more mindful present would result in the dominoes being placed correctly.

10. When the line of dominoes is completed, ask your client to tip the first one over so that all of them fall. If your client does not want to do so, this is OK; ask if he wants you to do it, or if he would just like to admire the lineup of dominoes. Leaving them standing is OK. You can say something like: "You created this beautiful line of dominoes. Nice job." Alternatively, the client could give the parent permission to tip over the first domino.

11. If your client is able to complete this exercise, you can experiment with different ways of lining up the dominoes. You can build "branches." Once again, attention to detail is needed. How does he need to place the dominoes in order to ensure that all the branches fall?

12. Summarize what you have done so far: You have learned and practiced strategies for task completion and affect regulation:

    - *Outlining the task.*

    - *Creating a strategy.*

    - *Completing the task one step at a time.*

    - *Using brain breaks to regulate affect.*

13. Assign homework of playing dominoes with the parent. Be sure to connect with the parent about not controlling the lineup and not scolding the child

for making mistakes. Coach the parent to teach the child to take brain breaks, if needed.

Ask the client and parent to pick a specific date and time to play dominoes together, and ask the parent to enter this in their electronic or paper calendar.

14. Closing. Encourage the client and the parent to learn together. You can say:

- *You can learn strategies through play.*

- *Remember your brain breaks.*

- *Be kind to each other.*

- *And enjoy the process. It's fun to play. If you are not having fun, be less serious about the activity!*

Psychotherapy Interventions

Psychotherapy Interventions target distorted thinking about ADHD symptoms and the ability to impact them, as well as the effect of those symptoms on the client's sense of self in relationships and in the world. They target the understanding and interpretation of symptoms of ADHD and seek to change them. Psychotherapy interventions are always provided by a licensed mental health professional.

Here is an example how the interpretation of a symptom can be helpful or harmful to a client:

> Brian is a 17-year-old high school student with ADHD. His grades are poor. He rarely does homework, and he struggles in relationship with this girlfriend, who accuses him of never listening. He brushes off all criticism or attempts to help, stating, "It's just my ADD. Leave me alone."

Brian is aware of his ADHD diagnosis but does not understand or accept that this diagnosis does not have to define him. It's become an excuse for not making much-needed changes in his life. He is stuck in an unproductive interpretation of his diagnosis and symptoms. Psychotherapy can help him examine his thoughts and beliefs about his symptoms and develop more realistic ways of thinking about and addressing them.

Here is another example of how the interpretation of a symptom can be harmful:

Six-year-old Kelsey is always in trouble. Kelsey has ADHD. She can't sit still at school and is constantly in trouble with her teacher. At home, she bounces around from activity to activity and leaves a trail of toys throughout the house. She loves to play outside but has few friends because she can get quite intense during play and has pushed and hit her peers. Kelsey does not feel good about herself. She often cries and says things like: "I am so bad. No one likes me."

Kelsey is not aware of her ADHD diagnosis. It could be helpful for her to learn, in an age-appropriate way, that her difficulties are rooted in symptoms, that she is not "bad." Psychotherapy can help Kelsey explore and understand and change how she thinks and feels about herself. Because Kelsey is very young, her primary caretaker needs to be involved in her psychotherapy to ensure that she receives healthy and helpful messages about herself. Additionally, Kelsey should receive school-based interventions to ensure academic and social success at school.

INTERVENTION 33

More Than Good Enough

The following intervention seeks to address feelings of shame that can accompany symptoms of ADHD. These feelings of shame can result in a sense of self as "bad" or "not good enough." This can then result in an amplification of symptoms.

Target skill: Reduce impact of mental health symptoms on school/work, home, community.

Method: Client will develop compassionate and realistic ways of thinking about self and symptoms.

What you will need: Index cards. Writing and drawing tools.

1. Begin with empathy. Ask:

    - *How are you feeling today?*

    - *Who did you connect with today?*

    - *In what way did you connect with yourself today?*

2. Introduce today's task: identifying core feelings, beliefs, and thoughts about oneself and examining them to ensure they are compassionate and reality-based. If you are working with a child, you can say this:

    Today we are going to think about how you feel and think about yourself. We are going to ask:

    - *Do you like yourself?*

    - *When do you not like yourself?*

    - *What does making mistakes feel like?*

    - *How can you be nice to yourself?*

    - *What do you need others to say to you and do for you to feel good about yourself?*

3. Work on today's task. Provide a stack of index cards. Ask:

    - *How do you feel when it seems you can't do anything right?*

    - *What are you saying to yourself?*

    - *What are others saying to you?*

    Record the answers on the index cards. Answers can be written or drawn. If your client is a child, the parent can serve as a scribe or the child can draw the answer, whichever works best.

4. Take a look at the index cards together. Go over each card and help your client reflect by asking:

    - *What does this mean about yourself?*

    - *Is this a kind way to think about yourself?*

- *Is what you are thinking really true, or is it just a fear/bad feelings about yourself?*

If your client drew the answers, look carefully and ask about details of the drawing. They may be able to give you more information about how she thinks and feels.

5. Help your client develop more realistic and compassionate ways of thinking about herself. If your client is a child, it is imperative that the parent is involved in this process. Parental messages about the child should consistently communicate unconditional love and acceptance of the child as well as the willingness to help her learn from mistakes and grow.

   If the client's parent struggles with this due to the intensity of symptoms, you can say: *Your child is so much more than her ADHD symptoms.*

6. Transform the messages from the original index cards into new, more realistic and compassionate messages and write those messages on new index cards. Again, those index cards can be illustrated to make the message come to life. Here are some examples:

Original message:	Compassionate and realistic message:
I can't do anything right.	I make mistakes. That's OK. I learn and I grow like everyone else.
I am so bad that no one loves me.	I am so much more than the things I do. I am loved.
I am stupid.	Some things are hard for me. That's OK. There are so many things I do well!

Figure 78

Again, if the client is a child, it is imperative the client's parent is involved in the process of developing compassionate and realistic messages. The parent will need to deliver these messages in a consistent way.

7. Summarize what you have done so far: You have explored the impact of ADHD symptoms on your client's thoughts and feelings about self. You have identified harmful and unrealistic thoughts and feelings and replaced them with compassionate and realistic messages to self.

8. Assign homework: Send the index cards with compassionate and realistic messages home with your client. Ask her to carry those cards and read them when negative messages about self and symptoms take over. If your client is a child, create a second set of index cards for the parent to use. The parent should use those index cards when she hears the child give harmful and unrealistic messages to self, or when the parent is at risk of giving the client harmful and unrealistic messages due to being emotionally reactive.

Ask your client and the parent to bring the index cards to your next meeting.

9. Closing. Send your client home with sincere words of encouragement. You can say: ***You are so much more than your ADHD symptoms. You are*** [positive characteristics of client].

INTERVENTION 34

Accepting the Beauty of Imperfection

This intervention addresses the need to accept imperfection in oneself. It also seeks to help your client identify the "up" sides of ADHD and how they relate to his sense of self.

Target skill: Reduce impact of mental health symptoms on school/work, home, community.

Method: Client will develop accepting, compassionate, and realistic ways of thinking about self and symptoms.

What you will need: Paper and drawing tools.

1. Begin with empathy. Ask:

   - *How did your week go?*

   - *What good things did you notice about yourself?*

   - *What good things have others noticed about you?*

2. Introduce today's task: accepting the beauty of imperfection in oneself and appreciating those parts of symptoms that translate into talents. Here is an example you may want to talk about:

   > *Indra was a child who could not focus. She struggled academically all through high school because she just did not think like other people. Her thoughts were jumpy, elusive, and connected in ways others did not understand. In her final year of high school, Indra was diagnosed with ADHD. She started to see her differences as a gift and began to make art. Her artwork was different because she thought differently. She made connections no one else would. She combined techniques and materials in new and exciting ways. Ultimately, she became a nationally known artist. Indra had found her niche!*

   If you are working with a child, you may want to say this: *Your attention works differently. This can make life at school hard. But you are creative and inventive. You are enthusiastic and energetic about the things you value. You don't have to be perfect. You can just be you and find what you do well.*

3. Review last week's homework. Ask your client or the parent to take out last week's index cards containing compassionate and self-affirming statements. Ask your client to recall when she used the cards. Ask:

   - *When did you use these cards? Tell me about the situation or thought that prompted you to use them.*

   - *In what way were the cards helpful? How did it change the way you thought or felt?*

   - *How could the cards be improved? What needs to be added?*

   Ask your client to continue to use these cards as needed to stop unrealistic and unhelpful thoughts about self.

4. Work on today's task. Provide paper and drawing materials. Ask your client to draw a tree with many branches. If your client needs inspiration, you can provide the following tree to start.

Figure 79

Then ask your client to add all the branches of his talents and difficulties. Creativity could be one branch. Ask: ***What grows on this branch?*** Then ask your client to draw the "fruits" of creativity on the branch. Ask your client to include branches that indicate areas of difficulty, such as academic performance. Help him explore these areas with compassion and kindness instead of judgment.

5. Take a look at the finished tree together. What does it look like? Ask your client to describe the tree in its entirety and be mindful of his emotions while doing so. Help him acknowledge difficult emotions and move away from judgment about imperfections.

6. You can say: ***This tree represents who you are. You have many branches. They are all needed. You never know what talent you will find in a branch that looks troublesome.***

7. Review what you have done so far. You have explored the different branches of your client's life, talents, and difficulties. You have explored the importance of valuing self as a whole person with all branches, even if imperfect. You have helped your client mindfully explore and accept feelings about self.

8. Assign homework: Send the tree drawing home with your client. Ask him to add branches throughout the next week, be they talents or imperfections. If your client is a child, the parent can also add branches but should do so only when emotionally nonreactive. In other words: The parent should not add branches of imperfection because she mad at the child. Close friends can

also be invited to add to the tree. Ask your client to bring the tree drawing back to your next meeting.

9. Closing. Send your client home with words of encouragement. You can say: *You are like a beautiful tree. You are still growing. All trees grow toward the light. Sometimes you have to stretch toward the light. That's OK. Just keep growing.*

INTERVENTION 35

Recognizing and Accepting Needs

Children and adults who have ADHD often have a greater need to move. This is a biologically driven trait, not a character flaw. There are other needs as well: being able to quickly do something without having to wait and having variety/change when it comes to daily tasks. Meeting these needs can be difficult. Children at school often have to sit for hours at a time. Adults who work in an office setting struggle with the same issue. The following intervention is designed to help clients (and parents) move toward acceptance of needs.

Target skill: Reduce impact of mental health symptoms on school/work, home, community.

Method: Client will develop accepting, compassionate, and realistic ways of thinking about self and symptoms.

What you will need: Paper. Writing and drawing tools.

1.   Welcome your client. Ask:

   - *How was the last week?*

   - *What did you do that you are proud of?*

   - *When and how did you enjoy yourself in the company of others?*

   Highlight experiences of normalcy, accomplishment, and relational joy. It's easy for a child or adult with ADHD to become hyperfocused on symptoms and problems, so it's important to draw attention to what is going well.

2.   Introduce today's task: recognizing and accepting needs. You can tell the following story to help your client think about needs:

   There once was a chicken. This chicken was quite wonderful. It had beautiful yellow feathers and walked with a proud spring in its step. This chicken lived on a farm until it was sold to a city dweller. The city dweller fed the chicken twice a day, in the morning and in the evening. But there was nothing in between. So when the city dweller went to work, the chicken searched for food everywhere in the apartment. It pecked and pecked and pecked. All day. Because that is what chickens do!

   When the city dweller came home, he saw the pecking marks all over floor and the couch and became very upset. He decided to stay home the following day to teach his chicken not to peck. Every time the chicken pecked, he told it to stop.

3.   Review last week's homework. Take a look at the tree drawing together. Ask:

   - *What did you add and why?*

   - *Who else added things?*

Take a look at what was added together. Explore what was added with the goal of increasing acceptance of imperfection and beauty in imperfection. You can say:

> *We are all a work in progress. Growth takes time. A tree does not grow a whole new branch in a day. But it may grow a new leaf or two. Pay attention to the leaves! Water the tree. Make sure you create conditions in which you can grow and thrive.*

4. Work on today's task. Help your client reflect on the story. Ask:

   - *Do you think this can work? Can you tell a chicken not to peck?*
   - *How frustrated do you think the city dweller will become?*
   - *How frustrated do you think the chicken is?*
   - *What does the chicken need?*
   - *What is missing for the chicken?*

5. Now, help your client make the connection between the chicken's needs and her needs. You can explain that it's natural for a chicken to peck. It's just the way it looks for food. You can ask:

   - *What are your needs?*
   - *What comes naturally to you?*
   - *What is difficult for you to stop because it is just in your nature?*

6. Help your client recognize and accept that ADHD-related needs are not personal flaws. Help her recognize areas of conflict between these needs and expectations she may encounter on a daily basis. You may want to use the following chart:

My ADHD-Related Needs	Conflict between Needs and Expectations

Figure 80

7. If you are working with a child, it is important to help the parent understand and validate the child's needs (such as the need to move about, stand up during the school day), as well as recognize how difficult it can be for the child to maneuver between needs and expectations.

8. Summarize what you have done so far: You have explored how your client may have needs related to her symptoms. You have helped your client recognize those needs as valid, as opposed to personal flaws. You have also explored the conflict between needs and expectations.

9. Assign homework: Send home the ADHD Needs and Expectations chart. Ask the client to use the chart during the next week to explore areas of conflict between ADHD-related needs and expectations at home and school. Ask the client and parent to make notes of those conflicts on the back of the chart and verbally acknowledge the conflict without getting caught up in the emotion of the moment. Ask the client and parent to bring the chart back to your next meeting.

10. Closing. As you close your session you can say:

> *Your needs are important. They count. You count. There is a way to get your needs met! Let's figure out what is difficult first.*

INTERVENTION 36

Balancing Needs and Expectations

This intervention builds on the prior intervention (Recognizing and Accepting Needs). It can be emotionally liberating to recognize and accept ADHD-related needs, as this removes self-blame and shame. But an emotionally difficult task lies ahead: recognizing that not all ADHD-related needs are a good "fit" for every environment. Your client will need to find a balance between legitimate needs and environmental expectations. Here is an example of how this may work:

Eli is an active third-grader with ADHD-related hyperactivity. His body tells him to move all the time. But at school he is often reminded to "sit still" and "sit down." Eli is frustrated. He understands that his need to move is a symptom. His mother has talked to his teacher about this, yet Eli's needs are tough to meet at school where desks designate work areas and silence is often required.

What can be done for Eli?

- His mother can advocate for appropriate accommodations, such as walking breaks and use of a fidget item.

- Eli may be eligible for a formal intervention plan, such as a 504 plan.

- Eli can learn to move in more subtle ways, such as moving his fingers instead of his whole body.

Ultimately, Eli will have to learn to balance his needs with expectations. This is not an easy task for a third-grader or anyone, really. This intervention addresses the emotional aspect of balancing needs and expectations.

Target skill: Reduce impact of mental health symptoms on school/work, home, community.

Method: Client will develop accepting, compassionate, and realistic ways of thinking about self and symptoms.

What you will need: Writing and drawing tools. Index cards.

1. Welcome your client. Ask:

    - *How was the last week?*

    - *When did you feel good about yourself?*

    - *What made you feel good about yourself?*

2. Introduce today's task: balancing ADHD-related needs and expectations. You can explain:

    It can be tough when needs and expectations clash. It's easy to be get angry when that happens. It's important to recognize anger and frustration. And it is possible to use anger and frustration in positive ways to create a new way of working with needs and expectations.

3. Review last week's homework. Ask your client and the parent to take out last week's ADHD Needs and Expectations chart. Check the back of the chart to see what is noted. Ask:

- *When did your needs and expectations clash?*
- *How did it feel when they clashed?*
- *How did you resolve the situation?*

Highlight areas of emotional competency, such as recognizing and letting go of emotional irritation about expectations.

4. Work on today's task. Begin by using the cognitive triad to help your client map out thoughts, feelings, and behaviors related to needs and expectations.

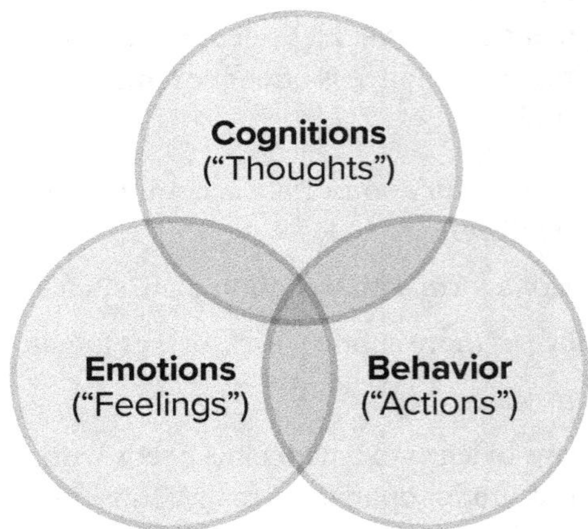

Figure 81

Help your client map out an incident during which needs and expectations did not line up. If you are working with a younger child, you can ask: *When did you feel like moving or making noise and got in trouble for it?*

You can use the following image to help your client map out the event/incident:

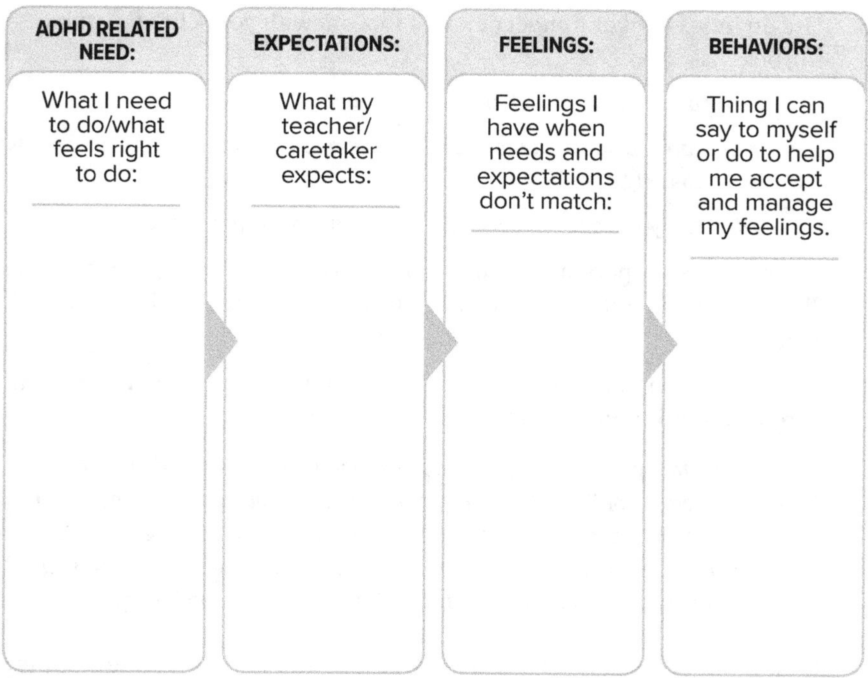

Figure 82

If your client is a younger child, he can draw in the columns. What is important is that your client begins to understand that feelings and behaviors relate, but feelings don't need to be acted upon right away and without reflection. In other words, there can be a break between feelings and behaviors. You can use the following image to illustrate this:

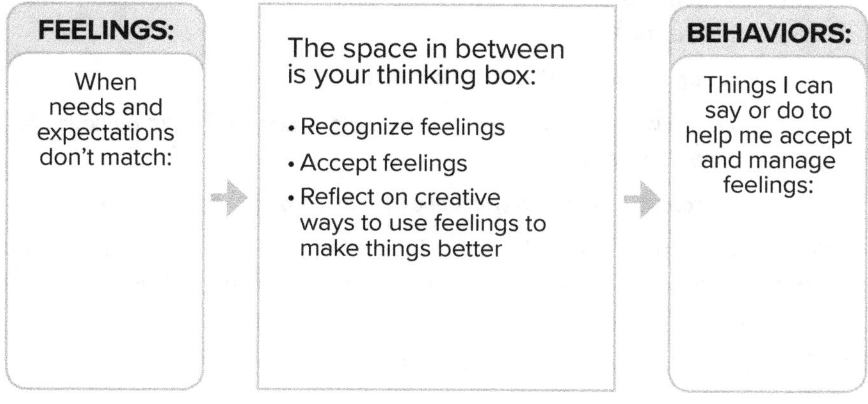

Figure 83

5. Use an index card or a sheet of paper to work with your client on the thinking box. Ask:

    - *How can you say "hello" to a difficult feeling?*

    - *What can you say to yourself or the feeling to calm the situation down, help yourself feel better?*

    - *What can you do to help you feel better and manage the situation?*

    Ask your client's parent to chime in. Here is an example: A parent could say "hello" to a difficult feeling or a need instead of being emotionally reactive to it.

6. Help your client reframe the struggle between needs and expectations as a careful and mindful balancing act. You can say:

    It can be tricky to balance needs and expectations. Feelings can make things more complicated, but they can also help guide your actions. When you don't think about needs and expectations and you don't reflect, it's easy to tip over. When you are aware of needs and expectations and you reflect on your feelings and behaviors, it's easier to stay in balance.

7. Summarize what you have done so far: You have reflected on the connection between needs and expectations, and you have explored how you can establish a thinking/reflecting space between feelings and behaviors.

8. If you are working with a parent, be sure to reiterate that the thinking space is not a punitive place and should not be used in that way. Rather, it is a place of acceptance and reflection, a place where mindful balance can grow.

9. Assign homework: Send three index cards labeled "Thinking Space" home with your client. Ask the parent to help the client use the index cards to create a thinking space when there is a clash between needs and expectations. Provide an index card with the following prompts written on it to assist with this task:

    - *How can you say "hello" to a difficult feeling?*

    - *What can you say to yourself or the feeling to calm the situation down, help yourself feel better?*

    - *What can you do to help you feel better and manage the situation?*

    Your client can use the index cards in any way that creates thinking space. He can: draw, write, make a collage, or even use the card to ask for help from an adult.

10. Closing. You can say the following at the end of the session:

    The thinking space is your friend. It helps you slow down. It helps you be kind to yourself. It helps you find balance.

INTERVENTION 37

What I Really Want to Say to You

This intervention is a variation of the "Empty Chair" exercise developed within Gestalt therapy. The intervention is simple: Your client sits facing an empty chair and tells it all the things she would like to say to herself or perhaps to someone who is deceased. In this case, your client (and perhaps the parent) will have a conversation with the other entity always in the room: ADHD.

This intervention requires the ability to think of ADHD as a person, sitting in the empty chair. Therefore, it may not be appropriate for very young children or those clients who struggle with imagination and creativity.

Target skill: Reduce impact of mental health symptoms on school/work, home, community.

Method: Client will develop accepting, compassionate, and realistic ways of thinking about self and symptoms.

What you will need: Additional chair.

1. Welcome your client. Ask:

    - *How was the last week?*

    - *Who helped you through tough times and how?*

    - *What was one thing/person that gave you joy?*

    Highlight experiences of support and joy. Help your client and the parent reflect on experiences of connection and support, and explain how these experiences can carry them through when times are tough.

2. Introduce today's task: talking to your symptoms/your ADHD. You can explain by saying:

    > *Sometimes people get angry with their symptoms. Or they get frustrated about having ADHD. Sometimes it can be helpful to talk to your symptoms. It's a good way to vent frustration. It's also a good way to reflect on your relationship with your ADHD. Are you at peace with it? Are you fighting it?*

3. Review last week's homework. Ask:

    - *In what way were you able to use the prompts to welcome difficult feelings?*

    - *What were you able to say to yourself to change the situation for the better?*

    - *What were you able to do to change the situation for the better?*

    Highlight any areas of success. Perhaps your client is not yet able to engage in positive self-talk but was able to welcome and sit with difficult feelings. This is progress!

4. Work on today's task. Set up the empty chair in front of your client. You can tell your client to pretend that her ADHD is sitting there. Explain that she can say anything she wants to her ADHD. If the parent is present, explain

to her that she will get a turn but should not interrupt the client or try to control what the client is saying.

If your client is struggling with understanding the exercise, you can give a few examples of what others have said to their symptoms. Here are a few examples:

- *I love the energy you give me.*
- *You keep getting me in trouble.*
- *I wish I had never met you.*
- *You make me giggle.*

Then give your client a chance to talk to the empty chair. Make note of important things she says to it.

5. Once the client is done speaking to the empty chair, ask:

- *How did it feel to speak to your ADHD?*
- *Did you like this exercise? If yes, why? If no, why not?*
- *What do you think was the most important thing you said to your ADHD?*

Help your client reflect on her relationship with ADHD. Ask:

- *Based on what you said to your symptoms, is there anything you want to change about the way you relate to your ADHD?*
- *What is needed in the relationship? More kindness? More acceptance? Or a little distance?*

6. If the parent is present and would like a turn talking to the symptoms, repeat the exercise with the parent (and the client listening). Explain that this is for the sake of the client. In other words, the client will hear and take in anything the parent says. In this case you do want the parent to "filter" a bit and say only things that are not harmful but will help client and parent connect. It's possible that parent and client can connect over their frustration.

When the parent has completed talking to the empty chair, turn to the client and ask:

- *What did you hear your parent say to ADHD?*
- *What did you think was helpful for you to hear?*
- *Is there anything you want to say to your parent right now? If there is, you can say it now.*

Highlight areas of connection between parent and client in how they relate to symptoms of ADHD.

7. Summarize what you have done so far: You have demonstrated a way your client (and the parent) can talk to ADHD symptoms. This creates both distance between your client and the symptoms (they are not personal flaws), and connection between her and the symptoms (by exploring how she can relate to symptoms in a meaningful way). Explain that both distance and connection are useful.

8. Assign homework: Ask your client to write a letter to her symptoms, outlining ways they can be friends and ways in which they need some distance. If your client can't or does not want to write, the parent can serve as a scribe (but not censor), or the client can draw the letter. Ask the client and parent to bring the letter to your next meeting.

9. Closing. You can say the following at the end of your session:

> *Having ADHD can be like having another family member. Family members are great to have, but sometimes they get on our nerves. It's good to be close to family, but sometimes we all need some distance. Remember the thinking space? The thinking space gives you distance when you need it.*

INTERVENTION 38

Conversing with Symptoms

This intervention builds on the prior one. Another chair is involved, but this time you, the therapist, will embody ADHD. You will "be" the symptoms and have a conversation with your client about listening to, attuning to, accepting, and working with symptoms.

Target skill: Reduce impact of mental health symptoms on school/work, home, community.

Method: Client will develop accepting, compassionate, and realistic ways of thinking about self and symptoms.

1. Welcome your client. Ask:

   - *How was your week?*

   - *When did you laugh this week?*

   - *When did you cry?*

   Highlight areas of emotional honesty and expression. Help your client understand that emotions can be listened to and honored.

2. Introduce today's task: having a conversation with your ADHD symptoms. Explain that in this case you, the therapist, will play the role of your client's ADHD.

3. Review last week's homework. Ask your client or the parent to take out the letter he has written to his symptoms. Ask the client to read the letter, or show and describe the pictures. If the client can't or does not want to read, ask the parent to read the letter for him. Help your client reflect on the letter by asking:

   - *How did it feel to write this letter?*

   - *In what way did you change the way you think about your ADHD by writing this letter?*

   - *Did you recognize something important about your relationship with ADHD? If you did, what was it?*

   Ask the parent to chime in with helpful reflection about the client's letter.

   Highlight the ability to step back and reflect. You can say:

   Sometimes it may feel like your symptoms are in charge of you. By writing this letter you are getting in the driver's seat. This puts you in charge of your symptoms.

4. Work on today's task: Set up a chair opposite your client. If the parent is present, instruct the parent to listen to the conversation. You can explain that at certain times you will invite her into the conversation.

5. Ask your client to begin talking to his ADHD. You can give prompts such as:

- *How you are feeling about me being with you every day?*

- *Do I ever get on your nerves?*

- *When do you like me?*

- *When would you like to hide from me?*

6. Then respond to your client's comments. Have a conversation. Here are some things you may want to weave into the conversation:

    - *I know I can be a pest.*

    - *I know you did not invite me into your life.*

    - *Sometimes it feels like you just want to get rid of me.*

    - *Here are some of the good things I bring with me: Creativity, energy, intense focus on things you really love, enthusiasm.*

    - *You can learn to manage me and live with me.*

    - *I understand that I am not always your best friend.*

    - *I wonder if you can relate to me with kindness.*

7. Continue the conversation. Highlight areas of connection and compassion. Help your client explore and understand that there is a way to connect with symptoms even when they are not always loved. You can say:

    Some people have allergies. You have me. Some people need glasses. You have me. It's just a fact of life. But I am very manageable when you give me a try.

    Then invite the parent into the conversation. Ask: *Is there anything you want to say to me?*

    If the parent is angry with the ADHD symptoms, this is OK because the symptom is now externalized. It's not the client who is causing the symptoms; it's the symptoms that are causing the problems.

    Still, you want to respond by suggesting that over time it may be more helpful to make peace with the symptoms.

8. Summarize what you have done so far: Your client has had a conversation with his symptoms. You (as the symptoms) have explained yourself as best as you can. You have explored different ways of relating to the symptoms and introduced the idea of making peace with them, much like anyone would make peace with a physical illness over time. You have helped to externalize the symptoms of ADHD and suggested that acceptance is the key to a peaceful life together.

9. You can explain that, of course, medications can help manage symptoms, but they usually do not make them completely disappear.

10. Assign homework: Ask your client to talk to his ADHD symptoms for a few minutes each night. Ask the parent to "be" the symptoms and talk back in a helpful manner. Ask the parent to take notes as to what important

things come up in the conversation and then bring those notes to your next meeting.

11. Closing. You can say this to your client and the parent before they leave:

> *The conversation with your symptoms is ongoing. It's good to check in with your ADHD every day. It's good to be kind to yourself and your symptoms.*

INTERVENTION 39

Just Be with Me

This intervention addresses the emotional impact ADHD symptoms can have on family and other relationships. When symptoms get in the way of emotional connection, the therapist asks the client and parent to make the emotional connection primary. When this is done, symptoms, of course, are still there, but they can be held and addressed within the relationship as opposed to destroying the sense of connection.

Target skill: Reduce impact of mental health symptoms on school/work, home, community.

Method: Client will accept, practice, and utilize co-regulation techniques with a support person or caregiver.

What you will need: Index cards. Writing and drawing tools. Legos.

1. Welcome your client. Ask:

    - *How was the last week?*

    - *Did anything stand out? If yes, tell me about it.*

    - *When were you kind to someone else?*

    - *When were you kind to yourself?*

    Highlight areas of emotional competency, such as the ability to stop impulsive emotionality and be kind to self and others. You can explain that being kind to self and others is an incredible tool for having a better day. Yes, your symptoms are still there, but you are having a good day in spite of them because of your kindness.

2. Introduce today's task: staying relationally connected when symptoms strike. You can explain why this is important by saying the following:

    Imagine that you are completely absorbed in building a Lego sculpture. Your mother comes in and asks you to do something and you say, "Yes, of course." You keep on building because you love to build things. And your project is growing and beautiful. You can't wait to show it to your friends. Suddenly the door opens. Your mother is asking you, loudly, why you haven't taken out the trash yet. You do remember her coming into the room, but you don't remember what she said. You were busy building. You say: "Mom, it's no big deal. I'll do it later." You mom is not having it. She loudly talks about the trash truck already having left. You argue with her. Why is she mad? There is always another trash truck. You raise your voice and before you know it, you find yourself grounded.

    What went wrong? Both you and your mother got swept away in an argument that was triggered by ADHD-related symptoms.

What can be done? You and your mother could be focusing on connecting and maintaining your positive relationship. This relationship will help you negotiate the problem at hand: the remaining trash.

Help your client and the parent explore their responses to this story. Have they had similar experiences?

3. Review last week's homework. Ask:

   - *What was it like to talk with your symptoms every night?*

   - *What did it feel like?*

   - *Did you learn anything?*

   Then ask the parent (if present):

   - *What did you learn?*

   - *Was there anything your child said that stuck with you? If yes, what was it, and why did it stick with you?*

   Highlight your client's ability to step back, to disengage from the symptoms of ADHD. You can explain that, when you are talking to your symptoms, you can better understand and manage them as well as your emotional responses to them.

4. Work on today's task. Ask your client and the parent to role play the scenario outlined above. If the parent is not present, you, the therapist, will play the role of the parent.

   Once you get to the point the parent returns and is angry, stop the role play. Take out the index cards and help your client (and parent, if present) identify things to say and do that will reestablish a relational connection to each other. Ask:

   - *What would help you feel emotionally closer in this situation?*

   - *What do you think your mother needs to hear about your feelings for her?*

   - *What do you need to hear from your mother?*

   - *What can you do to emotionally connect?*

5. Once you have identified meaningful phrases that reestablish emotional connection, write them on the index cards. Phrases should be short because you eventually want the client to remember them. Collect three to four. Here are some examples:

   - *Be with me.*

   - *This is just a bump in the road.*

   - *Let's stay connected.*

   - *Can we hug before we argue?*

   If your client is a young child or a creative older child, he can illustrate the connector cards with drawings.

6. Once you have identified your connector phrases, role play the situation one more time. This time, when the door opens for the second time, take out the connector-phrases index cards and ask your client to pick a phrase and use it. Once the phrase has been used, check in with your client and the parent. Ask:

    - *What changes when you use a connector phrase?*

    - *What happens to your state of mind?*

    - *What kind of resistance do you feel, if any, about softening your emotions and focusing on emotional connection? What would it take to let go of this resistance?*

7. Ask your client and the parent to continue their role play by reestablishing their emotional connection. If needed, you can coach the parent to open up emotionally, be present, take a breath, and approach the subject of taking out the trash once she feels emotionally connected again. You can explain that mindful emotional connection and presence can reduce emotional reactivity. If the parent is not present, you, the therapist, will play the role of the parent.

    You may want to explain: Connecting phrases do not ask you to ignore and push aside the conflict. They simply refocus you to address the conflict within the context of a solid emotional connection. You can have conflict in relationships. It's just more likely to be addressed effectively when you stay emotionally connected.

8. Summarize what you have done so far: You have explored a situation using role play in which there is a relational tear due to ADHD symptoms. You have identified connector phrases and explored using them.

9. Assign homework: Send the connector cards home with your client. You may want to send a second identical set for the parent. Ask client and parent to carry the cards with them and use them when conflict appears as a result of ADHD symptoms. Ask them to use the cards mindfully, not mechanically. Simply reading the card is not the same as using the card! When you use the card, you are emotionally present and ready to connect.

10. Closing. You can send your client home with the following words:

    Connection is the key! Connections can tear. These connector cards can help you reconnect with each other. This will help with resolving whatever the problem may be.

INTERVENTION 40

States of Mind

This intervention is designed to help your client reflect on what is driving his communication: Is it ADHD-related emotional reactivity or mindful presence and connection?

Target skill: Reduce impact of mental health symptoms on school/work, home, community.

Method: Client will engage in activities to improve inhibition of responses, working memory and processing speed in complex situations; and to build emotional control.

What you will need: Index cards. Writing and drawing tools.

1. Welcome your client. Ask:

    - *How was the last week?*

    - *How did you maintain connections to those close to you?*

    - *What stood in the way of connections?*

    - *How did you connect again if necessary?*

2. Introduce today's task: examining the difference between emotional reactivity and mindful presence. You can show the following image to help with this:

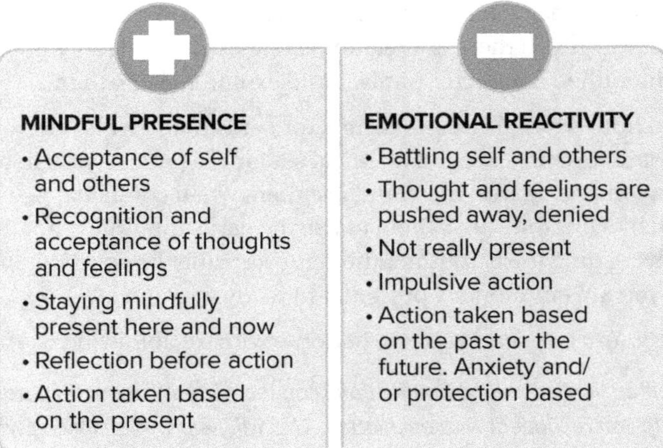

Figure 84

You can give the following example to illustrate the different mindsets:

Ian had forgotten to do his homework, and it was already 9 p.m. When his mother came into the room to ask him about it, he felt "caught" and under pressure, but he did not think about this. Instead he immediately lashed out at his mother by saying, "You never leave me alone. You are always on me.

And now you are going to ground me again like you did last week. And I won't get to go to the game. My life is over! I hate you!"

What went wrong?

- *Ian felt guilty and ashamed about forgetting his homework.*
- *He did not acknowledge or reflect on this, and he did not express it nonjudgmentally.*
- *He lashed out at his mother based on overgeneralizing past experiences.*
- *He catastrophized about the future.*

In other words: He was emotionally reactive, and this drove his impulsive behavior.

What could he have done instead?

- *He could have acknowledged his feelings.*
- *He could have expressed his feelings.*
- *He could worked on staying connected with himself and his mother.*
- *He could have asked his mother what she was thinking and feeling.*
- *They could have solved the problem together.*

3. Review last week's homework. Ask your client/parent:

   - *When did you use the connector cards?*
   - *What happened when you used them?*
   - *Did you feel reluctant to use them? If you did, how did you manage this reluctance?*
   - *In what way were you able to return to connection when you used the connector cards? In what way were you not?*

   Highlight any attempts to use the connector cards. Simply attempting to use them can often interrupt negative relational patterns. Encourage your client and the parent to continue to use these cards. Explain that, after a while, they will internalize the connector phrases, and carrying the cards will become unnecessary.

4. Work on today's task: Ask your client and the parent to describe, in detail, a recent conflict they had that spiraled out of control. Then put the following image on an index card and give each person a copy.

Figure 85

Ask your client and parent to examine the interaction using the card. They can use the following questions:

- *Was I accepting of self and others?*
- *Did I recognize and accept my feelings and those of others?*
- *Did I stay mindfully present?*
- *Did I reflect before I acted?*
- *Were my actions based on mindful presence?*

5. Help your client and parent explore ways in which they can increase mindful presence during times of conflict, keeping in mind that those ways should be concrete. Here is an example of concrete action to increase mindful presence:

   - *Ian uses connector cards to stay present in the relationship with his mother.*
   - *Ian takes a reflection break before responding to his mother.*
   - *Ian's mother writes out what she wants to say to Ian before she goes to his room, as this helps her reflect.*
   - *Ian uses the phrases "right now I feel/right now I need/right now I want."*

6. Make a note of those concrete action steps on the back of the mindful presence index card. Again, make sure that both the client and the parent have a copy.

7. Summarize what you have done so far: You have explored the difference between mindful presence and emotional reactivity using a real-life example. You have identified specific activities your client can engage in to increase mindful presence during difficult situations.

8. Assign homework: Send home a Mindful Presence card with your client and the parent. It may be helpful to use the card like this:

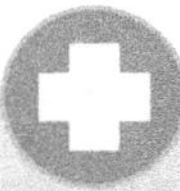

MINDFUL PRESENCE

- Acceptance of self
  and others
- Recognition and
  acceptance of thoughts
  and feelings
- Staying mindfully
  present here and now
- Reflection before action
- Action taken based
  on the present

SPECIFIC MINDFUL STEPS:

Figure 86

Ask your client to carry the card and use it when difficult situations arise. Remind your client to:

- *identify state of mind: mindful presence or emotional reactivity?*

- *move toward mindful presence by taking mindful steps outlined on the card.*

9. Closing. Remind your client that being mindfully present takes practice. There is no simple switch to mindful presence; it's a process that is learned. When there are bumps in the road, they should simply be acknowledged.

INTERVENTION 41

Soothing the Reactive Mind

This intervention outlines ways in which your client can acknowledge intense emotional reactivity and learn to soothe it by having a mindful and caring conversation with the emotional reactivity. The key here is to help your client acknowledge the reactivity instead of denying it, to think of the reactivity as both being a need and having a need (to be heard).

Target skill: Reduce impact of mental health symptoms on school/work, home, community.

Method: Client will engage in activities to improve inhibition of responses, working memory and processing speed in complex situations; and to build emotional control.

What you will need: Index cards. Writing and drawing tools.

1. Welcome your client. Ask:

    - *What was different in your life this week? What new activities did you engage in? Who did you meet?*

    - *How did doing new things or meeting new people change your life?*

    - *What did you learn?*

    - *How did you express gratitude about new things or people in your life?*

    Highlight mindfulness about new experiences and people. You can say:

    New things can be scary. And they can greatly enrich our lives. Sometimes both of those things can be true. Just be present with all your experiences of new things and people.

2. Introduce today's task: soothing the reactive mind. You can explain the task like this:

    Think of your emotionally reactive mind as a small child. When a small child is upset, it needs to be soothed. You need to be kind to the child. If you are not, the child will probably become more upset. Your emotionally reactive mind is very much like this. It needs your attention and compassion.

3. Review last week's homework. Take out the Mindful Presence index card indicating the mindful steps. Ask:

    - *When did you use this card?*

    - *When were you able to recognize emotional reactivity?*

    - *What steps did you take to move toward mindful presence?*

    - *What changed as a result of those steps?*

    - *How did you acknowledge and manage frustration and reluctance in the process?*

Highlight any attempts to move into a more mindful process. Explain that the process of becoming mindful can take time and practice. Encourage your client to take steps towards mindfulness every day and let go of perfectionism. You can explain that perfectionism is rooted in the nonworkable belief that we must be perfect in order to be loved.

4. Work on today's task. Tell your client the following story:

> *Little Shayla is upset. She is crying with all her might. Her cries are loud and forceful. She is upset. She wants help and she wants it now. She does not understand that her troubles will be short-lived. She is just very, very upset. So upset that she takes her little fists and begins to hit her head with them. Just then, you walk in.*

Now, ask your client:

- *What can you do to make things better for Shayla?*

- *What can you say?*

- *What should your tone of voice be and why?*

If your client is a young child, she will be able to relate to this story in a very immediate way. Ask: *What do you need to hear when you are this upset?*

5. Next, ask your client to think of a situation in which she was very emotionally reactive. If your client is a young child, you can ask her to think of a situation in which she became sad or angry very fast. Ask her to describe this situation in detail. Then, ask your client to think of his emotional response as a small child and to talk to that small child in a manner that will soothe it. You can say: *Say helpful things. Say them in a helpful way to make the child feel better.*

6. Once this is completed, help your client reflect by asking: *How emotional is the child now? Is the child comforted and calm?*

If the parent is present, repeat this activity with the parent. Ask the client to coach the parent to give only helpful responses.

7. Make a note of helpful responses (both nonverbal and verbal) on an index card.

8. Explain to your client again that intense emotions are like a small child. It's not a good idea to ignore them when they are crying. They must be acknowledged, and we must help soothe them.

9. Review what you have done so far: You have explored ways in which intense emotions are like a small child, and you have identified soothing and comforting ways to respond to them. You have made a note of those responses on an index card.

10. Assign homework: Send your Soothing Responses index card home with your client. Be sure to send the identical card with the parent, too. Ask your client to use the card to "talk to" her intense feelings when they occur.

Instruct the parent to use the card to help soothe the child's intense feelings if she does not do so herself.

11. Closing. As you send your client home you can say:

> *It's good to be kind to yourself and your feelings. Your feelings want to be heard. They are waiting for comfort. You can give that comfort!*

INTERVENTION 42

Team Effort

This intervention will help your client explore and understand the need to seek and accept help from others. This can be difficult for children (and adults) with ADHD. Although they are full of ideas and enthusiasm, they may lack the ability to create and follow a plan, especially in conjunction with others. This intervention reframes connection and support as something that is essential and beneficial, not something to be ashamed of.

Target skill: Accept support/structure in day-to-day life.

Method: Client will accept structure and support to decrease impulsive, inattentive, and hyperactive behaviors.

What you will need: Writing and drawing tools. Paper.

1. Welcome your client. Ask:

    - *How was the last week?*

    - *What kinds of intense feelings did you have?*

    - *Who was there for you?*

    - *In what way were you there for yourself?*

2. Introduce today's task: accepting support from others as an essential element of making things work. You can explain:

    > *We all need each other. We all can't be good at everything. It takes courage to seek out and accept help. When we accept help, we get better at what we do. Seeking help sometimes makes us feel like a failure. That's just a thought. It's not a helpful thought. It's a faulty thought. As humans we are built to need each other. That's who we are, and that's a good thing. We seek help and we give help. This connects us.*

3. Review last week's homework. Take out the Soothing Responses card and ask:

    - *When did you use this card?*

    - *How did it feel to use this card?*

    - *What changed when you used this card?*

    Help both the client and the parent reflect on using the card. Inquire how the parent was able to help the client by using it. Highlight any attempts to respond to intense feelings by using soothing responses. Just attempting to use soothing responses will help with detaching from intense feelings and emotional reactivity. It's not necessary to succeed with reducing emotional reactivity right away. It's more important to recognize it and begin to soothe it.

4. Work on today's task: recognizing and accepting that the support of others is always essential. You can explain:

The support of others is essential for children (and adults) with ADHD. They may need support in very specific areas such as planning and focusing. But needing support is really part of the human condition.

Help your client identify members of his support team and the kinds of support each team member may give. You can use the following image to help:

Figure 87

Be sure to note on the line the name or role of the team member and the kind of support that person gives.

Your client may want to illustrate the image in colorful ways. If your client is creative, he can create his own support diagram or tree, much like a family tree.

5.   Once the image is completed, help your client reflect on each team member. You can ask:

   • *How easy is it to accept support from this person?*

   • *How do you feel when this person supports you?*

   • *How do you feel about receiving support from this person?*

If the parent is present, ask the parent to create a similar image for herself to reinforce the idea that we all need support.

6.   Summarize what you have done so far: You have explored ways in which we all need support. You have reframed support as an essential part of human life, one that helps us connect to each other. Your client has created an image of his support team, identifying team members and the kinds of support they give. The parent has reinforced the idea that everyone needs support by creating and sharing the image of her own support team. You

have explored how your client feels about accepting support and what changes when he does.

7. Assign homework: Send the image of the support team home with your client. Ask him to connect with each member of the team over the next week and do the following:

   - *Offer an act of kindness as thanks. This can be as simple as giving a hug or drawing a picture for that person.*

   - *Reflect together on their relationship. The client can ask: "How do I make your life better?" He can also talk about how the other person makes his life better.*

8. Closing. Send your client home with the following words:

   You created a beautiful picture of your team. It's great to have a team. And you were able to acknowledge that you, like all of us, need help. Good job. It's great to connect with your team. I hope you enjoy doing that over the next week.

What About School?

While it would seem that the skills a child with ADHD acquires through skill-building exercises and with parental support at home should transfer into the school setting, the research tells a different story. Evans, Sarno, Wymbs, and Ray (2017) point out that treatment is specific to a setting, meaning that skills acquired in a specific setting tend to "live" in that setting but not necessarily in another. This is why school-based interventions for children with ADHD are crucial. Children need to learn and practice skills in the school and classroom setting.

Looking at behavior from a relational perspective, this makes sense. Children develop behavioral skills in a relational context. Here is an example:

> Deondre and his mother have worked hard for the last three months to help him develop his ability to focus and to manage his impulsivity, hyper-activity, and intense emotions. They spent quality time together every day, and the relationship they now have makes both of them happy. Deondre still struggles with homework at times, but he has developed strategies for managing this, and his mother coaches him to use those strategies.
>
> At school, however, Deondre struggles with work completion and behavior problems. He is often off task and talks back to his teacher, who feels that Deondre is capable but just does not want to try. He is often sent to the office during recess as a punishment for his behavior. Deondre reports that his teacher does not like him and that he does not like school.

What might be going on in this situation?
1. Deondre's school is not aware of his ADHD diagnosis. His teacher knows that he struggles with focus and attention, but there is no formal plan in place to assist him.
2. Deondre's mother is reluctant to request assistance for him at school because she does not want him to be labeled as a special education student.
3. Deondre and his teacher have a poor relationship. Deondre receives a lot of negative reinforcement but almost no positive reinforcement and feels like he can never get things right.
4. Hence Deondre has already developed an aversion to school.
5. Deondre is now academically behind. He knows this and feels like he is "stupid."

What is needed?
1. Deondre's school should be made aware of his disability, but this can only be done with parental consent, and communication about the disability should come from the parent. OhioGuidestone can provide documentation of the

      diagnosis to the school if the parent requests this and provides a release of information form.

2. Deondre's mother needs to be educated about the different ways that school can assist children with disabilities. For example, she may be relieved to hear that Deondre does not need to become a special education student with an individualized education plan (IEP) to receive assistance.

3. Deondre's teacher's voice needs to be heard. She then needs to be educated about Deondre's disability and common classroom accommodations for children with ADHD. This needs to be done in a manner that respects her role as a teacher.

4. A team approach is needed. If the parent agrees, an intervention assistance team meeting can be convened at school to explore and document the ways in which Deondre can receive appropriate and well-documented interventions. Generally speaking, the team consists of the child's teacher, building principal, school psychologist, and special education teacher, though others can be invited as appropriate. You, the community mental health provider, should also attend if the parent requests.

5. Skills need to be taught and practiced in the school setting.

6. An attempt to improve the relationship between Deondre and his teacher should be made. Deondre is much more likely to learn from his teacher (academically and otherwise) if he respects her and feels respected by her.

7. The principle of positive reinforcement should be introduced to the intervention assistance team and should become a part of Deondre's intervention plan. The use of negative reinforcement should be decreased as much as possible and appropriate in a school setting. The following image can be helpful to illustrate what is needed for teachers and other school personnel:

Figure 88

8. If a school-based mental health provider is available and Deondre's mother is willing to use this resource, Deondre should be referred for additional

support in the school setting. The school-based provider can then serve as an effective advocate; can help Deondre's teacher establish a workable behavior plan that uses positive reinforcement; and can address any emotional issues related to Deondre's symptoms.

9. If the school is willing, an evidence-based program for building social and emotional skills can be suggested. These interventions are classroom-based and thus do not single out the student with the disability. The following are evidence-based programs for building social and emotional skills:

- *The incredible years. (2013) The Incredible Years. http://www.incredibleyears. com/programs/*

- *Second Step. (2018). Committee for Children. http://www.secondstep.org/*

The Golden Rule of Working in a School Setting

Remember, you are a guest in the building. Respect the building, its rules, and the people. We don't tell people what to do at school. We provide information, education, and advocacy.

For more information about special education and disability rights within the school setting, please refer to the Ohio Coalition for the Education of Children with Disabilities:

Ohio coalition. (2018). Ohio Coalition for the Education of Children with Disabilities. https://www.ocecd.org/

What Kinds of Classroom Accommodations Should Be Put in Place for a Child with ADHD?

Accommodations will be determined by the intervention assistance team or the IEP team. School psychologists and special education teachers are usually, but not always, familiar with interventions such as:

- preferential seating;

- use of a fidget item;

- frequent breaks;

- walking breaks; and

- checklists for organizational skill building.

Keep in mind that interventions should be tailored to the child's individual needs. Not all children with ADHD need walking breaks.

School psychologists and teachers are not always aware of the importance of relationship building in the provision of accommodations for children with ADHD. It is important to understand that schools are under tremendous pressure to produce results in the form of improved student scores on generalized tests. When this is the case, relationship building can fall by the wayside. But it is important that the mental health provider help school personnel understand the importance of relationships in skill building. You can say something like this (pick and choose as appropriate):

- Children with ADHD often feel that they are never good enough.

- Children with ADHD often feel that they can't ever do things right.

- Teaching children academic skills is what teachers do. But children with ADHD have often clocked out of the relationships with their teachers. Hence, they have clocked out of learning.

- It is important to build a relationship of acceptance with each student. The message should be: You are all right. You are accepted.

- All children should receive the message that they are valued for who they are and not for how well they perform.

- When you build a better relationship with your student, you are laying the foundation for better learning.

- Relationship building does not need to take a lot of time. Rather, you can convey acceptance of all your students through simple gestures and tone of voice as well as praise for being (vs. praise for doing).

- When you incorporate moments of joy into your classroom routine, all students— including your student with ADHD—benefit. Joy builds connection and a sense of acceptance.

The following image may be helpful with understanding how behavior management and relationships between teachers and students relate.

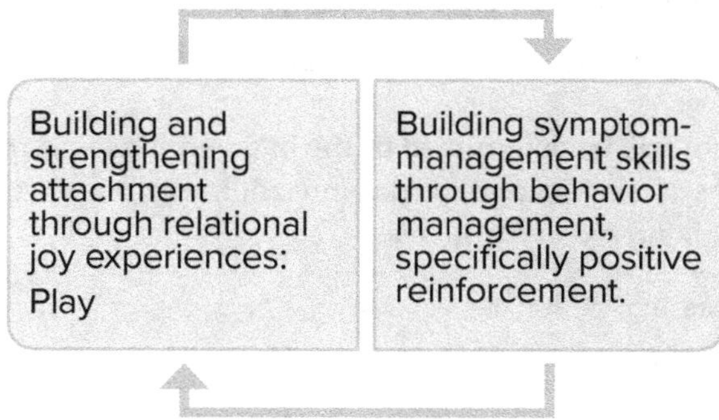

Figure 89

Remember that you, the mental health provider, are modeling relationship skills not just for the client, but also for the client's teacher and other school personnel. In other words: How you are when you are advocating for the client's needs is at least as important as the content of your communication. As such you should be:

- respectful;

- calm and composed;

- embodying kindness and assertive clarity;

- curious about everyone's perspective;

- accepting of people's different perspectives;

- asking open-ended questions about what could work, as opposed to telling people what they must do; and

- a team builder, not a lone wolf.

If the child's teacher requests suggestions regarding specific activities that will help your client with ADHD build symptom-management skills, you can suggest any of the skill-building activities from this manual. If the child's teacher requests suggestions about behavior management within the relational context, you can suggest any intervention from the behavior management section of this manual (other than those that are very parent-specific, such as interventions related to nighttime stories and family time). Many principles and interventions can easily be adapted for use in a school setting and build skills that can be useful to many children in the classroom, not just your client with ADHD.

Here is an example: Understanding the concepts of relational tear and repair can be extremely important in the school setting.

If a child with ADHD is in trouble at school for doing something impulsive, such as throwing an item that accidentally hits a peer in the head, there is a relational tear. It is important for teachers and all school personnel to understand that relational tears need to be repaired, and that the adults in the situation are in the best position for taking the first steps.

If the student with ADHD experiences a lot of relational tears and very little repair, he may stop caring about relationships and behavior.

The following image illustrates what can happen when there is a relational breakdown between client and teacher:

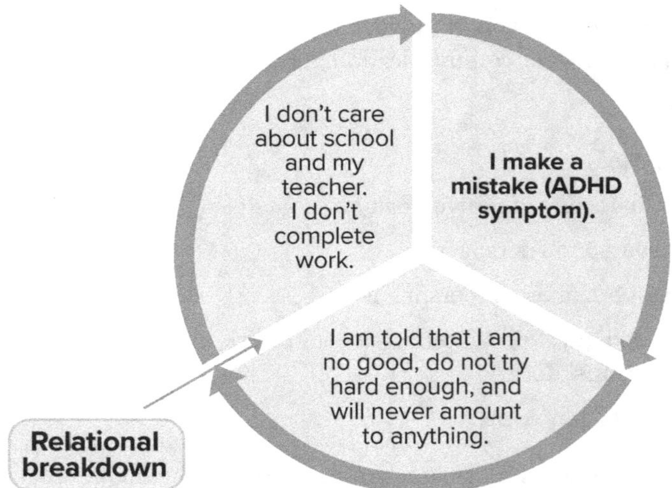

Figure 90

The concepts of attunement and co-regulation are also important for all adults who work with a child who has ADHD.

What Is Attunement?

Attunement puts teacher in touch with your client's emotional state. It gives the teacher an idea of how your client feels and what may be driving her behavior. When teachers are attuned to a student (or a classroom), they can:

- adjust how they are with a student. The teacher can lower her voice or create physical closeness or distance as appropriate;
- change the classroom atmosphere by playing soft music or creating spontaneous moments of joy; and
- adjust how they speak to the student.

When teachers are attuning, they are working with the emotional component of the cognitive triad.

Attunement by itself does not "fix" anything. It does help the student feel more comfortable. If the student feels more comfortable and trusts that the teacher is attuned with him and can handle the complex and intense emotions he is feeling, then he is much more likely to accept the teacher's help and guidance about completing school work.

What Is Co-Regulation and How Can It Be Applied in the School Setting?

Co-regulation is the use of emotional attunement plus the up-and-down regulation of emotional states in the presence of and with the student. That then impacts and changes the student's emotional state, which is up/down regulated with the adult's emotional state. Attunement can lead to co-regulation, meaning that student and teacher emotional states can impact each other positively. Co-regulation is a nonverbal and intuitive process. It nevertheless requires willingness to try.

It is important for teachers to understand that co-regulation can also go wrong. If a teacher is agitated, angry, and impatient, the student may pick up on this and begin to feel agitated, angry, and impatient, too. You can explain that this is not a conscious, willful process. Of course, no teacher wants to impact students in negative ways. You can explain that being aware of one's state of mind as an educator can be incredibly helpful with classroom management.

You can use co-regulation with your client and the client's teacher. Once the teacher gets it, you can provide psychoeducation about the process so that the teacher can use co-regulation with the student. This makes sense. You, the provider, are only with the client for a limited amount of time weekly, perhaps an hour or two. If your client's teacher can master co-regulation, your client can learn, much more quickly, that emotional states can be regulated because the teacher is there much of the time.

Appendix: Selected Figures

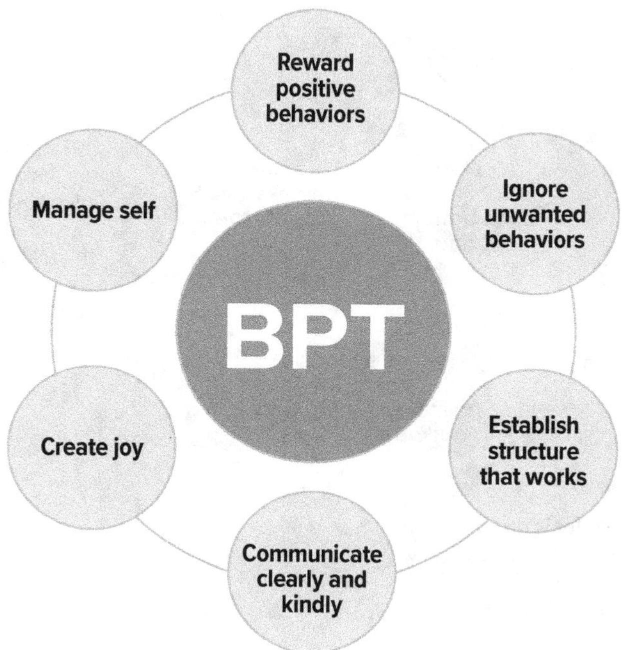

Figure 2

From *Treating Attention Deficit Hyperactivity Disorder....* © OhioGuidestone. Owners of this book are granted permission to reproduce pages for use with their clients.

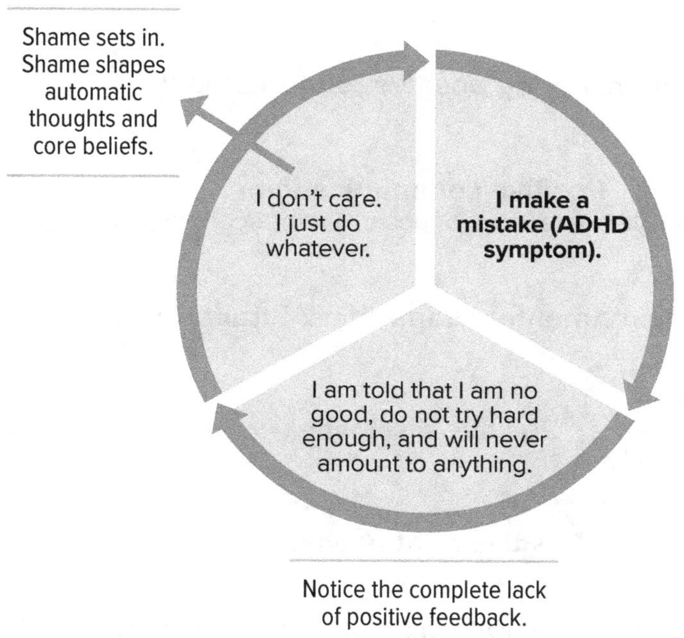

Figure 4

From *Treating Attention Deficit Hyperactivity Disorder....* © OhioGuidestone. Owners of this book are granted permission to reproduce pages for use with their clients.

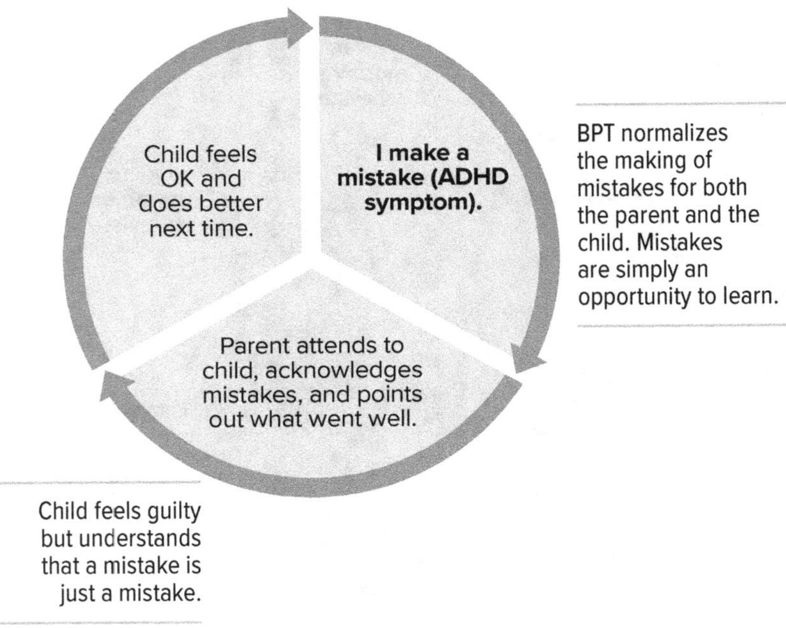

Figure 6

Figure 11 Adapted from: Behavior therapy for young children with ADHD. (2017). Atlanta, GA: Centers for Disease Control and Prevention.

Daily Dots: ________________________ used kind words:

Figure 12

POSITIVE BEHAVIOR	→	POSITIVE REINFORCEMENT	→	POSITIVE BEHAVIOR REPEATS
Child does the right thing, perhaps waits his or her turn, speaks kindly.		Parent notices. Parent acknowledges. Parent uses positive reinforcement.		Child notices and enjoys the positive reinforcement. Child is more likely to repeat the positive behavior.

Figure 13

Daily Schedule	Time?	Support needed:	Success?
Wake up / Breakfast / Bus			
School			
Back home: Rest and homework			
Playtime			
Activity together			
Dinner and Rest			
Nighttime			

Figure 14

Schedule: Morning	Time:	Support needed:	Success:
Get up			
Get dressed			
Eat breakfast			
Brush teeth			
Book bag and go			

Figure 15

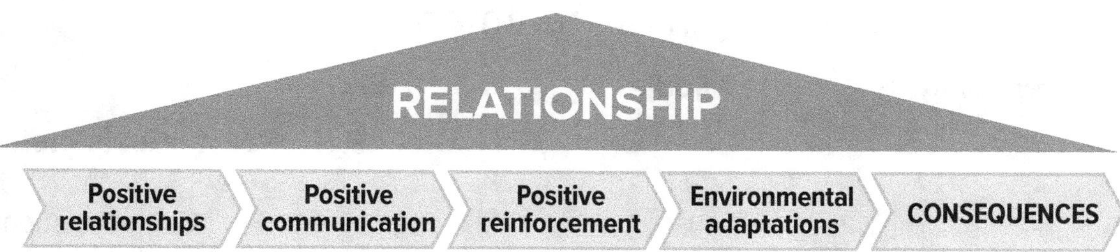

Figure 16: Discipline Continuum

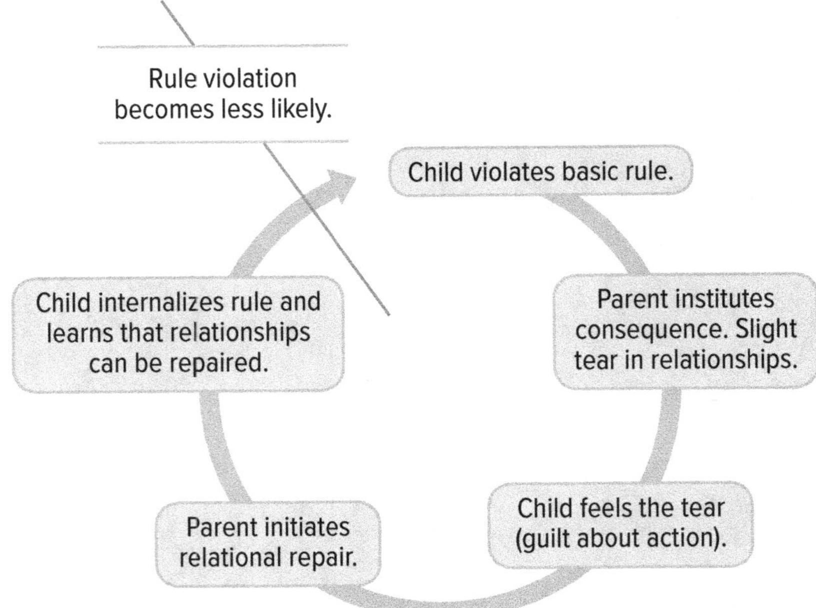

Figure 17

Course/Length of Treatment

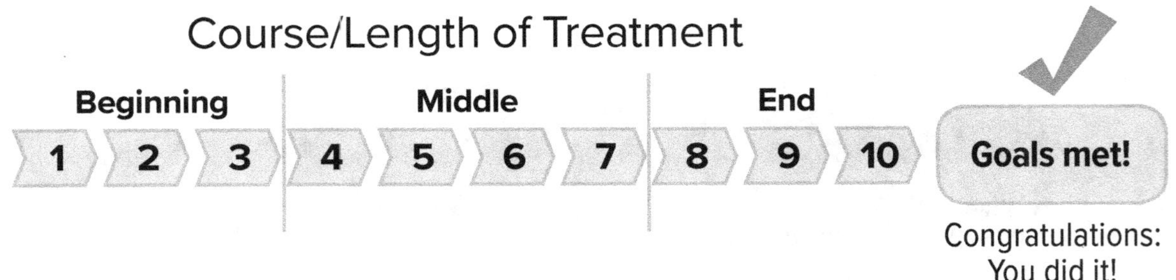

Figure 26

Session Structure
1. Check-In
2. Identify Today's Tasks
3. Homework Review
4. Work on Today's Tasks
5. Summarize the Work
6. Identify New Homework
7. Closing

Figure 27

	Mon	Tue	Wed	Thu	Fri	Sat	Sun
Complete 30 minutes of homework							
Hours of TV							

Figure 28

	Mon	Tue	Wed	Thu	Fri	Sat	Sun
Took 3 deep breaths before acting **X**							

Figure 29

	Mon	Tue	Wed	Thu	Fri	Sat	Sun
Morning							
Afternoon							
Evening							

Figure 32

Automatic Thought (AT)	Evidence for AT	Evidence against AT

Figure 35

Figure 36

Figure 37

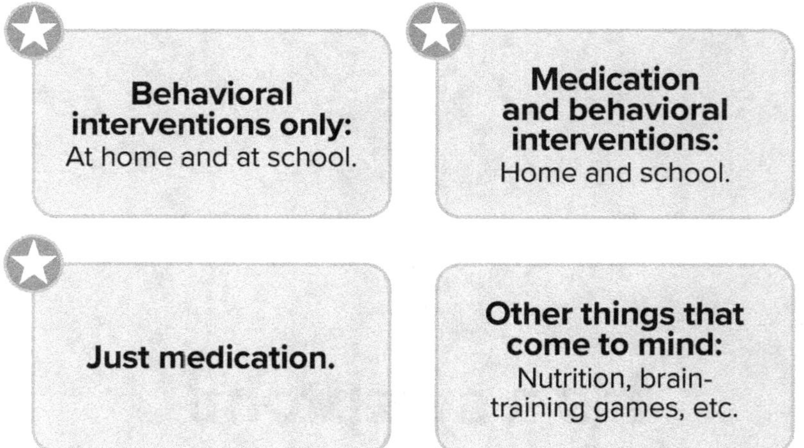

Figure 38

<table>
<tr><td>A job well done deserves a:</td></tr>
</table>

Hug
Wow!
Amazing!
High Five
To the park with mom . . .
. . .

Figure 39

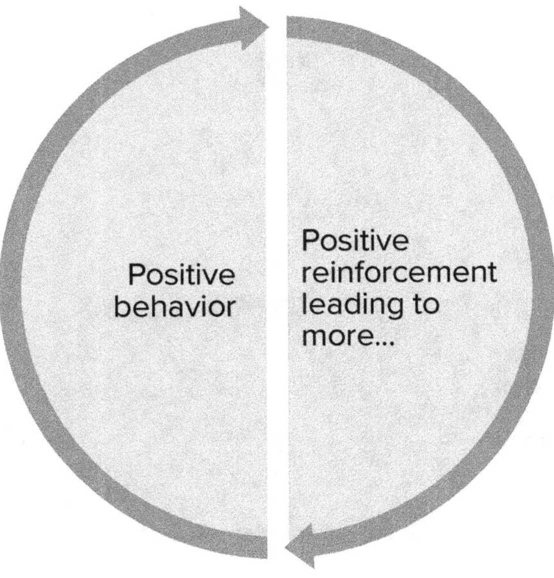

Figure 40

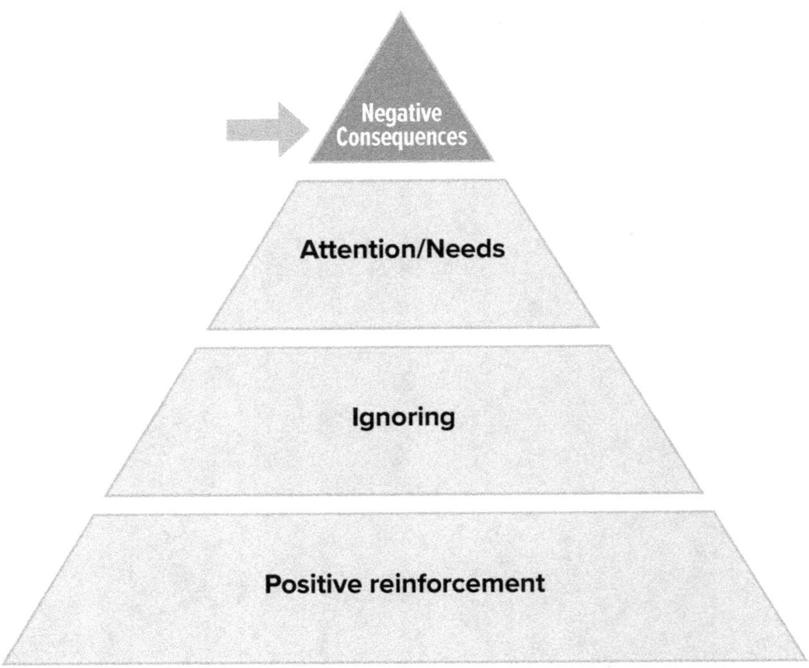

Figure 41

From *Treating Attention Deficit Hyperactivity Disorder*.... © OhioGuidestone. Owners of this book are granted permission to reproduce pages for use with their clients.

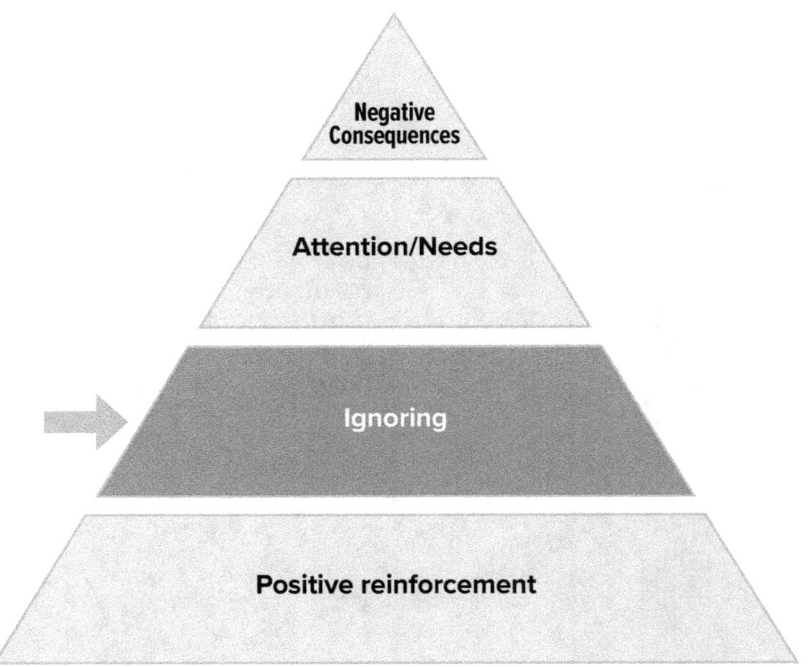

Figure 44

From *Treating Attention Deficit Hyperactivity Disorder*.... © OhioGuidestone. Owners of this book are granted permission to reproduce pages for use with their clients.

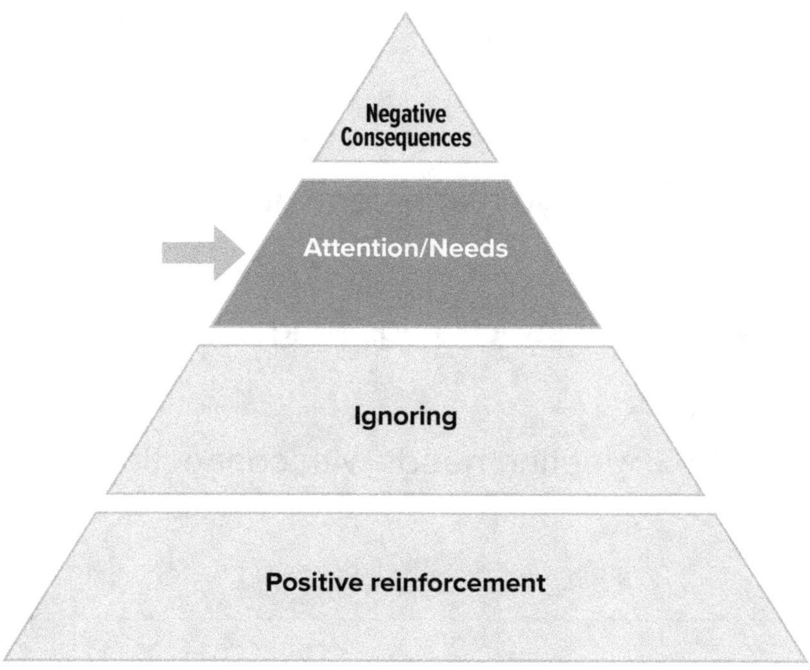

Figure 45

From *Treating Attention Deficit Hyperactivity Disorder*.... © OhioGuidestone. Owners of this book are granted permission to reproduce pages for use with their clients.

Connection Ideas
Hug
Quick story time
Playtime with a friend
Nap
Snack together

Figure 46

From *Treating Attention Deficit Hyperactivity Disorder*.... © OhioGuidestone. Owners of this book are granted permission to reproduce pages for use with their clients.

 1. Positive reinforcement

 2. Constructive ignoring

 3. Meeting needs with connection

Figure 47

Joy Box Activity
Monday
Tuesday
Wednesday
Thursday
Friday
Saturday
Sunday

Figure 48

Simple Things That Need to Be Done
Most important:
Least important, but still important:

Figure 50

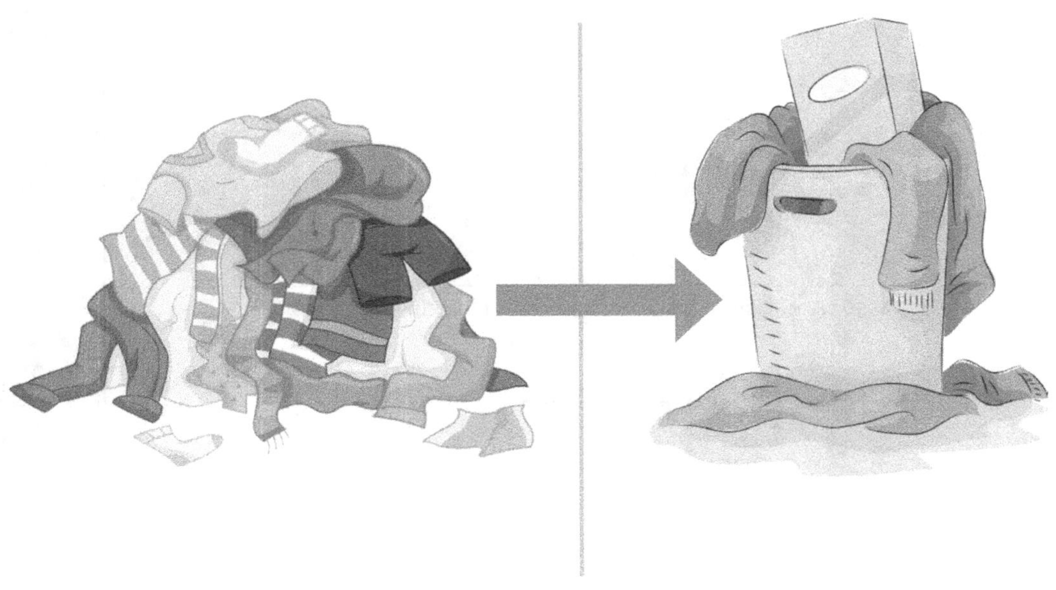

Figure 51

The Thing That Needs to Be Done
The thing that needs to be done is:
Here is what the job well done looks like (draw or insert picture):
When the job is done we will (insert relational positive reinforcement):

The Thing That Needs to Be Done
The thing that needs to be done is:
Here is what the job well done looks like (draw or insert picture):
When the job is done we will (insert relational positive reinforcement):

Figure 52

The Big Thing That Needs to Be Done
Step 1
The thing that needs to be done is:
Here is what the job well done looks like (draw/insert picture):
When the job is done we will (insert relational positive reinforcement):
Step 2
The thing that needs to be done is:
Here is what the job well done looks like (draw/insert picture)"
When the job is done we will (insert relational positive reinforcement):

Figure 54

Figure 56

Time:	Mon	Tue	Wed	Thu	Fri	Sat	Sun
Completed Stop and Go Activity							

Figure 57

	Mon	Tue	Wed	Thu	Fri	Sat	Sun
Practiced shifting attention							

Figure 58

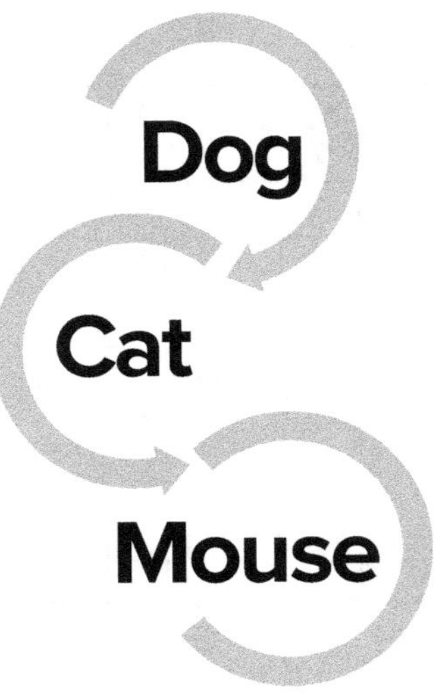

Figure 60

	Mon	Tue	Wed	Thu	Fri	Sat	Sun
Practice focus and memory							

Figure 61

Figure 62

Homework: 30 minutes	Dance together: 10 minutes

Figure 64

	Mon	Tue	Wed	Thu	Fri	Sat	Sun
Played fishing?							
Managed frustration?							

Figure 66

1. Take a breath.

2. Take a few steps back.

3. Walk away.

4. _______________________________

5. _______________________________

6. _______________________________

Figure 67

	Mon	Tue	Wed	Thu	Fri	Sat	Sun
Practiced anger management skills							

Figure 68

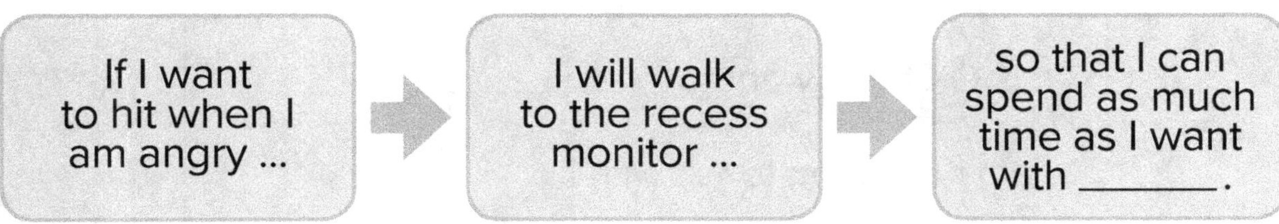

Figure 70

Figure 71

I see the ____.

I want to _______________________________________.

It is OK that I want to ____________________________.

I am just going to "sit with it."

It is OK to want, and it is OK to "sit with it."

Figure 72

1. Task:

2. Enjoyment:

3. Connection:

Figure 74

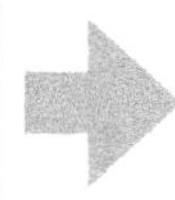

Do something that **has to** get done.

Then you get to do something that you **want to** do!

Figure 75

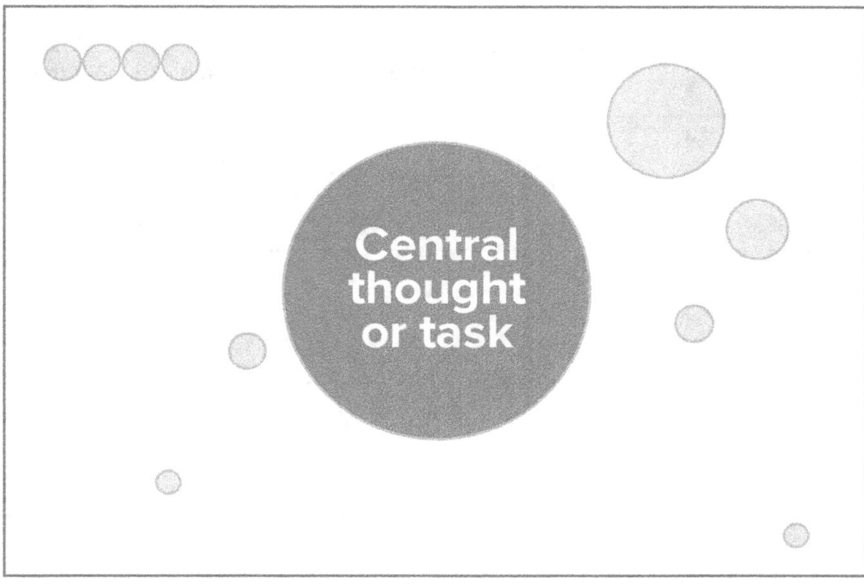

Figure 76

Figure 77

Original message:	Compassionate and realistic message:

Figure 78

Figure 79

My ADHD-Related Needs	Conflict between Needs and Expectations

Figure 80

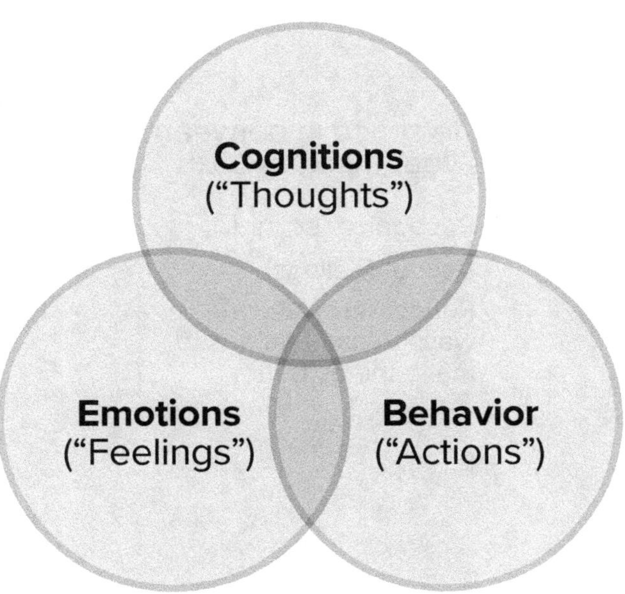

Figure 81

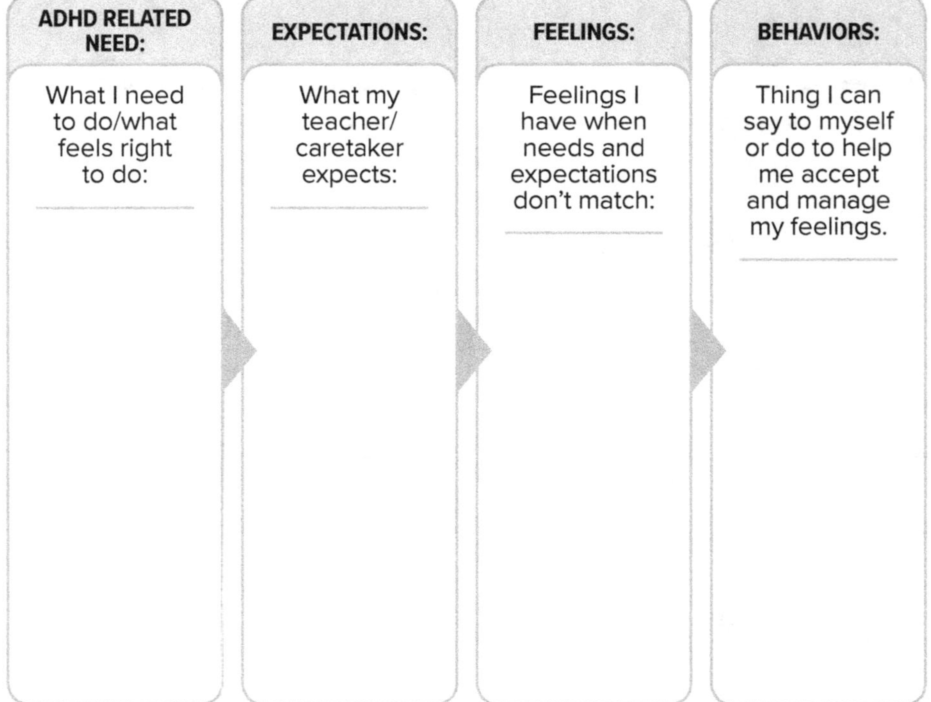

Figure 82

From *Treating Attention Deficit Hyperactivity Disorder....* © OhioGuidestone. Owners of this book are granted permission to reproduce pages for use with their clients.

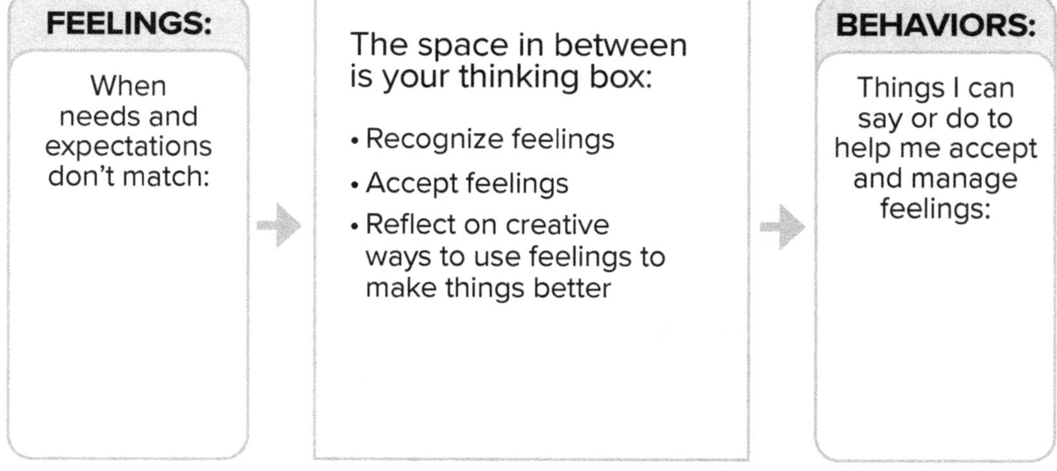

Figure 83

From *Treating Attention Deficit Hyperactivity Disorder....* © OhioGuidestone. Owners of this book are granted permission to reproduce pages for use with their clients.

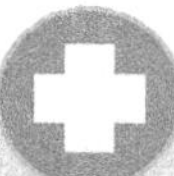

Figure 84

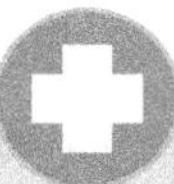

Figure 86

Figure 87

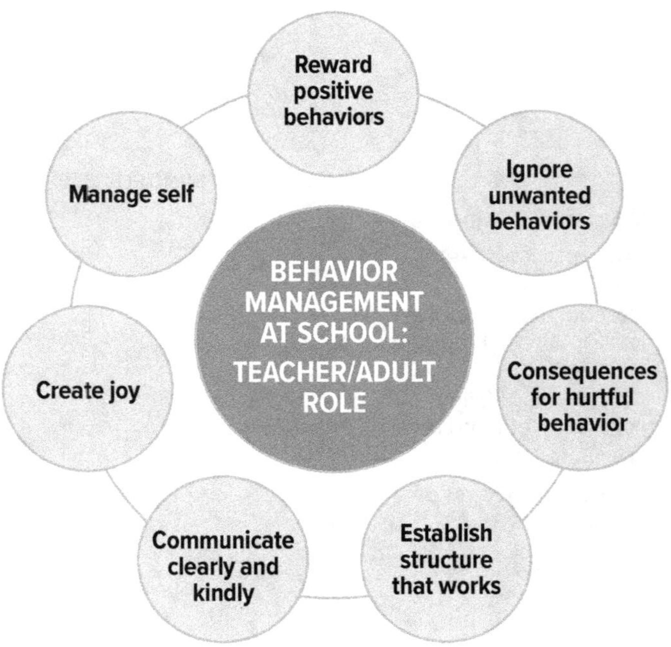

Figure 88

Building and strengthening attachment through relational joy experiences: Play

Building symptom-management skills through behavior management, specifically positive reinforcement.

Figure 89

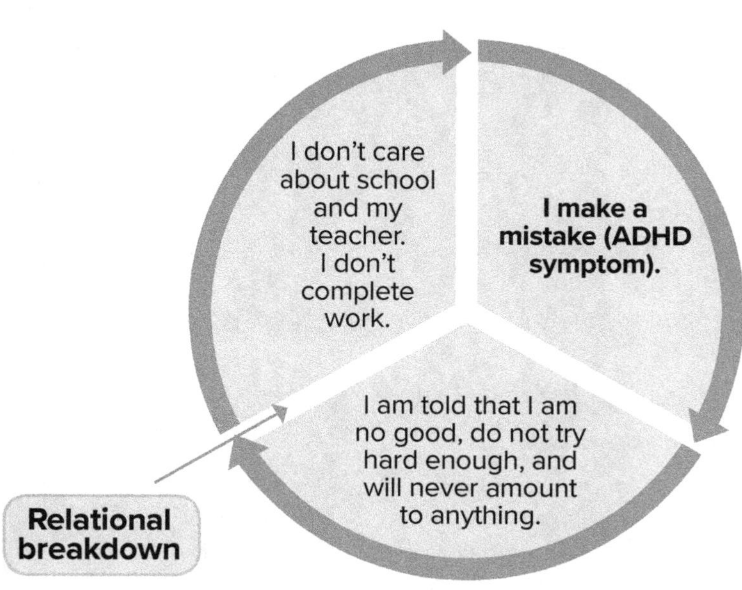

Figure 90

References

ACES too high (2017). ACES too high. Retrieved from https://acestoohigh.com/aces-101/

American Psychiatric Association. (2013). Diagnostic and statistical manual of mental disorders (5th ed.). Arlington, VA: American Psychiatric Publishing.

ABCT fact. (2018). Association for Behavioral and Cognitive Therapies. Retrieved from http://www.abct.org/Information/?m=mInformation&fa=fs_ADHD

Beck, A. T., Rush, A. J., Shaw, B. F., & Emery, G. (1979). Cognitive therapy of depression. New York, NY: Guilford Press.

Behavior therapy for children with ADHD. (2016). National Center on Birth Defects and Developmental Disabilities. Atlanta, GA. Retrieved from https://www.cdc.gov/ncbddd/adhd/behavior-therapy.html

Behavior therapy for young children with ADHD (2017). Atlanta, GA: Centers for Disease Control and Prevention. Retrieved from http://www.cdc.gov/ncbddd/adhd/behavior-therapy.html

Behavior therapy for young children with ADHD. (2017). Atlanta, GA: Centers for Disease Control and Prevention. Retrieved from https://www.cdc.gov/ncbddd/adhd/documents/adhd-behavior-therapy-overview-all-ages.pdf

Bunge, E., Mandil, J., Consoli, A., & Gomar, M. (2017). CBT strategies for anxious and depressed children and adolescents: A clinician's toolkit. New York, NY: Guilford Press.

Centers for Disease Control and Prevention. ADHD attention deficit/hyperactivity disorder fact sheet. Retrieved from https://www.cdc.gov/ncbddd/adhd/documents/adhdfactsheetenglish.pdf

Committee for Children. (2018). Second step. Retrieved from http://www.second-step.org/

Davis, K. L., Panksepp, J., & Solms, M. (2018). The emotional foundations of personality: A neurobiological and evolutionary approach. New York, NY: W.W Norton & Company.

Dimeff, L., & Linehan, M. (2001). Dialectical behavior therapy in a nutshell. *The California Psychologist, 34,* 10–13.

Dobson, D., & Dobson, K. (2017). Evidence-based practice of cognitive behavioral therapy. New York, NY: Guilford Press.

Evans, S. W., Sarno Owens, J., Wymbs, B. T., & Ray, A. R. (2017). Evidence-Based psychosocial treatments for children and adolescents with attention deficit/hyperactivity disorder. *Journal of Clinical Child & Adolescent Psychology, 2014;43(4):527-51.*

Fefergrad, M., & Maunder, R. (2013). Cognitive behavioral therapy for anxiety. *Psychotherapy Essentials to Go.* New York, NY: Norton & Company.

Fisher, J. E., & O Donohue, W. (2006). The practitioner's guide to evidence-based psychotherapy. New York, NY: Springer.

Hallowell, Edward M., MD, & Ratey, John J. (2011). Driven to distraction: Recognizing and coping with attention deficit disorder. New York, NY: Random House Inc.

The Incredible Years. (2013). Retrieved from http://www.incredibleyears.com/programs/

Kearney, B., Ritzenthaler, H., Gray, G., & Yoder, W. (2017). Using joyful activity to build resiliency in children in response to toxic stress. Berea, OH: OhioGuidestone Publication.

LAWriter Ohio Laws and Rules Section 5160-27-08. Retrieved from http://codes.ohio.gov/oac/5160-27-08.

The multimodal treatment of attention deficit hyperactivity study (MTA): Questions and answers. (2009). Bethesda, MD: National Institute of Mental Health.

Narváez, D. (2014). Neurobiology and the development of human morality: Evolution, culture, and wisdom. New York: W. W. Norton & Company.

Ohio Coalition for the Education of Children with Disabilities. (2018). Retrieved from https://www.ocecd.org/

Panksepp, J. (2008). The affective brain and core-consciousness: How does neural activity generate emotional feelings? In M. Lewis, J. M. Haviland, & L. F. Barrett (Eds.), *Handbook of emotions* (pp. 47–67). New York, NY: Guilford Press.

Persons, J., Davidson, J., & Tompkins, M. (2001). Essential components of cognitive-behavioral therapy for depression. Washington, DC: APA.

Schore, J. R., & Schore, A. N. (2008). Modern attachment theory: The central role of affect regulation in development and treatment. *Clinical Social Work Journal, 36,* 9–20. doi: 10.1007/s10615-007-0111-7

Sesame Street. (2012, October 19). Sesame street: common and colbie caillat—"Belly breathe" with elmo (video file). Retrieved from https://youtu.be/_mZbzDOpylA

Tolin, D. F. (2016). Doing CBT: A comprehensive guide to working with behaviors, thoughts, and emotions. New York, NY: Guilford Press.

Wehrenberg, M. (2017). Tough-to-treat anxiety: Hidden problems and effective solutions for your clients. New York, NY: Norton & Company.